Stephen Long
and
American Frontier Exploration

Stephen Long

and

American Frontier Exploration

by

Roger L. Nichols
and
Patrick L. Halley

Newark
University of Delaware Press
London and Toronto: Associated University Presses

© 1980 by Associated University Presses, Inc.

Associated University Presses, Inc.
Cranbury, New Jersey 08512

Associated University Presses
Magdalen House
136-148 Tooley Street
London SE1 2TT, England

Associated University Presses
Toronto M5E 1A7, Canada

Library of Congress Cataloging in Publication Data

Nichols, Roger L
   Stephen Long and American frontier exploration.

   Bibliography: p.
   Includes index.
   1.   The West—Description and travel—To 1848.
2.   Indians of North America—The West.   3.   Long,
Stephen Harriman, 1784-1864.   4.   Explorers—The West—
Biography.   I.   Halley, Patrick L., 1920-   joint author.
II.   Title.
F592.N48   917.8'04'20924   78-68878
ISBN 0-87413-149-9

Printed in the United States of America

To   Ruth L. Halley
and
To   Cynthia, Sarah, Martha, and Jeffrey Nichols

Contents

List of Illustrations and Maps

Preface

Readers who assume that any book with a man's name in the title is a biography will find that this book is not one. So few of Stephen Long's personal and family papers have survived that it is not possible to delineate his character or analyze his motivations with certainty. Therefore, this study concentrates on his actions as a promoter and leader of frontier exploration between 1816 and 1824. In doing so we have included a substantial narrative of his expeditions, believing that in order to understand what he and his companions reported about the frontier and why they did so it is necessary to know what they experienced at the time.

As is true in all scholarly projects, this one has been helped significantly by many people and institutions. It is unlikely that we could thank all who have contributed to this project without missing someone, so we will not try. A few people deserve special thanks, however, for the extra measure of assistance they provided. The staffs of several institutions helped immeasurably. Those at the Library of Congress and the War Records Branch of the National Archives cheerfully brought out vast numbers of documents to be read. The archivists and manuscript librarians at the Missouri Historical Society, St. Louis; the State Historical Society of Wisconsin, Madison; the Franklin Institute, Philadelphia; the Historical Society of Pennsylvania, Philadelphia; the American Philosophical Society, Philadelphia; the Academy of Natural Sciences, Philadelphia; the Minnesota Historical

11

Society, St. Paul; and the Nebraska State Historical Society, Lincoln, have all helped by answering inquiries, arranging for photocopy work, and making their material available to us.

Mrs. Chapin Hoskins of the New Hampshire Antiquarian Society, Hopkinton, provided information about the Long family; Mrs. F. C. Hawthorne of the Abbeyville County (South Carolina) Public Library helped locate a portion of the James Colhoun diary; and Mr. Edwin B. McDill of the Greensboro (North Carolina) Public Library graciously allowed the use of the part of the Colhoun diary which he owned. Professor Harwood P. Hinton, editor of *Arizona and the West,* critiqued the manuscript with his usual skill. Wiladene Stickel prepared the final copy of the manuscript pleasantly and with dispatch. Margaret P. Roeske and other staff members at Associated University Presses helped with the final editing and production tasks.

Some of the research for this project was done under a 1967 fellowship from the Penrose Fund of the American Philosophical Society. The University of Arizona Graduate Committee for Support of Faculty Research in the Humanities and Social Sciences also provided a grant during the summer of 1970. To all of these people and institutions we owe much, and we hope that the final product reflects their help and interest.

Introduction

On May 5, 1819, Major Stephen Long steamed out of Pittsburgh aboard the *Western Engineer* on what was hoped would be a highly successful voyage of exploration in the American West. This first of his major expeditions followed nearly two decades of explosive growth for the United States. Between 1803 and 1819 the nation had negotiated the Louisiana Purchase with France, the northern and western boundary settlements with Great Britain, and the Adams-Onis Treaty with Spain. These agreements pushed existing territorial limits west from the Mississippi River to the Pacific Ocean and south into Florida so that, by the 1820s, the United States spanned the continent.

As the government expanded the national boundaries, a vigorous and mobile population swept across the Appalachian Plateau, down the Ohio and Mississippi valleys, and into the southeastern Gulf and the northern Great Lakes regions. By 1820 hundreds of thousands of pioneers had overwhelmed the Indians and filled much of the countryside with farms and plantations. Cities such as Pittsburgh, Cincinnati, Louisville, and St. Louis, as well as hundreds of smaller towns, flourished where scattered Indian villages, herds of deer, and even forest solitude had existed a few years earlier.

Despite this floodtide of settlement, much of the West and South remained unpopulated and some of it unexplored. Like an early adolescent, the country needed time to adjust to

13

its new size and shape. Some federal leaders recognized this and strove to expand their knowledge of the vast new regions, as well as to strengthen American control over them. President Thomas Jefferson, in particular, sensed this need. Justly considered as the father of American exploration, during his administrations he began efforts to explore the West. The expeditions of Lewis and Clark and of Zebulon Pike, as well as several less important ventures, stand as reminders of Jefferson's efforts and interest.

Certainly Jefferson and others who followed his lead wanted explorers to draw competent maps and to gather accurate data, but this was only one aspect of the process. Broader policy goals also played an important role. The government sent expeditions to the frontier as part of its efforts to strengthen its claims in the international competition for North America. As a result, such probes had strategic, political, and economic goals, in addition to military and scientific ones. For example, nearly every explorer during the first half of the nineteenth century had orders to learn the extent of foreign influence among the Indian tribes of the region. Also closely related to this were commands to ascertain what trade goods the Indians wanted in order to strengthen the hand of American fur traders against their British and Canadian competitors.

Stephen Long's frontier explorations had these political, strategic, and economic objectives, but they must be recognized also as a part of the national effort of self-discovery then taking place. Most significant expeditions into the American West were planned, rather than chance, events. William Goetzmann's distinction between random discovery and organized, directed exploration is useful for understanding Long's work.[1] After much planning, Long entered unsettled regions with orders to map, observe, sketch, and collect specimens and information for the government. The scientists who accompanied him discovered the coyote, for example, as a new species while studying animal life near their camp, and not by accident while building forts or holding councils with the Indians. Long's companions gathered, examined, preserved, and recorded specimens of all types, a prosaic but necessary effort for that day. The results provided a solid foundation upon which later naturalists and explorers could build.

Long's career as an explorer began with a series of short journeys in the upper Mississippi Valley. There, between 1816 and 1818, he carried out five minor assignments into parts of Wisconsin, Minnesota, Illinois, Iowa, Missouri, and Arkansas. These expeditions included many of the duties that would occupy him on more important assignments later. He examined army forts, located potential sites for new ones, and reported the available resources he saw. His early frontier assignments whetted his appetite for more travel and led directly to his schemes for major expeditions into the West.

Stephen Long's growing enthusiasm for frontier exploration and the competence he demonstrated on his early assignments brought him to the renewed attention of his War Department superiors. From that point on, he served American exploration in two significant ways. First, and most obvious, he led several expeditions into the West. Less evident, but perhaps equally influential, was his role as a promoter and publicist who strove to interest the government in renewing large-scale exploration of the frontier. The work begun so well by Meriwether Lewis and William Clark and their contemporary Zebulon Pike had ended during President Jefferson's second term. International difficulties and the move toward war with Great Britain focused attention on other issues. Now Long hoped to rekindle the spark of curiosity that might cause the government to undertake further investigations of the frontier and give him the opportunity to lead expeditions into the West.

Long's first success came in 1818 when he convinced the War Department to authorize a water-borne expedition into the Missouri Valley to examine that stream and all its major tributaries. This became known as the Scientific Expedition of 1819. In 1820 he led a group of scientists and soldiers west across the Plains to the Rocky Mountains and then south and east back to Fort Smith, Arkansas. Three years later he organized and directed a similar expedition that followed the Mississippi, Minnesota, and Red River of the North into Canada. Then, in the spring of 1824, his superiors ordered Long to begin clearing obstructions from western rivers, and he never returned to the frontier as an explorer.

Despite these activities, few explorers have received so little credit and so much criticism for their work as has Stephen Long. In a recent popular book discussing the American frontier, the author wrote that "one official government explorer who might better never have gone west was Major Stephen H. Long. . . ."[2] That particular statement attacks him more vigorously than most, but, until recently, many frontier and western historians either failed to understand Long's activities, or described them negatively. As a result, Long stands near the bottom of their rankings for early frontier explorers.

Beginning the attack more than seventy years ago, Hiram Chittenden denounced the 1819 Scientific Expedition as "an unqualified failure. . .smothered in elaboration of method," while confusing it with the Missouri Expedition of the same year. In his popular text, *Westward Expansion*, Ray A. Billington also blasted Long's 1820 expedition for having "accomplished almost nothing." About the same journey, William Goetzmann stated that it is "comparatively easy to demonstrate that the scientific results. . .were negligible except for Long's important map."[3] It is true that Long disregarded orders, failed to achieve some of his assigned tasks, and usually hurried his men so much that they could not always do competent work. Nevertheless, the chief reasons for scholars to denounce him stem from his designation of the central Plains as the Great American Desert, and from his failure to locate the headwaters of the Red River.

Unfortunately, the negative view of Long's contributions overlooks what his early-nineteenth-century contemporaries saw clearly. He had explored competently vast portions of the Mississippi and Missouri valleys and the central Plains. Recently, a few writers have called for a more favorable assessment of his work. In 1963 John Tucker noted that the 1820 expedition across the Plains had made "substantial and noteworthy" accomplishments. Richard Dillon, although still somewhat critical, remarked that it "has received insufficient attention from historians." More recently, W. Eugene Hollon called Long the "most neglected of the early western explorers."[4]

In some ways, Long's specific contributions seem modest, but that is incorrect. He was the chief promoter of exploration following the War of 1812, and without his persistent efforts there is little indication that the government would have supported scientific exploration for another couple of decades. More than any other individual, Stephen Long helped to rekindle the spark of interest in frontier exploration that had gone out when Thomas Jefferson left the presidency. If Jefferson is considered the father of American exploration, Long should be remembered as one of its foster parents. Going beyond Jefferson, who depended on army officers and an occasional civilian researcher, Long's expeditions established firmly the practice of using competent scientists for explorations. Through his efforts the War Department accepted scientific data gathering as a legitimate corollary of military mapping and survey projects. In this respect the later expeditions of John C. Fremont, the Pacific Railroad surveys, and John Wesley Powell all built upon the foundations Long's efforts had laid.

The data that his expeditions collected was also important. It added to the growing body of knowledge American scholars were assembling about the natural and physical sciences. Recently Savoie Lottinville characterized the 1819 and 1820 explorations as "the most carefully organized, most satisfactorily oriented expedition from the point of view of science, that had yet been sent into the Trans-Mississippi West."[5] The naturalists who accompanied Long collected and reported much new information about the plants, animals, soil, climate, geological features, and the Indian societies they observed. In fact, their efforts caused Lottinville to claim that "for American science, the most electrifying information [about the West] was that contained in Edwin James *Account. . . .*" of the 1819-20 expeditions.[6] The knowledge gathered in those two years entered directly into the mainstream of American scientific thought of that day. Within only a few years books, articles, scientific papers, sketches and paintings, maps, collections of specimens, and, later, textbooks and general scientific treatises appeared. In fact, Long and his companions provided their contemporaries more new information about the frontier regions than had Lewis and Clark because the work of that famous pair lay virtually untouched for another three-quarters of a century.[7]

According to his own claim, during the eight years he crossed wilderness areas, Stephen Long traveled farther than the more noted Lewis and Clark or Zebulon Pike.[8] By his standards, perhaps, it was fitting that he summarized his achievements in mileage. The urge to travel vast distances in a short time was his most obvious weakness as an explorer. Perhaps curiosity about what lay beyond the next curve in the river or over the nearby range of hills caused him to hurry his companions' research work repeatedly. Nevertheless, his expeditions accomplished much. Stephen Long's work has been ignored, misunderstood, or criticised for decades. It is time to reexamine his contributions to exploration and to place him in the broader context of American geographical and intellectual growth during the early years of the nineteenth century.

Stephen Long
and
American Frontier Exploration

[1]

Apprentice Years, 1784-1817

On February 16, 1815, Stephen H. Long received a letter from the War Department of the United States. Dated the preceding December but misdirected to the wrong city, it offered him a commission as a second lieutenant in the Corps of Engineers of the United States Army. He accepted promptly, thus beginning a military career that lasted until the Civil War.[1]

Many of Long's earlier experiences had indirectly prepared him for service as an army engineer. Born on December 30, 1784, to Moses and Lucy Long, Stephen was the second child and also the first of their thirteen children to survive. His father had served in the Ninth Massachusetts Line Regiment and the Continental Army during the Revolutionary War. After his discharge in early 1780, he settled in Hopkinton, New Hampshire, where he practiced his trade as a cooper, or barrel maker, and operated a farm. In 1783 he married Lucy Harriman of Hopkinton. Although not a wealthy man, Moses Long became active in public affairs. His neighbors must have considered him honest and able because in 1800 they elected him a town selectman and six years later their tax collector.[2]

Thus it is clear that young Stephen Long grew to adulthood as the eldest son of a large and active farm family in a small New England town. Although there is little additional evidence from which to reconstruct the Long family life or activities, it seems likely that even as a farmer, cooper, and local officeholder, Moses Long could provide few luxuries for his large family. He did, however, teach Stephen and his other sons the skills of the cooper's trade and basic farming techniques. These experiences in working with his hands and in living on a New England farm proved valuable to Stephen Long later in his career as an army engineer and explorer.

As a New England farm boy, young Stephen received only the usual primary education offered in Hopkinton. Probably he attended the one-room school on Emerson Hill for several months each winter with the other neighborhood children. After that, work on the family farm must have kept him busy because there is no record that he attended any secondary school. In spite of this, Long did receive at least some informal postelementary school education because he applied to Dartmouth College in Hanover, New Hampshire. To be admitted, each would-be student had to demonstrate his understanding of "the Greek testament, Cicero's select orations, Virgil's *Aeneid* and *Georgics*, and the fundamental rules of arithmetic." This Long did, and he became a member of the class of 1809 when he was twenty-one.[3] Thus he entered college at the age when most young men had already completed their formal education.

By 1805 Dartmouth College's course offerings were of two types. The first included those usually part of a classical curriculum—philosophy, theology, history, mathematics, and languages. The other contained more vocationally oriented subjects—medicine, surveying, and navigation.[4] In spite of the obvious goal to educate prospective clergymen, lawyers, and physicians, the Dartmouth curriculum provided Stephen Long with valuable knowledge and skills for his later engineering career.

While an undergraduate at Dartmouth, young Long demonstrated a wide range of social and intellectual interests, as well as some qualities of leadership. He appears to have been a conscientious and able student. According to a biographer, he checked out and presumably read numerous books not required for his courses. In addition, the Alpha Chapter of Phi Beta Kappa elected him and three others to membership in 1808. Long also joined one of the two social clubs on the Dartmouth campus and the Handel Society, a student musical group. Either his popularity or his apparent abilities as a leader helped him become elected to several offices within these student organizations.[5] These academic and social successes must have strengthened his optimism and confidence in his own abilities. Certainly these two qualities remain important during his years as a frontier explorer. Still, this résumé of his boyhood and college experiences provides little indication that Stephen Long would achieve prominence as a technological innovator, surveyor, cartographer, or explorer.

Long left Dartmouth in August, 1809, after he and thirty-three classmates received their diplomas. He accepted a teaching position in Salisbury, New Hampshire, not far from his home. There are indications that he may have taught part time or temporarily on several occasions while still enrolled at Dartmouth but, whether he was teaching for the first time or not, Long proved competent. His students considered him to be firm but fair, and at least one of them remembered him as having been an "excellent mathematician."[6]

After teaching at Salisbury for a year, Long accepted an appointment as principal of the public school in Germantown, Pennsylvania. This small community lay within ten miles of Philadelphia, and during his years in Germantown Long met many educated people in Philadelphia. Among these were several members of the American Philosophical Society, then a sort of "Who's Who" of the American intellectual community. A few years later when he began his work as an explorer, Long submitted reports and papers to that organization. In addition, during the winter of 1818-19, the Philosophical Society cooperated with him and the War

Department to help get trained men for his scientific expedition. They even included research projects and lists of questions to be answered about the Indian tribes Long and his companions encountered.

Long's activities and correspondence during his three-year stay here provide insight into his wide-ranging interests and to a lesser degree some indications of his personality. He soon joined the local musical group, and through acquaintances there he became an honorary member of the Philharmonic Society of Philadelphia. These musical activities provided a welcome social diversion and gave him the chance to perform and receive the attention he craved. Whatever the reason, he tended to exaggerate the magnitude and significance of his efforts. For example, several years after he left Germantown, he bragged like a small boy about his participation in an oratorio performed in New York City. The performance, he claimed, had been the most ambitious of its kind ever tried there. Writing to a friend, he noted that the audience had included numerous wealthy and respectable people, "as you may well conclude from the price of the tickets, which was $3."[7] Although this musical effort was of little relevance to his later work as an explorer and army engineer, it indicated a tendency toward exaggeration and his craving for recognition.

In addition to his musical and social activities, Long retained an interest in agriculture. On one occasion he sent melon seeds to an acquaintance in Hopkinton for experimental planting. He warned that the melons needed special care because they could not survive the rigors of a New England autumn.[8] Another time Long reported to a friend that the soil around Germantown was richer than most of that at home in New Hampshire. The people, however, he complained, were "brutishly ignorant in everything but the art of amassing wealth," and to him their village seemed "mere sinks of dissipation and debauchery." As a result, he intimated, they were inefficient farmers.[9] It is in the context of

Stephen Long's experiences on his family farm in New Hampshire and of his limited travel and observations of agriculture in Pennsylvania that his later negative descriptions of some frontier areas must be considered.

Although employed in Germantown as a school principal, Stephen Long's activities demonstrate a dilettante-like interest in several kinds of study and work. For example, in 1812 a Philadelphia physician offered him tuition-free medical training and board if he would keep the office accounts. This proposal tempted Long, but he declined because he still owed money borrowed to pay for his Dartmouth education, and as a medical student he would have been unable to repay it.[10] The fact that he considered this offer indicates that even at age twenty-eight Stephen Long had no clear vocational objectives.

After declining this medical apprenticeship, Long turned his energies in other directions. He did some part-time survey work and, as a result, in late 1814 local officials asked him to prepare a cost estimate for a complete county survey.[11] Also, during this time he developed a device that he later described as a "Hydrostatic Engine" or some "successful hydraulic machinery." By 1814 his survey experience, reputation as a skillful mathematician, and success as an inventor attracted the attention of Major Isaac Roberdeau of the Army Topographical Engineers. Through this officer Long met General Joseph Swift, then chief of engineers of the United States Army. That same year Roberdeau persuaded his superior, Swift, to examine Long's hydraulic machinery. Apparently, both Long and his invention impressed Swift because he took an immediate interest in this new acquaintance.

The general described him as a "gentleman of large mechanical ingenuity" and later thought of Long as his protégé within the army. At the time, General Swift encouraged Long to resign his position as school principal and become an engineer. He offered to help obtain a commission as a second lieutenant in the army and, when Long declined, hired him as a civilian assistant engineer for the project of strengthening the Brooklyn harbor defenses. A few months later Swift convinced Long to apply for a commission in the Army Corps of Engineers.[12] Having the chief of engineers support his application helped, and in December 1814 the War Department issued a commission to Stephen Long as a second lieutenant of engineers. Because of some confusion about where to send it, he did not receive the commission for nearly three months. However, he accepted it promptly.[13]

Unlike thousands of young American men who left the military during the months immediately following the War of 1812, Stephen Long joined the army. Prior to General Swift's urgings that he become an army engineer, Long had exhibited no interest in either the war or a military career and there seems no way to be certain why, at age thirty, he made this choice. Once he joined the army, however, his decision was firm, and he remained an army officer for the rest of his life.

Long joined the army in part because of the urging of General Swift, and only a month after he made that decision Swift arranged to get the new lieutenant assigned to the faculty of the Military Academy at West Point. While there Long served as an assistant professor of mathematics for one year.[14] During that time he decided that the Topographical Engineers, an elite group of limited size within the Corps of Engineers, offered more challenge and he therefore applied for a transfer to that group. Long's request came late in 1815, after Congress had cut the army from its wartime high to 10,000 men and officers. In this reduction hundreds of veteran combat officers received discharges. Long, on the other hand, had not even entered the army until the war ended, yet now he wanted one of only eight choice engineering assignments. Realizing the weakness of his position, he included letters of support from General Swift and also from his friend Major Roberdeau. Through their assistance in May 1816, Long received notification of his transfer to the Topographical Engineers and of his promotion to the rank of

STEPHEN H. LONG by Charles Willson Peale. *Courtesy Independence National Historical Park Collection.*

brevet major.[15] This meant that he held the rank of captain but that he could assume the rank, duties, and salary of a major if circumstances or an assignment made that necessary. His success in getting this coveted appointment and a promotion of two full ranks and a brevet third one, in spite of his inexperience, proves that he had powerful friends within the army.

Long's brief career as an army explorer began soon after he became a topographical engineer. His first assignments occurred shortly after the War of 1812, when the United States moved to assert control over the Indians and the territory of the upper Mississippi Valley. The War Department had no stated policy of supporting formal exploration, but it did encourage topographical officers to gather nonmilitary information about the regions in which they worked. In Long's case, his first assignments included little more than minor topographical and engineering projects. What might be considered the first stage of his frontier experience lasted less than two years, from 1816 to 1817, during which his superiors gave him limited tasks chiefly in Illinois and Indiana. Although these assignments were minor, they provided a sort of apprenticeship for Long's later, more significant frontier duties.

In early 1816 Stephen Long left West Point and accompanied General Swift to New York City, where he began his topographic duties. Soon after his arrival in New York he received new orders that sent him west for his first frontier assignment. Secretary of War William Crawford directed him to report to General Thomas Smith, then commanding the Ninth Military Department. This included the states of Kentucky and Tennessee, as well as the territory north and west of Arkansas—or most of the frontier area that then belonged to the United States. Smith directed the activities of his department from his headquarters at Fort Belle Fontaine near St. Louis, but Long's orders indicated that the general was then at Prairie du Chien in southwestern Wisconsin. Situated near the strategic confluence of the Wisconsin and Mississippi rivers, this village had been occupied by both British and American forces during the War of 1812. Long's orders instructed him to join General Smith there and then to plan the construction of a new fort. After completing that, he was to travel from Prairie du Chien to St. Louis and to make a brief topographical survey of the river valley.[16] Thus his assignment was a part of the larger American effort to re-occupy the upper Mississippi Valley in order to secure control of the area and to assert dominance over the Indians there.

When he got these orders, Long requested some scientific instruments, and by late June 1816 he set out for St. Louis. Long's ride by stagecoach through Pennsylvania must have rivaled that described by Mark Twain half a century later. Certainly the coach operators failed to consider as necessities either ease of travel or the comfort of their passengers. The 240-mile trip lasted six days, each stretching from three in the morning until between nine and twelve at night for a total of at least eighteen hours. During these long days the coach inched its way across the countryside at an average speed of slightly more than two miles an hour—hardly a rapid pace. Perhaps his experiences on this journey helped to convince Long that the government should help rural and frontier regions overcome their transportation problems. At Pittsburgh he got a small skiff and floated down the Ohio River for twenty-three days until he reached Shawneetown, Illinois. There he left the river and rode overland to St. Louis, probably arriving in late July.[17]

General Smith had returned to St. Louis while Long travel-ed west, so instead of sending his new engineer north to Prairie du Chien the General directed Long to plan an arsenal building to store enough weapons and supplies to outfit the western army units. This project took until mid-August, when Long was free to begin his duties assigned by the War Department.[18] By then, however, his orders had been changed again. They directed him to travel up the Illinois River as far as Lake Peoria. There he was to inspect Fort Clark, built in 1813 as a defense against the British and their Indian allies, and to propose needed repairs or alterations. In addition, the orders required him to gather information about the navigable streams, the soil fertility, and what the Secretary of War called "the general face of the country."[19] Here, as they had since planning the Lewis and Clark expedition, government leaders wanted to use the army to achieve both military and nonmilitary goals. In his early assignments Long's military objectives dominated and therefore shaped both the work and the results.

Late in the summer of 1816 Long left Belle Fontaine and traveled north to the Illinois River, which flows south and west through a level, sometimes marshy valley lined with limestone bluffs. By the time he reached the Illinois in his small keelboat, the water level had fallen so much that often the stream resembled a series of nearly stagnant pools rather than a river. In places thick growths of wild rice impeded Long's movement upstream. Despite this, within a couple of weeks he traveled the 180 miles to Lake Peoria, a widening in the river. There, on the northwest bank of the stream stood his objective, Fort Clark, a squalid cluster of mud and log huts crowded inside a log palisade.[20]

Long denounced the structure as unfit for habitation and "illy calculated for defense." In addition to the barracks, the magazine or ammunition storage building and even the fireplaces and chimneys had been built with logs and mud, so that the whole garrison lived in constant danger from fire. The location of the fort was little better than its construction. Rather than enlarging or rebuilding the structure, he recommended that the troops tear it down and erect a new fort several hundred yards farther downstream. This, he claimed, would provide better control of the river, allow more protection for the troops, and make the post easier to supply than one served by overland transportation.[21]

To replace the existing structures at Fort Clark, Long pro-

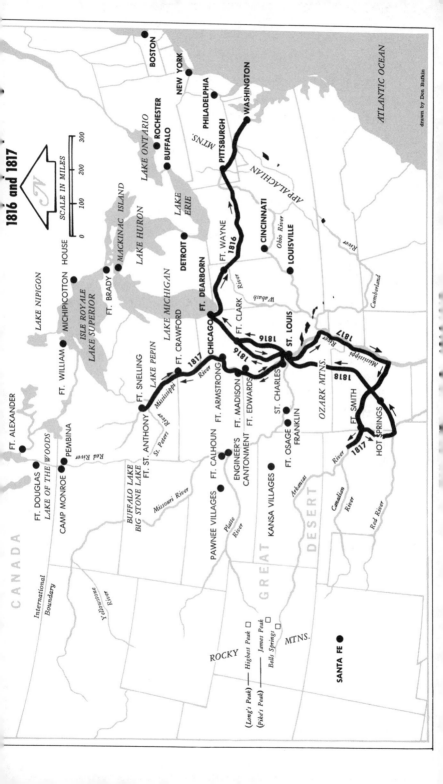

1816 and 1817

SCALE IN MILES
0 100 200 300

drawn by Don Bufkin

ATLANTIC OCEAN

BOSTON
NEW YORK
PHILADELPHIA
WASHINGTON
ROCHESTER
BUFFALO
PITTSBURGH
LAKE ONTARIO
ALLEGHENY MTNS.
APPALACHIAN MTNS.
CINCINNATI
LOUISVILLE
Ohio River
Cumberland River
River

LAKE ERIE
DETROIT
FT. DEARBORN
FT. WAYNE
1816
FT. CLARK
Wabash River
River

MACKINAC ISLAND
LAKE HURON
LAKE MICHIGAN
FT. BRADY
FT. CRAWFORD
CHICAGO
1816
1816
ST. LOUIS
1817
1818
1817
FT. SMITH
HOT SPRINGS
1817
OZARK MTNS.

LAKE SUPERIOR
ISLE ROYALE
MICHIPICOTTEN HOUSE
LAKE NIPIGON
FT. WILLIAM

FT. SNELLING
1817
Mississippi River
LAKE PEPIN
FT. ST. ANTHONY
St. Peters River
FT. ARMSTRONG
FT. MADISON
FT. EDWARDS
ST. CHARLES
FRANKLIN
FT. OSAGE

ST. ALEXANDER
CANADA
FT. DOUGLAS
LAKE OF THE WOODS
PEMBINA
CAMP MONROE
Red River
International Boundary

BUFFALO LAKE
BIG STONE LAKE
FT. CALHOUN
ENGINEER'S CANTONMENT
Missouri River
PAWNEE VILLAGES
Platte River
KANSA VILLAGES
Arkansas River
DESERT
GREAT
Canadian River
Red River

Yellowstone River

ROCKY
MTNS.
(Long's Peak) — Highest Peak □
(Pike's Peak) — James Peak □
Bell's Springs □

SANTA FE ●

N

posed a log and stone fort 264 feet on each side, with walls of earth and logs 18 feet high. When completed, it would include quarters for two companies of men and during a crisis might house twice that many. In addition, he submitted a plan for a stone tower about 30 feet high to be built on a nearby hill. Except for the bluffs lining the river valley nearly a half mile distant, this structure would stand on the highest ground and would offer control over much of the area. Long claimed that, by placing an eighteen-pound traversing artillery piece on top of this tower, the defenders would command "every inch of ground to the full extent of a 24 Pounder's range."[22] This proposal shows that he recognized two of the limiting factors in nineteenth-century American military planning: shortages of funds and of equipment. Not only were the fort and tower to be built of material in the area by the men who would garrison them, but the tower would enable the defenders to get a longer range from their weapons by raising them high above the surrounding terrain. On the other hand, Long showed his lack of military experience when he suggested that the fort and tower be placed 200 yards apart. This would divide the defenders and make a potential attack more dangerous. In spite of that flaw, General Smith appears to have accepted these suggestions, and later that same season the soldiers at Fort Clark began gathering timber and stone to use for building the new structures. By early 1817, however, the military frontier had moved farther north and west, so the War Department ordered Fort Clark closed.[23]

The second part of Long's assignment had been to gather information about the usable resources in the region around Fort Clark, and this duty provided experience for his later work as an explorer. While examining the fort he also "discovered and tested many specimens of Lime Stone," noted several beds of "Brick Clay," and reported that there was plenty of good timber near the fort. Anticipating a time when nearby timber and brush for firewood might be depleted, Long indicated that there was plenty of "Stone Coal," banks of bituminous coal, in the nearby limestone outcroppings. In his conclusion, Long estimated that the building material not available in the area would cost the government no more than $300 to buy and transport up the Illinois River.[24]

This first wilderness assignment lasted only a few weeks, but it provided in microcosm many of the duties and responsibilities that Long would experience on later, more significant expeditions. In this instance he traveled into a frontier area to examine an army fortification and to decide whether it needed to be rebuilt, abandoned, or moved. He had to consider the available means of transportation and communication, the natural resources of the area from which the structure might be built, and related tactical military matters. Also, he had to make topographical observations and to submit a report of his findings. Although this brief assignment had aspects of frontier exploration only as a secondary consideration, it placed Stephen Long in the forefront of American expansion on the northwest frontier and furthered his career. He enjoyed frontier travel and returned to St. Louis with increased enthusiasm for similar assignments. The trip up the Illinois enabled him to demonstrate ability as an engineer, a judge of military sites, and an explorer. His competent performance of these tasks appears to have impressed army superiors, because for the next seven years they kept him busy with similar projects.

After returning to St. Louis, Long had little time to relax. Within a month he was traveling north on a second expedition, this time to map parts of the unsettled areas in Illinois and Indiana. He took an interpreter to help in meetings with the Indians, and two enlisted men traveled along to offer some protection. The small party traveled overland to Fort Clark and then up the Illinois River Valley and along tributary streams to Fort Dearborn at present Chicago. Then they proceeded east and south across northern Illinois and Indiana to Fort Wayne, where the interpreter and two soldiers turned back for St. Louis. Long continued east to Washington, and there he submitted a tentative report to the War Department. While there he proposed to President-elect James Monroe a scheme to explore the Great Lakes and the major western rivers by steamboat, but he got no response. Then he traveled to engineer headquarters in New York City to write a formal report and to prepare a large map of the region through which he had just passed.[25]

If Long kept a journal or took notes of his experiences on this trip, they have not been found, so all that is known of his route and activities comes from the report he later sent to the War Department. This document is a sort of prototype for his later reports of other frontier expeditions. As did most army officers of his day, he wrote in dull, matter-of-fact prose and ignored or took for granted danger, discomfort, excitement, or significant events.

In some ways Long's report on the Illinois country was a logical expansion of his earlier discussion of the Fort Clark region. In it he gave primary consideration to the military aspects of the area, almost to the exclusion of anything else. Now, after this second and longer expedition, he enlarged the narrative to include a broader range of topics. Although his orders called for him to serve as a fortifications engineer and topographer, he went beyond these narrow limits to investigate and record items that would be included later in his instructions as an explorer.

In his report, Long discussed the Mississippi, Illinois, Des Plaines, Du Page, Kankakee, St. Joseph, and St. Mary's rivers. It is not known if he traveled on each of these streams or got some of his information secondhand, but in either case he recorded the estimated width and depth of the stream, noted how far each was navigable, and gave some description of the river valley.[26] Then he speculated about the future transportation needs of the region and how these streams might be utilized. He suggested opening canals between the Great Lakes and the Mississippi and Ohio river valleys. One such canal could provide a water route from Lake Michigan to the Mississippi via the Des Plaines and Illinois rivers. To complete this, he claimed, would require digging about two miles of canal through a marshy portage that already served as a connector between the two rivers at times of high water. Long estimated this would cost little to complete.[27]

Canals alone would be inadequate; the region needed roads, too. He thought that the government, as it moved the Indians west, should reserve portions of land east of the Mississippi from sale for future road use. He even predicted that "at no very remote period the public welfare will require a road leading from the seat of government to the northwestern frontier. . . ."[28] The Cumberland Road had been under construction for nearly a decade by 1816, and Long proposed that it or something similar be built from the upper Ohio to the Mississippi River. Whether Long shaped his ideas to existing federal policies or shared the nationalistic outlook of some of his War Department superiors about using the army to further national expansion matters little. His recommendation for the path of a major east-west road indicates his ability to predict future settlement, as well as his willingness to submit his own ideas to his superiors.

Another part of his task had been to examine existing army forts and to report on their condition. His chief recommendations included moving or enlarging Fort Dearborn at Chicago so that it would command the mouth of the Chicago River and building a major "military depot" on the north bank of the Ohio River some twelve miles above its confluence with the Mississippi. In addition to these suggestions, he noted the strengths and weaknesses of the other army posts in the northwest.[29]

Although his comments about army installations presented an objective description, it was Long's remarks about the resources and potential of the area that make this report important for an understanding of his growing experience and skill as an explorer. As already noted, he grasped the future need for roads and canals, but in addition he analyzed correctly the value of the land and the type of agriculture for which it was suited. For example, he described the area bounded by the Illinois, Rock, Kaskaskia, and Wabash rivers as nearly eighty percent prairie with interspersed woodland. Recognizing that this prairie was "well adapted to the pasture of cattle," he remarked that after a short time "the wild grass gives place to a luxuriant growth of blue grass, upon which the animals feed with greater avidity."[30]

Not only did Long describe the prairies as good pasture but he wrote also that the rich, deep soil was suited for raising "corn, grain, and most of the vegetable products common to the United States." In the areas cultivated by Indians, he reported corn yields varying from 40 to 100 bushels an acre.[31] This assessment is of particular significance in judging Long's competence as an explorer. In 1817 many frontier farmers moving into northern Illinois and Indiana tended to shun the treeless prairies because they shared a popular suspicion that land that did not support trees was infertile or at least inferior. The lack of forests on the Illinois and Indiana prairies did not blind Long to the agricultural potential of that area. Rather than denouncing the land, he praised its fertility. His correct evaluation of the farming and grazing potential of this prairie land reduces the validity of modern criticism of Long for not recognizing the grazing potential of the central and southern Plains or for not anticipating the development of dry farming techniques when he traversed the Plains in 1820. Given the degree of agricultural technology in use at the time, his description of the Plains as unfit for agriculture made more sense than it seems to today.

In addition to its value for understanding Long's growing skill as an explorer, the 1817 report shows the nearly universal scientific interest that he exhibited throughout his career. For example, it included a discussion of the geological resources of the region. He noted alluvial deposits, described the strata within rock outcroppings, and reported deposits of coal, sandstone, limestone, granite, clay, and gravel. He claimed that the soil was rich and deep and that large quantities of high-quality coal could be found. Clearly, his discussion left no doubt that this was desirable land and included nothing that might inhibit settlers from entering the area.

During the expedition, Long and his small party had met and talked with some Indians—perhaps his first experience with them. There is no indication how many tribes or bands he encountered, but Long claimed that many of the area tribes remained loyal to Great Britain. Some of this resulted from their alliances with the British against the United States during the War of 1812, but the Indians had more practical reasons for their pro-British views. Long reported that those Indians with whom he spoke claimed that the British gave them more presents, offered better quality trade goods, and were more honest and trustworthy than were the American traders.[32] These ideas about the influence exercised by British traders among the Indians of the Old Northwest coincided with those of incoming President James Monroe and of Governor William Clark of Missouri Territory. Whether Long knew this or not is unclear, but his report provided the sort of evidence that convinced the president and War Department leaders that the nation had to end British domination of the Indian tribes in the Old Northwest.

Stephen Long's first two frontier assignments included experience detrimental to his future contributions as an explorer. In particular, he became accustomed to crossing vast distances with a few men in a short time. Although this was necessary for certain military duties, speed of travel reduced the completeness of any scientific observations, and certainly in his later expeditions proved a major limiting factor. Another reason why Long's work sometimes added little new knowledge arose from the structure and nature of the army. Basically, it was a policing institution, and efforts to use it to expand knowledge, prepare maps, or encourage settlement in frontier regions were of secondary importance.

The practice of allowing junior officers to travel about the country caused confusion and anger among some army leaders. When Long completed his tour across the Illinois country and traveled east to Washington in January 1817, General Andrew Jackson, then commanding the Southern Division of the army, became incensed. Jackson thought that Long, who had been serving within the Southern Division, was still busy with topographic work in Missouri or Illinois. By traveling to Washington, Long had left Jackson's area of command and had entered another. This was not unusual, but, when issuing orders for Long's travel, the War Department forgot or ignored Jackson. In fact, it had not even sent a copy of the orders through Jackson's office, and the irascible general demanded an explanation for what he considered a breach in the chain-of-command procedures. Acting Secretary of War George Graham made matters worse when he replied, "[I]t is distinctly to be understood, that this department at all times exercises the right of assigning officers to the performance of special duties, at its discretion."[33]

Such a reply, coming from a man he considered little more than a paper-shuffling bureaucrat, enraged Jackson. Eventually, because of this dispute, Jackson complained to President James Monroe, challenged General Winfield Scott to a duel, denounced the newspapers, and issued an order prohibiting all officers within his command from obeying any War Department directive that had not first passed through his office. This squabble cast Stephen Long in the role of troublemaker. Jackson seemed to think that Long had been trying to avoid obeying orders or working within the Southern Division and, to mollify the quick-tempered general, Long visited Jackson's headquarters in Nashville on his return west. There, the two officers clarified their ideas about what had happened; later, Long reported that, although his superior had received him pleasantly, he remained worried that Jackson's continuing mistrust might ruin his hopes for other exploring assignments.[34] This example illustrates how army operations were unsuited for the independent work Long hoped to do.

On his first two journeys in the Old Northwest, Stephen Long carried out chiefly topographical and military work, or fortifications engineering, as he described it. Unlike Lewis and Clark or Zebulon Pike ten years earlier, Long had not been sent to the frontier primarily to bring back a description, but rather to examine military installations. Nevertheless, in July 1816, Secretary of War William Crawford had concluded his orders to Long by writing that everything in his report "should yield to the acquisition of this general knowledge" about the region. Therefore, Long did not hesitate to make judgments about the resources or the potential of areas through which he passed. His letters and reports indicate that he considered himself competent to evaluate such diverse topics as the correct location of a fort, the fertility of soil, the quality of coal, and the allegiance of the Indians with whom he talked. This seeming egotism is easily explainable. Long and hundreds of other educated Americans of that day believed that anyone with a smattering of chemistry, natural history, or geology was by definition a competent scientist. Clearly, Long's superiors wanted him to gather scientific information, even though his primary assignments remained military ones. The early emphasis on military goals affected his thinking about exploration and helped to limit his nonmilitary accomplishments on later expeditions.

When Stephen Long arrived in Washington in early 1817, the first stage of his career as an army explorer ended, at the same time as did American indecision about frontier military policy. Beginning in that same year, the government began planning a series of moves to gain strategic and economic control of the upper Mississippi and Missouri river valleys. Because Long had just come from that region, his report received wide attention from both administrative and congressional committees. In late March 1817 Acting Secretary of War George Graham published Long's description of the frontier in the Washington weekly paper, *The National Register*. The five-page narrative gave the explorer's findings and called for roads and canals into frontier areas. Two years later, in December, 1819, when the House of Representatives began considering the possibility of building a canal between Lake Michigan and the Illinois River, the War Department submitted a part of this same 1817 discussion to Congress.[35] Certainly, Stephen Long's first minor expeditions contained useful information and helped promote renewed federal interest in the West, thereby providing the rationale for his next assignments as a frontier engineer-explorer.

[2]

An Engineer-Explorer, 1817-1818

While James Monroe repeated his oath of office and became the fifth president of the United States during March, 1817, Stephen Long struggled west over muddy roads from Nashville to St. Louis. The new chief executive had served previously as secretary of war and retained an active interest in military matters. This and his subsequent appointment of John C. Calhoun as secretary of war made Monroe's years at the White House a period of opportunity for the army and for Stephen Long in the West. As the only experienced topographical engineer serving near the northwestern frontier during the first two years of the Monroe administration, he provided much of the information the War Department needed to make decisions about frontier problems. Long's duties included a wide variety of assignments in the Mississippi Valley, where he traveled north from St. Louis into Wisconsin and Minnesota, and south and west into Missouri and Arkansas. His new assignments not only called upon him to exercise skills developed during the preceding eighteen months, but also provided opportunities to command larger detachments, to travel farther, and to render independent decisions on a larger scale than he had done previously. These experiences whetted his enthusiasm for large-scale exploration.

Mounting American concern over the continuing influence of British agents and Canadian fur traders in the Old North-

JOHN C. CALHOUN. *Courtesy State Historical Society of Wisconsin.*

west brought increased army activity into that region and directly affected Stephen Long. Many Indians in the area had sided with the British or had remained neutral during much of the War of 1812. Following the peace settlement in 1814, some of the red men retained what seemed to white Americans as sullen, unrepentant attitudes. The Indians' obvious pro-British views encouraged North West Company traders based at Pembina on the Red River of the North to swarm south into the region between Lake Michigan and the Missouri River to keep alive the economic allegiance between the Indians and their northern neighbors. Frontiersmen and bureaucrats alike viewed this activity with alarm, and gradually the War Department strove to consolidate American strength in the upper Mississippi Valley. There, United States Army units labored to expand existing military facilities and to establish new forts in the wilderness.

As part of this effort, General Thomas Smith ordered Major Long "to proceed on a military and topographical reconnaissance of the upper Mississippi." After stopping at each army garrison near the river as far north as Prairie du Chien, he was to examine the Wisconsin River Valley to the portage between the river and the Fox River flowing east into Green Bay. Then he was to return downriver to the Mississippi and to ascend that stream, investigating possible sites for new army posts and talking with Indians he met along the river.[1] Once again, his major objectives were military ones.

To transport the expedition, Missouri territorial governor and former explorer William Clark gave Long a "six-oared skiff." The major took a crew of one non-commissioned officer with a small squad of soldiers, possibly a river pilot, and an interpreter for talking with the Indians. Their supplies and equipment included "a common tent, cooking utensils, a small supply of provisions, &c., &c." Long requested a few books, instruments, and maps to use in implementing the government policy of expanding and correcting existing knowledge of the area, but gave no indication how many of these items he received.[2]

It took the party several weeks to gather supplies and personnel. Not until the morning of June 1, 1817, did they board the skiff at the base of the bluff beneath Fort Belle Fontaine on the Missouri River. When all was ready, the crew pushed away from the shore and rowed downstream with the current. At the Mississippi they turned the craft to the left and headed north, upstream. The journey upriver was slow because of rain, high water, strong current, and adverse winds. After some days, Long ordered a halt at Fort Edwards across from the mouth of the Des Moines River. Authorized in 1816 to protect travelers and riverboatmen who slowed for the Des Moines Rapids from attack by roving bands of Potawatomi warriors, the square-timbered structure had not been completed when Long's men arrived. Although intended to house one company of men, the fort could not because it had been planned "on a scale too contracted for comfortable accommodations."[3]

From partially completed Fort Edwards the party continued north another one hundred miles to Fort Armstrong. This garrison, built on the southern tip of Rock Island in 1816, towered some thirty feet above the water. Here the garrison defenses included stone walls eight feet high, topped with log palisades and wooden blockhouses. According to Long, the location and construction of this installation were excellent. In fact, although nearly a thousand Sac-Fox and Winnebago warriors lived in nearby villages, they posed little danger to the post because it could withstand "the attack of an enemy armed with anything less than heavy artillery."[4]

Leaving this strong fort, the expedition continued north slowly. Intermittent bad weather and the visits to army posts near the river slowed their progress, and it took them a month to travel from the Missouri to Prairie du Chien. The village stood on river bottom land just north of the junction of the

Wisconsin and Mississippi rivers and included houses, stores, workshops and stables along a single street. Outside the settlement other houses lay scattered across a level prairie. Long's orders directed him to halt the upriver journey here and to make a brief side trip up the Wisconsin River.

Frequent depredations by the Winnebago living along the river had led to demands for an army post near the Fox-Wisconsin portage, and the major was to reconnoiter the area and locate possible sites for a fort. To accomplish this, some of the men hurried overland to the portage where Long examined the area briefly before returning to Prairie du Chien.[5] There they reorganized the party, added one more soldier to the crew, and gathered provisions for sixteen days of travel. It also became necessary to hire a new interpreter because the man hired for this task in Missouri spoke neither Chippewa nor any of the Sioux dialects. Long chose for this position Augustin Rocque, a half-breed who had served in the British Indian Department during the War of 1812. Unfortunately, because Rocque spoke little English and Long no French, it became necessary to get yet another man, Stephen Hempstead, Jr., to translate English into French so that Rocque could express Long's ideas to the Indians.[6]

In spite of this awkward situation, the party seemed undismayed. On the morning of July 9, after the sun burned away some of the mist along the river, the soldiers launched their skiff into the main channel of the Mississippi and headed north with a favorable wind at their back. Long's orders had directed him to make a "military and topographical reconnaissance," and to gather information that would increase the "general knowledge" of the region.[7] To provide himself with factual material from which to prepare his official report once the expedition ended, he kept a journal account of the voyage. Entitled "Voyage in a Six-Oared Skiff to the Falls of Saint Anthony in 1817," it included his description of the journey north to the falls and back downriver to Belle Fontaine. He noted each major stream they passed, commented on its size and navigability, and listed mineral deposits or large stands of timber along the river. From the narrative, however, the party evidently never traveled more than a few hundred yards from the Mississippi and therefore could not have gathered all of the information firsthand. Apparently, Long obtained some of it from his interpreters, from the Indians, or even from the accounts of earlier travelers such as Jonathan Carver and Zebulon Pike, whose books he carried aboard the skiff.[8] It is not known if he ever considered publishing this account, but it is one of his most extensive efforts to use anything but a simple military style and seems to be the most colorful and imaginative prose he produced.

Long spent most of his time, however, carrying out assigned duties. One of these was to meet and talk with Indians residing in the valley, but strangely, the party did not stop to talk with all the natives they saw. For example, on July 10, they passed a small Sioux village on the Iowa shore. When the Indians noticed the American flag flying over the skiff, they raised a flag of their own and exchanged salutes with the crew. In spite of this friendly sign, the major decided not to stop for idle chatter but wanted instead to take advantage of a "very fine wind." When the Indians realized that the soldiers had no intention of stopping, six warriors clambered into a canoe and paddled toward them. This persuaded Long to stop, and he ordered the sail slackened so the canoe could soon intercept the skiff. The two groups talked briefly in midstream. Then Long gave the braves some tobacco and a pint of whiskey and the soldiers raised their sail and continued upriver.[9]

Long's interest in Indians varied widely, and the next morning when they passed the site of present LaCrosse, Wisconsin, he ordered a halt to examine an Indian grave with a weathered American flag flying over it. Nearby, the soldiers visited a small Winnebago village that Long characterized as including "the most civil of any of that nation I have met with," probably because he mistakenly thought that this band had been the only one to remain at peace with the United States during the War of 1812. After their brief stop, the party traded some tobacco for a half-basketful of turtle eggs and then returned to their boat.[10]

Occasionally, Long inserted descriptions of the scenery into the narrative. These seem to indicate that he hoped to write a publishable account, rather than a mere report for his superiors. For example, on July 11, he pictured the bluffs lining the river as being "exceedingly wild and romantic. . . . some of them of mountainous size, while others in slender conical peaks, seemed to tower aloft till their elevation rendered them invisible."[11] Not only was this burst of rhetoric wildly inaccurate—most of the bluffs stood less than 500 feet tall—it was out of character for Long, who usually wrote in a dull, matter-of-fact style. Either the wilderness travel had exhilarated his imagination or he wrote this as a personal memento or for private publication and not for his superiors.

Although Long occasionally indulged in such flights of literary fancy, each day he recorded more mundane items such as the weather, his impressions of geographic features along the river, and, in particular, comments about the Indians. On Saturday, July 12, the skiff stopped at a Sioux village near present Winona, Minnesota, for the party to meet the chief Wabasha, or the Leaf, reputed to be "one of the most honest and honorable of any of the Indians." To Long's chagrin, the chief was absent. Nevertheless, the major held a meeting with the other village leaders to explain his purpose for traveling into their country. The Great Father President Monroe, he announced, needed "more information relative to his red children," and so he and his companions had come to collect this. Long promised to return for talks with the absent chief on his way back downstream.

When the council meeting dispersed, Long and one of the interpreters walked into the village, hoping to see a bear dance ceremony then in progress. This was a secret ritual for initiating young men into adulthood, however, so when the whites arrived, the Indians stopped the dance. In spite of this, Long described the rite for the first time, apparently from information provided by Wawzee-Kootee or Shooter from the Pine Tree, a minor chief who voluntarily accompanied the soldiers farther up the river. There is some question about this Indian's reliability, and at least some of the Indians considered him to be a "known babbler" ten years later.[12] In any case, Long's account of the ceremony provided information not previously recorded.

For the next few days, while the soldiers rowed their craft northward, Long ordered frequent stops in order to examine high points of land, bluffs, prairies, and land at the mouths of important tributary streams. He assessed the military value of sites for future military posts, and measured the elevation of hills, the width of the river, and the size of islands. These activities may appear insignificant, but they contributed bits and pieces of knowledge that helped to fill the blank portions of existing maps and increased the store of information about the region available to the Washington bureaucrats. The experience of examining and evaluating unsettled portions of American territory also increased Long's skills as an explorer.

At the midway point of Lake Pepin, a twenty-one-mile-wide section of the river, stood a hill that the Indians called Lover's Leap, named for an Indian maiden who committed suicide there rather than marry an unloved suitor. As in his discussion of the Sioux bear dance, Long's record gives the fullest early written account of this legend. Just beyond Lover's Leap stood a large Sioux camp, and as the skiff came up to the shore the Indians raised an American flag and fired a salute of welcome. The soldiers landed, visited briefly, passed out a little tobacco, and then hurried back to their boat in order to take advantage of a strong wind.

On July 16, the skiff sailed past the village of Sioux chief Little Crow. This settlement included fourteen "stockade buildings. . .of a better appearance than any Indian dwellings" the party had seen along the upper Mississippi. Little Crow and his warriors were hunting when the soldiers reached the village, and Long expressed no regret at having missed them. "This band," he remarked, "are said to be the most notorious beggars of all the Sioux of the Mississippi." Little Crow's men went beyond the usual Indian methods of begging, however. One of their sturdy cabins stood near the river bank, and, through loopholes cut in its heavy walls, the Indians threatened passing travelers. To avoid attacks by the well-protected Indians, most boatmen stopped and gave the villagers large presents.[13] Once past this village, the party encountered few other Indians.

Throughout his journal, Major Long commented frequently on the geological features of the Mississippi Valley. He was surprised that above the Des Moines Rapids the river valley did not lose its "alluvial and secondary character" gradually, because he expected to see "mountains of vast height and magnitude." These did not appear, however, but rather the land changed from rough limestone bluffs to rolling prairie and forested plains. Long thought that the country north of Lake Pepin once lay under an enormous lake several hundred feet deep that had covered the entire upper Mississippi Valley. This water carved and shaped the banks, islands, and shorelines of the valley. Then, sometime in the past, a "tremendous convulsion that must have shaken the earth to its centre," caused the water to drain away and exposed the valley with a "rich and fertile alluvion, well adapted to vegetation of all kinds." As the water receded, the heavy current cut through the soft rock layers, leaving limestone and sandstone spires thrust up from the valley floor and wearing a deep channel between the bluffs that remained.[14]

Long halted the party frequently in order to examine interesting features of the valley. They stopped at Carver's Cave, named for the English traveler who claimed to have visited it during the 1770s. The soldiers found the entrance to this cavern nearly blocked and entered it with difficulty. Disappointed that it was both plain and small, the explorers stopped at the more impressive Fountain Cave later that same afternoon. With each man holding a candle, the party stepped through the entrance into a hall-like room 8 feet high, 15 feet wide, and about 150 feet deep. At the rear of this chamber the soldiers found a narrow passage that led them into a "most beautiful circular room, finely arched above, and about forty feet in diameter." From there they followed the passageway deeper into the rock and found two more small rooms about 150 yards from the cave entrance. By that time the damp, sixty-degree air had chilled everyone and, with their candles burning low, they scrambled back to the entrance.[15] The value of these brief cave visits was probably minimal, except to provide an escape from the routine of rowing the skiff and to give the men a chance to exercise their curiosity. For Long these simple tasks increased his experience in examining, evaluating, and recording what he encountered in the wilderness.

By mid-afternoon that same day, July 16, the party reached the mouth of the St. Peter's River (the Minnesota), and two miles farther upstream they came to the first in a series of rapids. There, even with a strong tail wind pushing them, they found the current so strong that they had to pull the skiff upstream with a towrope the rest of the afternoon. The exhausted crew struggled along the riverbank until seven that evening, when they reached their destination, the Falls of St. Anthony.[16]

The falls are "the most interesting and magnificent of any I have ever witnessed," Long noted the next morning during his survey of the area. This comment suggests that he had little experience with waterfalls because in 1806 Zebulon Pike had measured them as only 16½ feet high. The major agreed, but suggested that another 4 or 5 feet be added to that figure because of the sharp drop in the stream bed at the foot of the falls. While Long measured the width of the stream and estimated the speed of the current, his men poked through the rocks lining the riverbanks and splashed in the shallows. The next morning the party loaded the tent and other equipment aboard the skiff and later that day started back down the river.

When they reached the mouth of the St. Peter's River they stopped so that Long might examine the area for a potential fort site. He decided that the best location for a military installation there was a high, level point of land between the Mississippi and St. Peter's. There, 120 feet above the water, "a military work of considerable magnitude might be constructed," he noted. Only a couple of years later, the men of the Mississippi Expedition did camp there and built what became Fort Snelling.[17]

The voyage downstream brought some discomfort to the soldiers. On July 17, the whiskey supply ran dry. The army food ration then included one gill or a half cup of whiskey each day, and Long worried that the lack of it would injure his crew because whiskey was necessary for "life to those employed in the navigation of the Mississippi in hot weather." The crew had emptied the keg ahead of schedule because their corporal let each man fill his own cup. The corporal's trust or ineptitude extended to other food items, too, and a few days later the party ate the last of their meat. This shortage had to be remedied at once, Long noted, because "my men have hard duty to perform." Consequently, he ordered a daily halt so the crew could fish. This kept them supplied with catfish until they got back to Prairie du Chien.

These incidents raise questions about Stephen Long's capabilities as an explorer and a leader. Obviously, he was interested in the well-being of his men and did what was possible to help them. On the other hand, the shortages of both food and drink on a small expedition indicate some carelessness or inefficiency in handling routine matters. Apparently, he did not intend to have the soldiers depend on hunting or fishing for part of their food, yet this became necessary several days before they completed the assignment. At first Long misjudged his corporal's ability to manage the supplies, but after the whiskey shortage he recognized the problem. Nevertheless, the major seems to have given the corporal no supervision with the rations, even after the whiskey shortage. These difficulties show that Long had much to learn about leading men through the wilderness successfully. In this respect he stood midway between Lewis and Clark, who had led their men with patience and skill, and the later John C. Fremont, who brought one of his expeditions to disaster because of inept leadership.[18]

Late on the evening of July 18, a storm hit just as the skiff reached Lake Pepin. The wind churned the large expanse of water into rough waves and a driving rain hid the shore and threatened to swamp the craft. Driven before the gale, the men struggled to get their boat ashore. When they reached the riverbank, they clambered out of the skiff and ran to high ground. Sudden gusts of wind and a steady downpour made pitching the tent difficult, but the men finished before everything got soaked. At first the shivering soldiers found nothing dry that they could use to start a fire, but soon Long tore some lining from his coat sleeve and one of the others brought a partially rotted log that would still burn. When they found that the tent provided little shelter from the storm, the men spent the rest of the night hunched around the sizzling fire in their soaked, mud-spattered clothes. When daylight appeared, the tired soldiers packed their wet baggage, bailed the water from their skiff, and pushed out into the storm.[19]

The next several days passed uneventfully, and on July 21, the exploring party sailed up to the shore at Prairie du Chien. They had traveled the 420 miles from there to the Falls of St. Anthony and back in just thirteen days for an average speed of about 32 miles each day. This rapid pace resulted from good weather most of the way, but Long's leadership played a part, too. He made certain that the skiff crew began

each day "at an early hour," which usually mean
sunrise, and occasionally as early as 4:30 A.M.[20] By tra
until evening, or even all night, the party could spend b
tween twelve and fifteen hours each day on the river and still
have time for visits with the Indians, stops to measure hills or
distances, or searches for minerals. The speed with which he
moved along the Mississippi, however, forced Long to give
only cursory attention to some of the region. In spite of frequent comments on the obvious physical features, he had
little time to examine the river valley carefully. Consequently,
some of his information repeated available material, although he did gather some new facts about the Sioux and the
military potential of numerous sites as well. Long's apparent
compulsion for rapid travel, demonstrated so clearly on this
voyage, remained with him throughout his career and reduced his potential contributions as an explorer.

At Prairie du Chien, the boat-weary soldiers had five days
to rest while their commander inspected nearby Fort Crawford. That unfinished structure included a log palisade 340
feet on each side, with blockhouses two stories high at
alternate corners, and barracks, hospital, officers' quarters,
and a magazine within the walls. According to Long, only the
magazine was of stone. Construction had been under way for
a year, but much work remained to be done because little of
the building material was available nearby. The nearest
timber and stone were several miles away in the hills and
then, because no roads existed, once the soldiers gathered
what they needed, they had to drag it to the river and load it
on steamboats for transportation to the fort.

Despite the continuing work at the post, the War Department planners thought that it should be moved. Its general
location near the junction of the Mississippi and Wisconsin
rivers was a good one and placed the garrison in a strategic
position between Fort Howard at Green Bay and Fort Armstrong at Rock Island. Also, it offered military and Indian
Office personnel ample opportunity to meet the frontier

t before
eling
e-

...less, these considerations did not out-
...s of the fort site. Stagnant pools near-
...several large marshes lay nearby. This,
...nual flooding of the river bottom land
...post a sickly one. Ague, or intermittent
...eteenth-century terms for malaria, deci-
...by late summer each year. Added to this
...vere several military ones. Nearby islands
obstruc..... ...w so that the fort did not command the
river. In addition, a small valley several hundred yards north
of the post offered ample concealment for attacking troops,
as shown by the successful British and Indian attack there
during the War of 1812. A line of bluffs rising 420 feet above
the entire area also made the fort site untenable if attacked.
"The military features of the place are so faint and obscure,"
Long concluded, "that they would hardly be perceptible,
except by occupying several of the neighboring heights. . . ."[21]

In spite of these valid reasons for shifting the post site,
Long failed to put forward any other location as better suited
for military purposes. Instead of listing alternate fort sites, he
filled his narrative with descriptions of "curiosities that have
baffled the ingenuity and penetration of the wisest" people in
the community. The curiosities included earth mounds and
ridges, parapets, and burial grounds, all considered to be of
non-Indian origin by local inhabitants. Surprisingly, he
related one citizen's story, that while digging a basement he
found eight skeletons "of gigantic size, measuring about
eight feet from head to foot." Perhaps this demonstrates
Long's gullibility, although it is strange that he would accept
this report from one of the villagers, whom he considered
inferior because "there are very few of them that have not
savage blood in their veins."[22]

On July 27, their business at Fort Crawford completed, the
explorers boarded the skiff for their return to Belle Fontaine.
They paddled south to Fort Armstrong, arriving there four
days later, and after a two-day stop continued on down-

stream. On August 4, they halted briefly to visit the ruins of Fort Madison, abandoned after an Indian attack during the War of 1812. The explorers found only a few stone chimneys protruding above the tall weeds, and some peach, apple, and nectarine trees in what had been the post orchard. Downstream a short distance, the skiff hit a rock ledge while passing through the Des Moines Rapids, and the crew had to bail constantly to keep their craft afloat. Fortunately, they were near Fort Edwards, where they halted for repairs. Leaving the post on August 11, they began the last portion of the journey, and on Friday, August, 15, 1817, the skiff sailed up to the dock at Belle Fontaine.[23]

After returning to General Smith's headquarters, Major Long was supposed to prepare a report of his work, but before he could do this, Smith ordered him on still another frontier assignment. This one took him into Arkansas, then the scene of the Osage-Cherokee War. President Thomas Jefferson had sowed the seeds of this conflict on January 9, 1809, when he encouraged the Cherokee to send a delegation west to explore portions of eastern Arkansas that the Osage tribe had ceded to the United States the preceding year. The Cherokee did this, and, when they found an area to their liking, began a gradual migration to it. Consequently, by 1814 nearly 2,000 Cherokee had moved west. Instead of escaping from the pressures of land-hungry frontiersmen and illicit whiskey vendors, however, the migrants met similar difficulties in the west. Then, when game and fur-bearing animals became scarce in their area, the Cherokee shifted their annual hunting expeditions to the west, intruding on Osage lands. This brought immediate and violent resistance from the Osage, and by 1814, raids and counterraids had become common.

Indian Office personnel asked repeatedly for an army fort to be built in the area to maintain peace, but got little response. By 1817, however, increasing Cherokee migration and an intensification of the war seem to have convinced the

War Department that action was necessary. In July of that year, Acting Secretary of War Richard Graham ordered General Andrew Jackson to despatch troops to build a post where the Osage boundary line met the Arkansas River. Jackson, in turn, relayed the order to General Smith, within whose department the fort would stand, and Smith assigned Stephen Long to choose the location and design the structure of the new garrison.[24]

Long and a five-man engineering party were to accompany Major William Bradford, who led a company of Rifle Regiment troops that would garrison the new post. In mid-September, Long and his men boarded the skiff he had used earlier that summer on the Mississippi, while Bradford's command traveled in a larger army keelboat. The two boats floated downstream from Belle Fontaine until October 1, when they met a second contingent of riflemen traveling north to join them. Over twenty of the new men were sick, and Bradford and Long found that treating them slowed their movement. So on October 15, when they arrived at the mouth of the Arkansas, Bradford halted, hoping that his men would recover.[25]

Here the troops rested, while Long took time to write General Swift at Engineer Headquarters. He repeated his earlier proposal to President Monroe for exploring parts of the West by steamboat and indicated that he and General Smith had discussed the matter that summer. Then the engineering party continued upstream to survey possible fort sites. Long led his men west and north as far as the Verdigris River, well beyond the Osage line. Then they returned to the region where the boundary and river met. There the major noted a tree-covered bluff, standing about fifty feet above the water, which seemed best suited for the fort. Further examination convinced him that his first impression was correct, so while his men built shelters he surveyed the site at the confluence of the Arkansas and Poteau rivers. Then he drew plans for a fort to house the seventy riflemen who would soon begin their journey up the Arkansas. A square structure 132 feet on each side, the post would have walls of logs 10 feet high placed on top of stone foundations and surrounded by a moat 4 feet deep. In alternate corners Long designed block-houses nearly 30 feet square that offered a "commanding and picturesque view" of the nearby terrain. Within the stockade walls he planned for barracks, officers' quarters, a hospital, guardhouse, magazine, saddle shop, carpenters' and wheel-wrights' facilities, and storerooms for a sutler and the quartermaster.[26]

Long's orders directed him to explore the region between the campsite and the Red River when he completed his survey and planning work, so he left two men with the building plans for Major Bradford and, taking the others, ascended the Poteau to the Kiamichi Mountains. There he followed the Kiamichi River down to the Red, near the future site of Fort Towson. During the last days of December, 1817, the party traveled along the north bank of the Red and then turned northeast to Hot Springs, where they spent the last day of the year examining the thermal springs. A few days later they crossed the Arkansas at Little Rock and, continuing in the same direction, reached Herculaneum on the Mississippi. Then the party traveled north to Belle Fontaine.[27]

With the establishment of Fort Smith, as the new post was soon named, government officials hoped for an end to the Cherokee-Osage fighting. Nevertheless, War Department plans called for continuing Cherokee removal from the Southeast into the disputed area, a policy that increased rather than decreased the friction. As a result, when Colonel Henry Atkinson succeeded General Smith as commander of the Ninth Military Department in 1819, he ordered that Fort Smith be tied into the evolving system of army forts along the frontier by surveying a road from it to Fort Osage on the Missouri River. This was done, and Fort Smith remained in active use until after the Civil War, demonstrating the wisdom of Long's choice of location.[28]

When Long arrived at Belle Fontaine in January, 1818, he had to report his activities of the previous year. While doing this, he resubmitted his plan to explore parts of the frontier by steamboat, this time to General Smith. His superior sent a copy of Long's ideas to the War Department within a few days, but got no immediate response. Describing his 1817-18 travels took the major until May, 1818, and the result demonstrates his growing maturity as a military engineer and an explorer, as well as his weaknesses in judging frontier problems. After a brief geographic discussion of the river valleys through which he had traveled, Long considered the relationship between British and Canadian traders and the Indians living along the northern border of the United States. Repeating earlier ideas about the strong influence these foreigners had on the Indians, he wrote that this could not be ended or even reduced without continuing action by the government. In fact, he predicted that in any future war with Great Britain, "strenuous attempts would be made to wrest a portion of [the Northwest] from our possession." Therefore, he proposed that a well-organized system of frontier forts be maintained to deter the British and to influence the Indians.[29]

His proposal included retaining forts Howard at Green Bay, Dearborn at Chicago, and Armstrong at Rock Island on the Mississippi. Forts Crawford, Edwards and Clark, however, he considered less important, so they could be abandoned. To replace them, Long recommended building a new fort at the confluence of the Mississippi and St. Peter's rivers. These comments Long based on his travels and personal knowledge of the region. General Smith, however, asked him to suggest locations for forts in the Missouri Valley, a region that the major knew little about because he had not traveled there. Long's shortage of firsthand information failed to deter him, however, and he recommended locating forts at the Kansas and Platte rivers, at the Mandan Villages in North Dakota, and at the Yellowstone River some 1,800 miles up the Missouri. For strategic reasons, he considered the

Mandan Villages site the most important and noted that any fort built there should be a permanent one.[30]

At the end of this lengthy report, Long added a few random suggestions to improve American military strength in frontier regions. He recommended that each garrison located on a major river have armed and fortified keelboats for use against attacking parties. Each post needed enough horses to carry at least one company of men, he claimed, if the troops were to campaign effectively against the Indians. He also proposed that the men at each frontier fort maintain company vegetable gardens in order to supplement the inadequate army diet. Certainly he was not the only officer to complain about the poor food provided the troops, but within a few months after his report reached Washington, Secretary of War John C. Calhoun ordered frontier commanders to use their enlisted men as farmers whenever possible.[31]

Shortly after he completed this report, Long set out for Washington to discuss his activities and to get a new assignment. Arriving there in midsummer, he met with War Department superiors to reiterate some of his proposals, and in particular he stressed the need for an organized system of frontier forts from which to control the Indian trade. When these discussions ended, he traveled to Engineer Headquarters in New York and began work on a large map of the central United States.[32]

It is difficult to prove whether Stephen Long's ideas and information on frontier military matters provided the basis for War Department decisions or merely reflected known interests within the army. Probably some of both occurred. In either case, the War Department implemented some of his proposals soon after he submitted them. He had suggested that a fort be built at the mouth of St. Peter's River, and in 1819, American troops occupied that place. In the Missouri Valley he had recommended forts at the Platte, the Great Bend, the Mandan Villages, and the Yellowstone, and within a few months the so-called Yellowstone Expedition was being planned. During 1818, Secretary of War Calhoun proposed building temporary forts at either Council Bluffs or the Great Bend, and when the troops started up the Missouri he supposed that they would halt at the Mandan Villages—just the place Long recommended as the best site for a permanent army post in the Indian country.[33]

The similarities between Calhoun's plans and Long's earlier recommendations are many, and certainly the secretary knew of the major's reports. Long was the only topographical engineer doing fortifications work and exploring along the northern frontier, and he cautioned his superiors repeatedly that the Indians retained strong ties with the British. Even if Stephen Long's letters and reports did not provide the specific ideas that evolved into the Yellowstone Expedition, they at least lent supporting evidence to existing fears of continuing British dominance in the Northwest. In this way Stephen Long's work supported Calhoun's ambition to extend American control up the Mississippi and Missouri river valleys to the edge of Canada and west to the Rocky Mountains.

Organizing the Scientific Expedition, 1818-1819

When Stephen Long returned to Washington during the summer of 1818, he noticed an extra urgency among the War Department clerks. Their activity resulted from the plans of newly appointed Secretary of War John C. Calhoun to have American troops occupy a position at the mouth of the Yellowstone River. This stream joined the Missouri near the present boundary between North Dakota and Montana, deep within the area thought to be controlled by British and Canadian fur traders. Calhoun wanted United States troops to end this foreign influence and his plan was a logical outgrowth of American fears, interest, and activity along what was then called the northwestern frontier.

Ever since most of the northern tribes had joined the British against the United States during the War of 1812, frontier newspaper editors had clamored for protection from Indian attacks. At the same time, American fur traders pressed for government assistance in ridding the fur trade of their British and Canadian competitors. Continuing intertribal warfare also kept some frontier areas in a state of turmoil, making trade, travel, and settlement unsafe. For these reasons, the United States government had decided to take steps to end foreign influence along the northern frontier and to pacify the Indians.[1] Stephen Long's previous assignments in the Northwest had been a part of the limited American effort to do just that. Now, under Calhoun's direction, actions to reassert national dominance in the upper Mississippi and Missouri valleys became a major part of the Monroe administration's western and Indian policies.

While Long worked on his reports during the winter months of 1817-18, Secretary Calhoun had taken the first steps to put his project into motion. On March 16, 1818, he ordered General Smith to prepare troops to ascend the Missouri River as far as the Yellowstone River. Because of this original goal, the resulting military operations came to be called the Yellowstone Expedition. This name, however, soon ceased to describe either the goal or the activity, and even as he wrote Smith, Calhoun realized that the troops could not travel to the Yellowstone that same year. Instead, he suggested that they halt and build an intermediate post at the Mandan Villages in North Dakota or even farther downstream at the Council Bluffs in Nebraska.[2]

By October, 1818, the secretary expanded his original concept of a single fort deep within the Indian country. He added two other military installations to meet his objectives: one at the junction of the Mississippi and St. Peter's rivers and the other at the mouth of the St. Croix. Once built, these forts, in addition to those already occupied or planned, would form a line of army posts stretching from Green Bay in the east to the Yellowstone in the west. Working from these locations, Calhoun expected that army officers and Indian Office personnel would expel foreign traders and pacify the Indians.[3]

To build these forts, several expeditions had to be organized. Thus, the Yellowstone Expedition faded from view, except to some newspaper editors who were apparently captivated by its romantic-sounding name. In its place two new troop movements emerged: the Missouri Expedition, commanded by Colonel Henry Atkinson; and the Mississippi Expedition, commanded by Colonel Henry Leavenworth. During 1819, federal officials expected these two movements to get at least 1,000 troops up those two rivers.[4]

The large-scale War Department effort to move hundreds of American troops to the northwestern frontier prompted Stephen Long to resubmit his earlier proposals for a topographical and scientific expedition to that same region. In March, 1817, he had written to President-Elect James Monroe, proposing to explore the western rivers and the Great Lakes. Long claimed that such explorations were needed to overcome the "extreme dearth of information" about that frontier, and suggested using a specially designed steamboat to explore and map the northern waterways. With a craft forty feet long, seven feet wide, drawing about fourteen inches of water, and costing about $5,000, he claimed it would be possible to navigate the major tributaries of the Mississippi, "meander their courses, and take the Latitude and Longitude of their mouths and heades [*sic*] of navigations." Then, with characteristic over-optimism, Long stated that he could steam up the Illinois River and enter the Great Lakes during the spring high-water season. Once there, he proposed to explore the coasts, islands, and streams entering the lakes—all by steamboat. Working from such a craft, he claimed, "a correct plan of the country may be made, with less trouble and expense, probably, than by any other method that would be devised."[5] Although Monroe had been concerned about western defense when he served as secretary of war some years earlier, as the newly inaugurated president he failed to answer or even acknowledge Long's letter.

Despite this, the major did not abandon his idea of using a steamboat for frontier exploration. In the late summer of 1817, he had discussed the ideas with his superior, General Smith. Smith suggested that he ask for a vessel large enough to carry at least a company of soldiers, but Long disagreed. A boat that size was too large and heavy for navigation on the small western rivers. During October of that year Long had repeated his plan in a letter to Chief Engineer Joseph Swift and at the same time expressed his doubts about further exploration. General Andrew Jackson's "rigid adherence to military rule," he noted, would probably prevent him from getting the kind of independent command he thought necessary for successful exploration.[6]

There is no record of Swift's reply, but a few months later, in February, 1818, Long resubmitted his proposal for water-borne exploration to General Smith. He in turn forwarded the plan to Secretary of War Calhoun with a recommendation supporting the idea. When there was no immediate response, General Smith wrote Calhoun a second time, praising Long as "the most skillful, industrious and enterprising officer I have known" in the Engineers.[7] What influence, if any, this note had on Calhoun's thinking about western exploration is unknown. Nevertheless, Long's plan reached the War Department at a time when the secretary was busy organizing troop movements into the Northwest.

In June, 1818, Long traveled to Washington to discuss his frontier assignments in person before returning to Engineer Headquarters in New York. There he had a chance to present his ideas directly to Calhoun. Describing what he thought should be done and how he proposed to accomplish it, Long outlined the size and cost of the steamboat; listed what books, instruments, and armaments would be needed; and even discussed the size of crew needed. Envisioning a lengthy expedition, Long suggested that members of the party enlist for four years. Then, although he admitted that the plan seemed ambitious, he cautioned that it might be "viewed as too limited rather than too comprehensive." Calhoun wasted no time in accepting this latest proposal. The same day that he received Long's letter, he approved the plan and authorized the major to superintend construction of the steamboat he had described.[8]

Stephen Long was not the only army officer to use such a vessel. As early as December, 1814, Andrew Jackson had moved munitions and supplies by steamboat at New Orleans. Also, within a few months after Long started his project,

Quartermaster General Thomas Jesup let a contract for transporting the troops and supplies of the Missouri Expedition by steamer.[9] By that time, enthusiasm for steamboats had spread rapidly throughout the army and in February, 1819, Colonel Henry Atkinson suggested using such craft to move the Sixth Infantry from Pittsburgh down the Ohio River to St. Louis. These boats, he claimed, would cost less, be faster, and would "save all that fatigue & indisposition incedential [*sic*] to troops who have to be on the water in Barges for several months."[10] From these examples it seems clear that Long's interest in steamboat travel was not unusual, nor were his expectations unduly optimistic by existing standards. That Americans of all positions might have overestimated the capabilities of steamboats and the benefits coming from their use seems not to have been considered.

The decision to use steamers on the Missouri River came from Calhoun's obsession with impressing the Indians with American strength. This objective was legitimate, but the means used to accomplish it proved faulty. Steamboats would impress the Indians only if they could navigate the western rivers successfully. The War Department, however, had little evidence that they could. In fact, while the decision to use them was being made, no steam-driven craft had even attempted to navigate the Missouri River. Nevertheless, Calhoun foolishly based the success of both the Missouri and Scientific expeditions and the prestige of the United States Government upon an unproved technological device. This was a mistake, because the steamers proved unable to navigate the Missouri, and their inability to do so certainly limited their impact upon the Indians.

Such problems lay in the future, however, and the day after Calhoun accepted Long's proposal to use a steamboat for frontier exploration, the Engineer Department notified the would-be explorer of the decision. He was to go to the Allegheny Arsenal, located on the bank of the Allegheny River about two miles above Pittsburgh.[11] As the upriver terminal for most steamboat traffic on the Ohio River, Pittsburgh received hundreds of other river craft as well. This heavy traffic and the demand for building and repairing boats of all types had attracted boatwrights and steam engine mechanics to the city. Their presence seemed to make the nearby arsenal the ideal place for Long to construct his vessel.

When he first proposed a steam-propelled craft for exploring the shallow western rivers, Long estimated its dimensions as forty feet long and seven feet wide. He hoped that it would need only fourteen inches of water for navigation. This was not to be, because by late 1818 the scope and size of his forthcoming expedition had grown. As a result, the craft he designed was almost twice his original estimate. It grew to seventy-five feet in length and thirteen feet in width. Then, having increased the size and weight, he had to enlarge the keel as well. Instead of drawing fourteen inches of water, the craft, Long hoped, would float in nineteen inches. This latter figure came either from his optimism or described the boat prior to loading the equipment, supplies, and crew, because when completed, the craft needed two-and-a-half feet of water for navigation.[12]

The *Western Engineer*, as Long named the steamer, included several important technological innovations. Although there is some question about whether or not it was the first stern-wheeler built in the United States, it was indeed the first steamboat to have the paddle wheels entirely aft of the hull. This allowed the builders to maintain a reasonably narrow beam and at the same time afforded some protection for the buckets or paddles from damage by snags and floating debris. A second new device was the cam cutoff that used a valve to regulate the flow of steam from the boiler into the engine cylinder. This allowed the engineer to use full or partial power, depending on the navigational conditions.[13]

In addition to designing the new craft, Long had to supervise all aspects of the construction, hire workmen, and even order parts and material. During the autumn of 1818, he gathered at least fifty different items—from the obvious, such as lumber and engine parts, to whale oil for the lanterns. Even with this personal attention to each detail, delays in construction occurred. For example, seasoned wood was scarce at Pittsburgh, and after unsuccessful efforts to get enough of this lumber, it became necessary to complete the *Western Engineer* with much "green" timber. This warped as it dried, causing leaking and related problems. In spite of such delays and the difficulty of hiring competent workers at the wages he was authorized to pay, by late 1818 Long expected the boat to be completed by the next March.[14] As usual, his optimism outran his performance.

From the day he submitted his plan for western exploration to Secretary Calhoun, Stephen Long anticipated that the expedition would serve both military and scientific purposes. Others outside of the government hoped that this would be the case, too. In fact, even before Long's plan had been approved, the American Philosophical Society of Philadelphia had urged that the forthcoming Yellowstone Expedition include scientists among its members. Both Thomas Say and Thomas Nuttall, members of that organization, wanted to join the explorers and the society appointed a committee to achieve that goal. On August 21, 1818, one member of the committee wrote to Thomas Jefferson asking him to use his "influence with Mr. [President James] Monroe to send" the two men as zoologist and botanist with any army movement into the Northwest.[15]

It is unclear what President Monroe or Secretary of War Calhoun thought of such suggestions at first, but by October, 1818, *Niles Register* reported that Long's group would include men it described as "scientific characters."[16] The news story was premature and it was not until December, 1818, that Calhoun wrote that he hoped the expedition would enlarge general knowledge about the West, as well as gather military and geographic information. Then he authorized Long to recruit scientists and to forward applications from

WESTERN ENGINEER by Titian R. Peale. *Courtesy American Philosophical Society.*

"such characters" to Washington. The secretary noted that he had received letters of inquiry from several would-be explorers, and asked what the major wanted to do about these individuals.[17]

Long replied promptly, submitting the names of three men who had been recommended by friends in Philadelphia. That city stood as the intellectual capital of the nation, and the faculty of the University of Pennsylvania, as well as the members of the American Philosophical Society and the other scholarly groups there, took an active interest in the forthcoming expedition. Only four years earlier when

Stephen Long had lived in Germantown, less than ten miles from Philadelphia, he had met many of these men. Therefore, it was natural that he turned to them now for advice and nominations for his expedition. Only a week after Calhoun requested nominees, Long chose Thomas Say as zoologist, Dr. William Baldwin as botanist, and Dr. John Torrey as geologist. He had met and liked Titian Peale, one of those who had written directly to Calhoun, but made no commitment about him at this time.[18] Of these men, two came from Philadelphia and the other two had been recommended by friends there and in New York City.

There seems to have been little question about Stephen Long's ability to organize and lead a scientific expedition. Although he lacked a public reputation, this proved no hindrance because the nation's military, engineering, and scientific leaders knew of his work and considered it competent. Contemporary newspapers labeled him as "well qualified for the command," and as "an intelligent and perservering man. . .an excellent engineer." Dr. William Baldwin, the expedition botanist and surgeon, wrote a friend after he learned that Long would command the expedition that "with this gentleman I am acquainted; and a better [man] could not perhaps be selected."[19]

Some scientists remained skeptical, particularly when Long received no authorization to offer participants a salary. In fact, the major acted as if this were a minor matter, even though he would draw his regular salary as an officer. Replying to one query about this matter, he wrote that the volunteers would have to serve "without any further assurance of being remunerated, than that of having their board, passage, &c. . .afforded them, free of expense." Not only did the major propose that the scientists labor without pay, but he noted that the expedition would last from three to five years. The prospect of serving without compensation on an expedition lasting that long dimmed the enthusiasm of some. For example, Dr. John Torrey, noted New York botanist and physician, lost interest because "no compensation [would] be allowed the naturalists," and because the scientists would have to surrender their notes and papers to the government "who are to have the entire disposal of them."[20]

In addition to the lack of pay, the itinerary Long outlined for the first year of the expedition was enough to frighten all but the most reckless. He wanted to ascend the Missouri River to the Platte, explore that stream, then continue up the Missouri to the Yellowstone, where he expected to arrive before the troops of the Missouri Expedition. Then he planned to explore the Yellowstone, examine the Missouri up to the Great Falls in eastern Montana, and, finally, explore as many of the smaller tributary streams as possible before winter.[21] If carried out, this plan would take the scientists hundreds of miles into the Indian country and might well bring them into contact with tribes openly hostile to all United States citizens.

Long avoided a potential problem—that of having political favorites forced upon him—when Calhoun allowed him to pick the members of his party. He chose well. In recruiting he tried to attract prominent men who had made significant contributions to their fields. Although not always successful in getting his first choice, the staff Long gathered was a good one. Early-nineteenth-century scientists devoted most of their time to gathering, identifying, and classifying items, and frequently had little formal education in their disciplines. By present standards, these pioneer American scientists appear to have been amateurish and ill-equipped for their parts in the expedition. By the standards of their own day, however, the men comprised as competent a group as could have been assembled.

At a time when few Americans had more than a rudimentary education, the exploring party included men with substantial education, travel, and previous scientific experience to their credit. Of the nine scientists and army officers on the expedition, the educational achievements of six are known. Four had earned college or university degrees, one had taken university work but was too young to have finished, and only one had no higher education. Six of the men had extensive travel experience and of these, four had participated in other scientific or topographical expeditions. The ages of the seven explorers for whom birth data are available ranged from nineteen to forty-one, with an average or mean age of twenty-seven-and-a-half years.[22] These somewhat incomplete figures indicate a relatively high level of accomplishment and support the contention that Long gathered an able and experienced party, as may be seen in the following sketches.

Dr. William Baldwin, Long's first choice for the positions of surgeon and botanist, was among the most well-known scientists of the day. In fact, after sifting through the applications of several "gentlemen of Science," the major wrote Calhoun that according "to the best information I can obtain, [Baldwin] stands unrivalled" among the nation's botanists.[23] Born in 1779, the Pennsylvania Quaker attended a series of medical lectures given at the University of Pennsylvania and, in 1805, sailed as the surgeon aboard an American merchant ship bound for Canton and Wampoa. During that voyage he studied the diseases prevalent among the American sailors at Wampoa. After the voyage he returned to the university, where he submitted his findings, and in 1807 received his medical degree.

While a student, Baldwin became interested in botany, which he studied whenever he had time. After his graduation, the young physician moved to Wilmington where he practiced medicine and continued his botanical research. Suffering from "an hereditary predisposition to Pulmonary Consumption," from which all of his family died, he moved to Savannah, Georgia, in 1811. The mild southern weather failed to relieve his sickness, but it did allow more opportunity to gather botanical specimens. In 1817, he traveled to South America aboard the U.S.S. *Congress* as a member of a fact-finding mission, and the next year he returned to practice medicine. Baldwin had moved south to Georgia to regain good health, but did not meet with success. Now he applied for membership in the Scientific Expedition, hoping that a move west might help. Instead, living aboard the damp and leaky *Western Engineer* did more harm than good. Unfortunately for the expedition, his continuing sickness limited his research and contributions and he died of tuberculosis at Franklin, Missouri, during the summer of 1819. Nevertheless, when he applied for the position as botanist, the forty-one-year-old Baldwin was one of the most respected scientists in the country.[24]

When Long chose Baldwin as botanist he lost whatever chance he might have had to persuade Dr. John Torrey, a young New York physician, to join the expedition. Although only twenty-two years old, Torrey held an M.D. degree from the New York College of Physicians and Surgeons and was already an avid mineralogist and botanist. His later scientific accomplishments placed him among the most prominent men of science in America during the first half of the nineteenth century, and he certainly would have added luster to the group. Unfortunately, he and Long could not agree about which position the doctor should hold. This happened because Long did not learn of Torrey's interest until after he had appointed Baldwin to the post of botanist. Hoping to convince Torrey to join anyway, the major offered him the position of geologist, but the doctor declined. In his case, Long's assertion that the explorers would have to serve without pay cooled Torrey's ardor, and when he could not have the position he wanted, Torrey withdrew his inquiry. Nevertheless, when he learned of Baldwin's death, Torrey agreed to publish the botanical findings of the expedition and cooperated in several related matters during the next few years.[25]

When Torrey declined to serve as geologist, Long chose Augustus E. Jessup for the job. A native of Massachusetts, the twenty-nine-year-old Jessup was a wealthy Philadelphia merchant with an active interest in mineralogy and geology. Although an amateur, his sophisticated work received attention in 1818 when the Philadelphia Academy of Natural Sciences elected him to membership. He remained with the expedition only during the first year, but later assisted the expedition zoologist in gathering fossils and preparing a book on entomology.[26]

As zoologist for the expedition, Long appointed Thomas Say, a Philadelphia apothecary. A man of little formal education, Say nevertheless became a giant in the early American scientific community. Related to William Bartram, the famous botanist, Say's interest in animal and insect life brought him into the group that founded the Philadelphia Academy of Natural Sciences in 1812. He worked to make the academy a scientific group rather than a social one, and with several others Say helped start the *Journal of the Academy of Natural Sciences* in 1817. That same year he published the first volume of *American Entomology*. That winter he traveled to the Georgia and Florida coastal region as one of four members of a small scientific party led and financed by William McClure. The tiny group traveled to Savannah, from there to the Sea Islands, and then up the St. Mary's River into Spanish Florida. Having gathered a few specimens, they learned that Indian hostilities made it unwise to penetrate further, so they returned to Philadelphia in April, 1818. This premature return disappointed Say because he had missed many of the species he wanted to observe. When he learned of Long's expedition, Say applied for membership, and after participating during 1819 and 1820, returned east to become curator of the American Philosophical Society in Philadelphia and professor of natural history at the University of Pennsylvania. In 1823, he accompanied Long again, this time on the expedition up the Mississippi. Between expeditions and while teaching at Pennsylvania, Say continued work on his *American Ento-*

mology, and from 1824 to 1828, published the last two volumes of that study. Then he moved west to New Harmony, Indiana, where he lived until his death in 1843.[27] From this résumé of his career, it appears that Say, along with Dr. Baldwin, was probably the most qualified scientist to serve with the expedition.

To assist the scientists in gathering and preparing specimens and to sketch what they gathered, nineteen-year-old Titian Peale received the appointment as assistant naturalist. The youngest son of Charles Willson Peale, Philadelphia artist and museum proprietor, Peale worked in the family museum, at the time the most comprehensive in the nation. It included hundreds of mounted mammals, birds, reptiles, and fishes, as well as "thousands of insects, shells, and other invertebrates. . . ." Competently prepared displays showed visitors habitat settings that combined plants, animals, minerals, and hundreds of oil paintings by the Peales. The exhibits were so well done that natural history classes from the University of Pennsylvania often met at the museum to study specimens. There Titian Peale got his introduction to the natural history of North America.[28] He learned taxidermy, practiced drawing, and attended classes at the University of Pennsylvania. In 1817, he left Philadelphia to take part in the previously mentioned McClure expedition to Georgia. This adventure proved an exhilarating experience because the party wandered through forests and swamps; collected Indian artifacts, birds, animals, and insects; hunted for its food; and even shot alligators. When the collectors returned home, Peale's father noted that he "not only preserves Animals with neatness but is also clever in drawing and is an indefatigible [*sic*] collector." As a result of this journey, Peale gained frontier experience to temper his curiosity and youthful enthusiasm. During the two years he participated in the Scientific Expedition, he kept a useful diary, gathered and prepared specimens, and made dozens of drawings and sketches, many of which are still extant. Most of Peale's fame, however, came from his later work. In 1820, he became assistant manger of the family museum in Philadelphia. Later, he traveled to Florida a second time to collect specimens, drew the plates for Thomas Say's books on insects, traveled to South America, and served as a member of the John Wilkes Expedition from 1838 to 1842.[29]

Long wanted an artist to gather a pictorial record of the region through which the explorers would pass, and for this post he chose Samuel Seymour, also from Philadelphia. Unlike the other members of the party, little is known about Seymour. An emigrant from Great Britain, the painter and engraver was an associate of Thomas Sully and other artists in Philadelphia. Despite Seymour's relative historical obscurity, Long liked his work. On the expedition he was to sketch landscape scenes and to make portraits of Indians the explorers met.[30] The artist and Long appear to have liked each other, and in 1823, Seymour accompanied the major on his last expedition.

In addition to these "scientific gentlemen," about whom the newspapers made frequent comments, Long filled the ranks of his party with two other army officers and a West Point cadet. As the official journalist for the expedition he chose Captain (brevet major) Thomas Biddle, Jr., a member of the famous Philadelphia Biddle family. The captain had begun his army career as an infantry captain in 1812 but soon transferred to the artillery. During the War of 1812, he was breveted as a major for distinguished service at Fort Erie, but during the lull in army activity following the war he became bored. When he learned of Long's expedition, he asked for permission to accompany it. Major Biddle, as he was called by the participants, soon came to regret his decision, because he and Long quarrelled bitterly several times. After visiting an Indian village with some of the scientists, Biddle and the party were robbed by a band of Pawnee warriors. The major claimed that this "defeat" would hurt his army career if he stayed with the expedition, so he resigned in mid-1819 to join the staff of Colonel Henry Atkinson. He remained in the army, serving as a paymaster, and died in 1831 during a duel with Congressman Spencer Petis on Bloody Island near St. Louis.[31]

To help with the topographic duties of the expedition, Long requested the services of two young men. Lieutenant James D. Graham, a twenty-year-old artillery officer and West Point graduate, was the first of these. He assisted with running the *Western Engineer*, and when the party traveled overland in June, 1820, he remained in command of the steamer. Graham served a long and varied career in the Topographical Engineer Corps and participated in several coastal and boundary surveys.[32] William Swift, a nineteen-year-old West Point cadet, was the second assistant topographer. Swift had not completed his studies at the Military Academy, but through the influence of his brother, General Joseph Swift, was able to retain his class position and to graduate on time. The youngest of the officers and scientists, Swift was to prepare a map of the explored territory. While traveling on the Missouri on July 1, 1819, Swift graduated from the academy with his class and became a second lieutenant. Later, he, too, spent many years as a military and civilian engineer working on coastal surveys.[33]

Attached informally to the group but not actually a member of the exploring party was Major Benjamin O'Fallon, the Indian agent for the Missouri River tribes. Much of the time he preceded the explorers to assure the Indians that the troops and scientists coming into their country were friends and came in peace.[34]

To do much of the manual labor and afford protection, Long took an escort of one sergeant and eight privates. He hired a "steam engineer" to operate the *Western Engineer*, but this person was only a mechanic because experienced steamboat engineers demanded sixty to eighty dollars a month, far more than the government would pay. The remainder of the crew consisted of a pilot, clerk, carpenter, and two boys.[35] Thus the party, excluding O'Fallon, numbered twenty-four people.

As the winter of 1818-19 slipped past, numerous tasks occupied Long's time. He continued to supervise the construction, but also had to gather equipment, books, and maps for use the next spring. Because of his difficulties with using inferior instruments in the past, he was determined to get high-quality ones for the expedition. He complained about the poor equipment to General Smith, and the general recommended that Long be allowed to buy what he needed. Actually, he had purchased some survey and navigational instruments prior to traveling west to Pittsburgh, but had not gotten everything he wanted. When the expedition left Pittsburgh some months later, he had gathered forty items, including a hygrometer, a measuring chain for survey work, a microscope, a theodolite, a glass horizon, a sea sextant, a watch, and several cases of "mathematical instruments." To supplement these and to provide reference material for the expedition personnel, Long also gathered numerous books that he described as "the works of a variety of Authors concerning the Western Country."[36]

When he first began to design the steamboat, Long had anticipated a small command. As the size of his party grew, he revised and enlarged the planned vessel, all of which took extra time. Other delays ensued, some unrelated to his military duties. While recruiting scientists and supervising the building of the *Western Engineer*, Long found time to court and marry Martha Hodgkins of Philadelphia. The wedding took place on March 3, 1819, and certainly did nothing to speed progress on the boat.[37]

Nevertheless, a few weeks later all seemed ready, and, on March 26, the boatwrights launched the steamer. "She entered the watery element in the most graceful manner under a national salute," a local editor noted. What the newsman failed to mention was that Long's calculations had failed to allow for the increased number of passengers. Their extra weight lowered the craft so far into the water that the paddle wheels could not turn properly. In addition, the new machinery was stiff and the crew had difficulty getting good fuel. Therefore, during the rest of March and all of April, the workers labored to alter and adjust the machinery. As the weeks passed with little apparent progress, Long apologized to Calhoun. Accepting responsibility for the delays, he wrote, "my ignorance of the time requisite for the construction of a Steam boat and my inexperience in that business" are to blame.[38]

While Long struggled with these difficulties, Secretary Calhoun issued an extensive set of orders for the explorers. These specific instructions demonstrate Calhoun's widened range of interests and yet show that questions of military activity, Indian affairs, the fur trade, and transportation held the top priorities. The secretary ordered the party to explore the region between the Mississippi River and the Rocky Mountains. "You will first explore the Missouri and its principle [sic] branches," he wrote, "and then in succession Red river, Arkansas and Mississippi above the mouth of the Missouri. . . ." Throughout the expedition, the explorers were to "permit nothing worthy of notice to escape" their attention. They had to locate the forty-ninth parallel, note soil, topography, vegetation, animal life, and mineral deposits, and record the latitude and longitude of prominent geographic features. Repeating his earlier warnings that they should exercise care when dealing with the Indians, Calhoun directed them to study the size, culture, and land claims of each tribe. As if all of this were not enough to keep them occupied, he suggested that Long re-read President Jefferson's instructions to Meriwether Lewis prior to the Lewis and Clark expedition in 1804. A few days later, Calhoun asked the American Philosophical Society for topics on which the scientists might gather data and for other questions and guides that might help their work.[39]

Soon after this flood of orders arrived, the *Western*

Engineer was ready for a second launching. On April 30, 1819, the boat headed out into the waters of the Allegheny again, but with little more success than at its first trial four weeks earlier. It soon ran aground on a sandbar, and when the crew tried to dislodge the boat, they found a defect in an engine cylinder and a leak in one of the boilers. Three days later, at 4:00 P.M., the steamer headed away from the arsenal dock, cheered by "great numbers of spectators" who lined the riverbanks to watch. The crew fired a twenty-two-gun salute that workers at the arsenal answered, and then sent their craft downstream to Pittsburgh. They remained overnight so that Long could confer with Oliver Evans, one of the developers of steamboats at Pittsburgh. While the designers compared notes, the crew continued making necessary minor adjustments in the machinery. On May 5, 1819, they completed the last-minute alterations, loaded their provisions, and began the journey down the Ohio River.[40]

The Scientific Expedition, 1819

At 4:30 P.M. on May 5, 1819, Stephen Long ordered the *Western Engineer* from her berth, and the vessel steamed away from the "gloomy repulsiveness" of Pittsburgh out into the Ohio River current.[1] Elated for the chance to follow some of the route traveled by Lewis and Clark with a well-equipped group of scientists, Long was to encounter little but disappointment, frustration, and criticism during the summer voyage west. The Scientific Expedition included both promising and experienced members of the American scientific community. It enjoyed the enthusiastic support of the Monroe administration, particularly of Secretary of War John C. Calhoun. And it received much favorable publicity in the nation's newspapers. Yet, the popular accounts of the expedition created unrealistic expectations of what might be achieved, and the resulting over-optimism made the real accomplishments of the scientists seem minor when they were recognized at all. During 1819, a combination of factors, usually beyond their control, limited the explorers to less than six months' work and curtailed the amount of data they could gather. Therefore, many contemporaries assumed that the Scientific Expedition had failed. Certainly, the explorers made no startling geographic discoveries, but they did obtain much new information about the lower Missouri Valley.

The scientists and crew of the *Western Engineer*, reportedly "in excellent spirits," except for the ailing Dr.

Baldwin, rode their novel-appearing steamer with enthusiasm. Designed to impress the Indians, as well as to navigate on the shallow western streams, the vessel appeared to ride on the back of a large water serpent. At the bow a black, reptilian head with a red mouth and protruding tongue belched smoke and steam from gaping jaws. To further the serpentine illusion, the engine and all other machinery rested below decks or out of sight, and even the paddle wheels had covers over them. "From under the boat, at its stern, issues a stream of foaming water," reported a contemporary. "To the eye of ignorance, the illusion is complete, that a monster of the deep carried her on his back, smoking with fatigue, and lashing the waves with violent exertion."[2]

From the mast flew a flag designed especially for the expedition. It portrayed a white man and an Indian shaking hands before a background of a sword and a calumet, or peace pipe. This demonstrated Secretary Calhoun's hope that the explorers would have friendly relations with the Indians. In addition, the flag provided a visible symbol to any red men who might be uncertain about the scientists' motives for entering the Missouri Valley. Although everyone associated with the expedition anticipated peaceful dealings with the Indians, Long equipped the steamer with one brass four-pounder mounted at the bow, four smaller howitzers—two on swivels and two on field carriages—and a bulletproof housing on deck for the steersman. Small arms and personal weapons included:

> two wall pieces carrying four ounce balls; twelve muskets, six rifles, and several fowling pieces, besides an air gun, twelve sabres, pistols and a quantity of private arms of various sorts and a great sufficiency of ammunition of all kinds. . . .[3]

Clearly, this amount of firearms was unnecessary for hunting or gathering specimens and had been taken for personal defense in case of attack.

As the *Western Engineer* steamed down the Ohio in the late afternoon of May 5, a spirit of excitement and adventure gripped the passengers and crew. Farmers and other onlookers stopped along the riverbank to gawk and wave as the strange craft slid past, spouting smoke from the bow and trailing foam from the stern. Steaming rapidly between banks lined with lush vegetation and occasional farms, the explorers met the first riverboat they had seen since leaving Pittsburgh fourteen miles upstream. The other steamer lay stranded on a sandbar in the river, but its crew exchanged salutes with the scientists, as was the river custom.[4] Long and his party appear to have been undismayed by seeing a steamer aground, and little did they realize that they too would suffer the same indignity many times before the end of their summer journey.

Continuing downstream into a steady head wind, the *Western Engineer* carried the explorers south and west. Either Major Long had decided to travel as far as possible each day or else there were few places to stop for fuel along the upper Ohio. In either case, the party continued downriver until 2:00 A.M., when they reached Steubenvile, Ohio, about seventy miles from Pittsburgh. While the crew loaded wood aboard the craft, the scientists wandered around the town and crossed the river into Virginia. Then, after an hour-long thunderstorm, they renewed their journey.[5] Each time they passed a town or another riverboat, the crew fired a salute to announce their presence and perhaps to break the monotony.

Arriving at Marietta, Ohio, at 4:00 A.M. the next day, Long ordered a stop for more fuel. They left that city at 11:00 A.M., an indication of how much time it took to load fuel aboard these early riverboats. Traveling at night proved only slightly more hazardous than during the daylight hours, at least on this first portion of the trip. During the night of May 8, a severe thunderstorm and strong wind drove the vessel ashore, but artist Titian Peale reported that the loss of the flagstaff and a lantern hanging from it was the only damage.[6]

In late evening, May 9, the steamer arrived at Cincinnati,

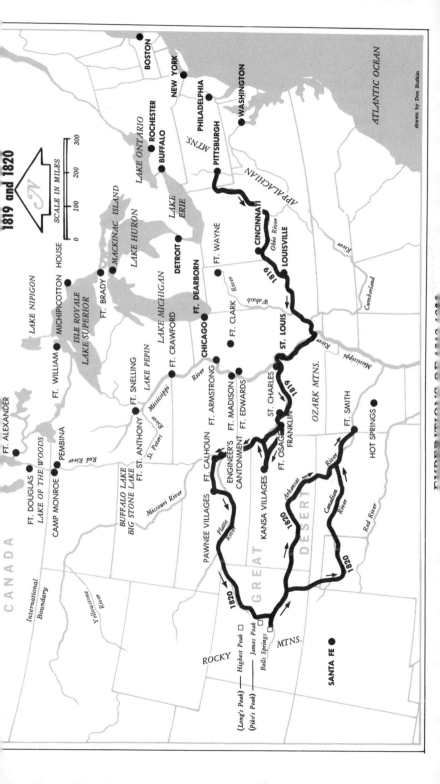

EXPEDITIONS OF 1819-1820

1819 and 1820

SCALE IN MILES

0   100   200   300

drawn by Don Bufkin

CANADA

International Boundary

ATLANTIC OCEAN

APPALACHIAN MTNS.

GREAT DESERT

ROCKY MTNS.

OZARK MTNS.

BOSTON
NEW YORK
PHILADELPHIA
WASHINGTON
ROCHESTER
BUFFALO
PITTSBURGH
CINCINNATI
LOUISVILLE
DETROIT
FT. DEARBORN
FT. WAYNE
CHICAGO
FT. CLARK
ST. LOUIS
ST. CHARLES
FRANKLIN
FT. OSAGE
FT. SMITH
HOT SPRINGS
SANTA FE
FT. ARMSTRONG
FT. MADISON
FT. EDWARDS
FT. CALHOUN
ENGINEER'S CANTONMENT
PAWNEE VILLAGES
KANSA VILLAGES
FT. CRAWFORD
FT. SNELLING
FT. ST. ANTHONY
PEMBINA
CAMP MONROE
FT. DOUGLAS
FT. ALEXANDER
FT. WILLIAM
MICHIPICOTTON HOUSE
FT. BRADY
MACKINAC ISLAND

LAKE SUPERIOR
LAKE NIPIGON
ISLE ROYALE
LAKE HURON
LAKE MICHIGAN
LAKE ERIE
LAKE ONTARIO
LAKE PEPIN
BUFFALO LAKE
BIG STONE LAKE
LAKE OF THE WOODS

Mississippi River
Missouri River
Yellowstone River
Red River
St. Peters R.
Wabash River
Ohio River
Cumberland River
Platte River
Arkansas River
Canadian River
Red River

(Long's Peak) — Highest Peak
(Pike's Peak) — James Peak
Bell's Springs

1819
1820

one of the fastest-growing cities in the nation. Here extensive docks and repair facilities existed, and Long decided that the party should stop for several days to have "some alterations in the machinery of the boat" made. It is not certain what problems had arisen, and except for Titian Peale's remark about storm damage, none of the narratives describing the trip noted any specific trouble. On the other hand, Dr. Baldwin complained later that the inadequate machinery had caused all of the early downriver stops. Whether this was true or not, the steamboat had not performed as Long expected. He informed Secretary Calhoun that defects in the machinery "required rectification before it could be deemed prudent to venture upon the rapid current of the Missouri."[7] Long obviously recognized the potential difficulties ahead, yet he remained confident that the *Western Engineer* could navigate the Missouri once adjustments had been completed.

The stop at Cincinnati had a second purpose. Dr. Baldwin had gotten so sick that he needed a few days of rest on shore. It was unfortunate that the sickly surgeon had become a member of the expedition in the first place. Baldwin's existence aboard the steamboat must have been wretched. Suffering from tuberculosis, he needed warm, dry quarters. The vessel, however, built of green timber, failed to provide these. It was "so leaky and Wet," Baldwin complained, "that we have not a dry locker for our clothes." His health worsened gradually, and in spite of occasional days of good spirits and increased energy, he grumbled that it took all his strength merely "to crawl on shore" at each stop.[8] As a result, he was unable to perform his duties as botanist and had to ask the other scientists to do them. Not only did this cause resentment and lower morale, but it limited the botanical achievements of the expedition as well. Had a healthy man served as botanist, the explorers could have avoided the delays caused by Baldwin's sickness, and the other investigators could have spent more time doing their own work, rather than helping him.

After a nine-day halt, the last three spent waiting for Baldwin to get well enough to resume travel, the party left Cincinnati. Long tried to regain some of the lost time by traveling all night, so they reached Louisville, about 120 miles downriver, the next day. Here they expected to meet Major Benjamin O'Fallon, the Indian agent who was to accompany them west. Apparently the agent had tired of waiting for the explorers because he had left for St. Louis before they got to Louisville. Continuing mechanical trouble kept the steamer there another four days. Then, once they passed through the rapids known as the "Indian Chute" without incident, they proceeded under a full head of steam at ten miles an hour. This was probably the fastest speed for the boat on the entire expedition, but the pace was short-lived. At the mouth of the Wabash, the engine failed and the steamer had to drift with the current for ten miles to Shawneetown. There, while Long searched frantically for parts and mechanics, the scientists tramped through nearby river bottom land gathering specimens.[9]

Two days passed before the engine was repaired, and on May 28 the *Western Engineer* continued down the river. After a few hours, however, the craft ran aground and the members of the party worked most of the afternoon to extricate it. Using ropes, poles, and the engine, they pushed and tugged, rocking the steamer loose only with the greatest difficulty. At Cave-in-Rock, a few miles below, they halted for fuel, then took the wrong channel of the river and so got stuck again. Finally, on May 30, 1819, Major Long's party reached the mouth of the Ohio, ending the downstream leg of their voyage.[10]

Their progress from Pittsburgh to the Mississippi was slow: it took twenty-six days to cover that distance. True, extended delays at Cincinnati and Louisville accounted for much of that time, but continuing mechanical difficulties turned what should have been a brief and easy journey into a month-long struggle. The easiest part of the expedition was over. Both the

Mississippi and Missouri rivers presented far greater obstacles for Long's poorly designed craft than any encountered thus far. Although several of the explorers noted the differences between the quiet Ohio and the more turbulent Mississippi, if any of them worried that the boat might not be able to stem the latter stream, they kept such doubts to themselves.

After heading north, up the Mississippi, a few miles, Long halted to allow the scientists ashore to observe and collect specimens. The gloomy forests swarmed with mosquitoes, and hundreds of "enormous nettles" tore the explorers' clothing and stung their flesh. Discouraged, they fled back to the boat practically empty-handed. Continuing engine difficulties, however, caused further delay, and the dispirited group went ashore to hunt. Because of their limited skill as woodsmen, they made so much noise stumbling through the forest that they frightened all the game, and so they returned to the boat without any fresh meat.[11]

The *Western Engineer* made poor progress against the strong Mississippi current from the outset. Members of the party could keep pace with the boat easily when walking along the shore, so when they became bored or felt venturesome, they tramped the riverbanks. On June 5, a brisk tail wind encouraged Long to raise the auxiliary mast and use a sail for the first time. This helped but only briefly, because the vessel struck a submerged log that damaged the hull. For the next two days the crew and passengers worked to plug the leak. Instead of moving rapidly once the damage had been repaired, the craft struggled feebly against the current, so Long stopped to reexamine the engine. To his dismay, he found that mud and sand from the turgid river water had clogged the boilers. To remove this sludge it was necessary to extinguish the fires, cool the boilers, remove the head of each, and have a man crawl inside to scrape out the unwanted mud. Then the crew reassembled each boiler, restarted the furnaces, and waited for the steam pressure to rise. The hot, dirty process took nearly half a day to complete and cut potential speed drastically for the rest of the voyage.[12]

On June 9, the boat steamed up to the docks at St. Louis. The arrival of another steamer at the city usually would have created little excitement because forty-three other vessels had preceded it that year. Nevertheless, western interest in the so-called Yellowstone Expedition ran high, and as the scientific party neared the dock, salutes from shore batteries and guns aboard some of the docked steamboats roared a welcome. That same day, Long and his associates attended a public banquet given to honor the expedition leaders.[13]

For the next two weeks the exploring party stayed at St. Louis. Major Long conferred with his superiors there and took several days to survey proposed locations for military buildings in the city. While he worked on these routine duties, the naturalists hiked up the valleys of nearby creeks, examined geologic formations, and spent much time digging into Indian mounds for artifacts and skeletal remains. Titian Peale even had time to renew his acquaintance with an Osage Indian he had met earlier at Philadelphia while his brother Rembrandt painted the Indian's picture.[14]

Considering the slow pace of the *Western Engineer* on its journey from Pittsburgh, Long's two-week stop in St. Louis appears unwarranted. While there, however, the major seemed to have decided that he should not out-distance the Missouri Expedition, then preparing to bring troops up that stream, so there was no need to hurry. Continuing difficulties in getting supplies and adequate boats for that expedition stymied all efforts to get the troops moving up the river quickly. As a result, Colonel Atkinson, who led the Missouri Expedition, decided that the main body of troops would spend the 1819-20 winter at the Council Bluffs, about 600 miles up the Missouri.[15] By keeping pace with the large but slow-moving military expedition, the explorers cut their ambitious itinerary to a realistic length.

While the leaders of the Missouri Expedition quarreled with their contractor about missing supplies and slow steamboats, Long gathered his small party and at noon, June 21, the scientists left St. Louis. For a change, the *Western*

Engineer had no difficulty moving upstream against the powerful current, and that evening the explorers halted just below the mouth of the Missouri. The next morning they entered the Missouri. The craft churned ahead and with both relief and pride the scientists noted their ability to navigate on steam power alone. Progress remained slow, however, because their fuel burned badly and gave so little heat that the engineer could not keep the steam pressure high enough for rapid movement. The muddy water hid many sandbars, and twice that first day the craft grounded on such obstacles. As a result, the party traveled less than five miles before stopping at Belle Fontaine late in the afternoon.[16]

Difficulties similar to those encountered this first day on the Missouri continued to hinder the explorers' headway throughout the summer. For example, between Belle Fontaine and St. Charles, the first settlement of any size on the Missouri, the *Western Engineer* struggled against the current, dodged piles of driftwood, and grounded on sandbars. The chief obstacle to successful navigation, however, proved to be the silt-laden water of the stream. The vessel used river water, which clogged the boilers in fifteen hours. Every day or two the craft had to stop so that the crew could clean out the mud. After much grumbling about this disagreeable task, the crew members improvised a better method for removing the mud. Instead of stopping the engine and dismantling the boilers, they attached a hose to each boiler and, by using steam pressure, blew the sludge out through the tube. This innovation reduced the time it took to clean the boilers, but it failed to get rid of all the sand and mud. Consequently, the remaining grit wore some engine parts excessively and further reduced the effectiveness of the craft.[17]

Despite their ability to clean the engine faster, the party took one and a half days to travel the twenty-one miles to St. Charles. There, the realization that the steamer lacked sufficient power brought the explorers' growing frustrations into the open. Unlike Lewis and Clark, who had cooperated well, Long seemed unable to avoid frequent disputes with

Major Biddle. When they arrived at St. Charles, the two officers refused the speak to each other, and Biddle demanded a duel to settle the matter. Long ignored or rejected the challenge.[18]

At St. Charles, Long met Indian Agent Benjamin O'Fallon and his interpreter John Doughtery for the first time. O'Fallon was then the agent for the Pawnee, Oto, Missouri, and Omaha tribes of the upper Missouri region. Dougherty, an experienced frontiersman and trader, served as his deputy. These two men expected to accompany or precede the scientists up the Missouri that summer so that they could prevent difficulties with the Indians, and for a time they traveled aboard the steamer.[19]

Before leaving St. Charles, Long decided to send some of the scientists overland for several days so that they might have more time to carry out their tasks. When Thomas Say, Augustus Jessup, Samuel Seymour, and Titian Peale volunteered, the major appointed Say the leader and assigned the clerk, L. R. Kinney, to accompany them. Dressed in enlisted men's fatigue uniforms and leading a hastily purchased pack horse loaded "with a tent and blankets, and a few biscuits together with 2 canteens," early on the morning of May 26 the men trudged out of the city.[20] By sending some of the explorers overland, Long accomplished two goals. He lightened the load that his under-powered steamer had to carry, and, at the same time, he gave the scientists a chance to explore beyond the immediate vicinity of the river.

While the remainder of the scientific party struggled against the Missouri current in their undependable steamboat, Say's party encountered obstacles of its own. They suffered from a shortage of food and water, excessive heat, fatigue, and sickness on this first overland march. Hiking across prairie land dotted with bushes, the scientists looked in vain for a few shade trees under which they might escape the hot sun. After walking for ten miles, they drank their last water and for the rest of the afternoon trudged through the heat and dust without any. Then, when they stopped to hunt for water, the pack horse "took fright, threw his pack, and made off full speed toward St. Charles." Two of the party tracked the beast four miles before they overtook it, and then they succeeded only because other travelers had stopped the runaway.[21]

Later, the reunited but weary hikers stopped at a settler's cabin to buy food and water. Their bad luck continued, however, because the frontiersman refused to sell or give them anything. After much urging and with "apparent reluctance" and "a bad grace," he consented to give them some water. The explorers guessed that the fatigue uniforms that some of them wore caused this hostility and remarked that even enlisted men were "entitled to some respect." As they walked a half-mile to their camp, Mr. Jessup shot a hawk that, along with their biscuits and water, provided "a slight, but good supper."[22]

The next day brought no lessening of hardship. The men rose early and at sunrise, without any breakfast, set out across the prairie with only two canteens of water. By eleven o'clock they had gone nine miles and stopped at another frontier cabin. These settlers proved hospitable and gave the scientists water, buttermilk, and cornbread. After their morning-long fast, this meal made Mr. Say sick, so the party rested until late afternoon. That evening they camped near a small creek and "made supper on some squirrels, and larks," supplemented by more buttermilk and cornbread.[23]

The region through which the explorers passed now consisted of rolling prairie cut by small streams. Along the creek bottoms a heavy growth of trees and bushes sheltered turkeys, partridges, sandpipers, and many song birds. On the prairies, however, the party noted little wildlife, except to complain about a species of green-headed fly with such a painful bite that it drove the livestock nearly crazy and tormented daytime travelers. These flies caused an unexpected delay because when the men stopped for breakfast on June 28, the pests bit their pack horse, which ran off again. Leaving one man to guard the camp, the rest began an all-day search. At evening, exhausted and still without the horse, they rented one from a cooperative farmer and sent Mr. Kinney back toward St. Charles to continue the search. When he returned empty-handed the next morning, they decided to forget the horse and to hurry ahead so they would not miss the *Western Engineer*. Dividing their gear and using the inner bark of some young hickory trees to fashion rude packs, the men set out after breakfast. As they tramped across the dusty prairies, the blazing sun sapped their energy, and even with careful rationing, they had consumed their water long before they reached the river at evening. The combination of "rough roads, a hot sun, and heavy loads" left the travelers exhausted and footsore.[24]

The explorers needed to have no fear about being left behind by the balky steamboat, however, because it was another three days before the *Western Engineer* puffed into view. While they waited for their tardy waterborne companions, Say and the others visited nearby Otter Island. Immense numbers of deer, rabbits, squirrels, and wild turkeys made the island a hunter's paradise, and one morning Titian Peale killed four turkeys, "two of them with a single shot." Fertile soil and abundant water produced the enormous trees dotting the island. According to the inhabitants, a single walnut tree had provided enough timber for 200 fence rails, while a giant cottonwood "produced thirty-thousand shingles."[25] The veracity of such claims is difficult to ascertain, but had the existing trees not been huge, it seems unlikely that the explorers would have bothered to record such tales.

The overland journey from St. Charles to Otter Island seems to have given the naturalists more time to observe, to collect specimens, and to record their findings than they would have had aboard the steamer. Dr. Baldwin disagreed, however, and complained that once they had lost their horse, the men had "to carry their equipage upon their backs." Because of this, he claimed that Titian Peale "has ever since been confined, with inflammation in his feet. . . ." When Baldwin wrote this he had left the expedtion and was dying so his comments may have been inaccurate. Whether ashore or on the boat, the explorers wrote little about their duties. They did list observed animals, birds, trees, and plants, but made few references to their work of gathering specimens, making drawings, preserving skins, or keeping notebooks. Occasionally, Titian Peale mentioned setting traps in the evening and gathering them the next morning, but usually he failed to describe the traps, indicate his desire to get living or dead subjects for study, or even note which creatures he hoped to catch, except to mention his inability to get any "wood rats."[26] Apparently, working at close quarters, the scientists saw everyone's work and therefore no one bothered to record such activities. Consequently, the expedition narratives include much descriptive material about scenery, weather, and settlements, but from them it is difficult to know how much time each man spent carrying out his assigned tasks. The descriptions do make clear that the party spent most of its time traveling and that scientific activity occurred usually in the morning and evening.

On the evening of July 2, the *Western Engineer* steamed past the small camp on Otter Island and stopped a mile beyond it. Those remaining on board had continued to have difficulties with the engines and the current, but except for an accident that broke the arm of one of Major O'Fallon's black slaves, they had nothing unusual to report. Two days later the reunited explorers celebrated national independence by dining on roast opossum and "a few glasses of wine," but otherwise continued their regular duties. The next day they anchored at the French village of Cote Sans Dessein on the north bank of the river and there bought leather moccasins, leggings, and hunting shirts for tramping through the wilderness.[27]

Here, for the first time in some days, Dr. Baldwin felt well enough to make several short trips into the woods. These excursions weakened him, however, and during the next few weeks his health failed noticeably. Baldwin was able to make some observations and appears to have discussed his findings with his companions at length. He noted, with surprise, finding plant and bird species in the lower Missouri Valley that also inhabited regions along the southeastern coast of the United States. What seemed to puzzle him most was that many "southern birds" seen in Missouri were "never seen in the same latitudes east of the Alleghany [*sic*] Mountains." For example, the white pelican was "a most rare bird in Virginia," yet the explorers saw hundreds of them along the Missouri. Large numbers of the minute tern, "rarely seen 100 miles from the sea" along the East Coast, also mystified him.[28] Regardless of the seeming insignificance of these questions, they indicate that the scientists exchanged ideas about their findings.

The week after the party left Cote Sans Dessein was one of the most difficult of the long summer. Strong current, frequent sandbars, floating debris, and continuing engine trouble limited their speed upriver. Not only did these obstacles make travel difficult, but heat and physical exhaustion also began to take their toll. Dr. Baldwin was no longer the only sick man aboard the steamer. Titian Peale limped about on painfully swollen feet, apparently infected while on the overland trek some days earlier. Others suffered from the heat, and the boat crew complained that they could not work on deck without an awning. Corporal Joseph Norman "was seized with a violent cramp" that left him "quite delirious" for the next few days. On July 10, Sergeant Samuel Roan fell overboard and swam ashore to escape injury from the paddle wheels.[29]

Such incidents slowed but did not stop the expedition. On July 13, the *Western Engineer* puffed its way up to the dock at Franklin, Missouri. A crowd of nearly 100 spectators lined the riverbank to gawk and cheer the explorers and their strange-looking craft. This vessel was only the second steamer to ascend the Missouri as far as Franklin, and the pioneers probably cheered its arrival as a welcome break in their routine activities. Some anticipated better transportation links with the East and saw the explorers' upriver trip as one demonstration that technological improvements would soon fulfill that desire. Nevertheless the inhabitants' cheers could not hide the fact that it had taken the expedition eighteen days to travel the 140 miles from St. Charles to Franklin. That was a speed no better than the men of the Rifle Regiment had made the previous year on their trip up the Missouri by keelboat.30

Long realized this, and, reporting to Secretary Calhoun from Franklin, he tried to gloss over the mediocre performance of the steamer. "The frequent delays," he explained, "were occasioned in consequence of the boilers' becoming overcharged with mud" and because the current had been stronger than anticipated. Then he tried to show that the craft had traveled faster than the figures indicated by noting that the voyage from St. Charles to Franklin had taken only ninety-seven running hours. In other words, had he been able to navigate twenty-four hours a day it would have taken only four days and nights.31 Apparently, Long was already working to keep War Department support for the expedition beyond that current year, and he tried to anticipate criticism before it came.

Despite Long's forced optimism, his frustration must have been apparent to Calhoun, and the secretary tried to cheer his harried subordinate. He reminded the major that although the *Western Engineer* had not performed as hoped, there was no reason to worry about long-range success. Calhoun reminded the scientists of the enthusiasm their work had created and urged them to "use every exertion" to achieve their goals. When news that Major Biddle had refused to obey Long's orders because he outranked the expedition leader reached Calhoun, he became furious. "The question of rank," he raged, "had been so distinctly adjusted" that it was inconceivable any problems might develop on that issue. The secretary feared that Long's expedition had "excited too much interest to fail, without producing unhappy consequences" for the War Department, and with good reason. By late summer of 1819, a rising tide of criticism threatened to engulf him, and Calhoun needed to mollify Congress. He hoped that the Scientific Expedition would serve this purpose. In an effort to underline the urgency of the situation and to raise the explorers' sagging morale, Calhoun reminded Long that "the cause of Science as well as the interest and reputation of the Country is involved in the success of the expedition."[32]

Long's colleagues knew that his usual optimism had given way to bitter disappointment. According to Dr. Baldwin, the major had "entirely despaired of success on this river." Certainly Baldwin thought that transporting the explorers by steamboat had been a mistake. He denounced the plan to use the craft as hastily conceived and the boat itself as the least safe and most expensive means of transportation. Baldwin suggested that the disgruntled Major Biddle also would object to further use of the *Western Engineer* because of its poor construction. Yet the doctor feared that Long's pride would cause him to insist on operating the craft again. "I should wish him to have the command of the exploring party," Baldwin wrote, "in anything but a steamboat."[33]

The explorers remained at Franklin for six days repairing the steamer, investigating nearby salt springs, and visiting with townsfolk. During that time Dr. Baldwin decided that he was too sick to continue with the expedition, so he resigned. Long thanked him for his work that summer and wished him a speedy recovery, but the physician died within two months. The expedition was now without a botanist.[34]

Leaving Franklin on July 19, the *Western Engineer* moved upriver to Fort Osage, where the party stopped for nearly two weeks. There Major Long sent out a group to explore the region between the fort and the Platte River in Nebraska. This party included Say, Jessup, Seymour, Peale, Swift, and Biddle—who apparently had tired of life aboard the balky steamer—and an escort of five or six soldiers. Taking some minimal rations and equipment on three pack horses, the explorers left Fort Osage on August 6. From there they moved west across a treeless region cut by small creeks and

ravines. Excessive heat and thousands of blowflies irritated
men and animals alike, and the tall, coarse plains grass not
only "greatly impeded [sic] their progress," but also
shredded their clothing and moccasins.[35] Dysentery struck
several of the men, and a number of unexplained "accidents"
slowed their march to a mere couple of miles in one two-day
period. After ten days they reached the Kansas River and,
following that stream, on August 20 the footsore travelers
came to the main Kansa Indian village.

When the explorers first sighted the village of 120 lodges,
they stopped to inspect their weapons. This proved unnecessary. As the whites trudged across the level prairie, they could
see Indians on top of their earth lodges, waving and peering
at them. Then a group of painted chiefs and warriors rode
out from the village, followed by other tribesmen afoot.
Before this crowd reached the travelers, however, the chiefs
started arguing among themselves, and ten or twelve of them
returned to the village. In spite of this, any apprehension the
scientists may have had when they first saw the noisy throng
left when the Indians greeted them.[36]

Only a few days before the scientists arrived, the Kansa had
received a warning from Indian Agent Benjamin O'Fallon to
treat the visitors with kindness. Under most circumstances
such a message would have had little effect, but Kansa leaders
feared military reprisals for their recent depredations upon
the soldiers at Cantonment Martin on the Missouri. Therefore, they did everything possible to make their visitors comfortable. First, they led the tired travelers to the council lodge
where Indian leaders smoked with the explorers and discussed
the reasons for the whites traveling through Indian country.
Apparently satisfied that their visitors meant no harm, the
red men served a ceremonial meal of jerked buffalo meat and
boiled corn. A short time later, they invited their guests to six
more such "feasts" in succession.[37]

While at this village, Say questioned the Indians about
every aspect of tribal life. As a result of this conscientious-
ness, he gathered much accurate ethnological information

"WAR DANCE" IN A KANSA LODGE. Engraving from a drawing by Samuel Seymour. *Courtesy Smithsonian Institution Office of Anthropology.*

and in only a couple of days was able to get answers to all of the questions that the American Philosophical Society had sent the explorers. While Say and his interpreters talked with the Indians, the others rested, took notes, and bought clothing and souvenirs from the villagers. On August 23, the party decided to resume their march toward the Platte and traded for two more horses as well as for jerked buffalo meat, ground corn, large chunks of buffalo fat "put up like sausages," and some Indian spoons and dishes.[38]

Early the next morning when they prepared to leave the villages, the explorers found that their horses had strayed. It took hours to catch them, so they left the Kansa in midafternoon. After traveling for seven miles, they camped for the evening, and John Doughtery and another man left to hunt. Soon a party of nearly 140 armed Pawnee warriors rode up to the camp, and when the nervous scientists prepared to defend themselves, the red men shook hands and showed the open-handed peace sign. Nevertheless, the explorers feared that individual braves might steal their equipment, and their suspicions proved correct. While some Indians talked with the whites, others rifled their tent and still others rode off with their three pack horses. The explorers huddled together trying to protect their equipment, but the Indians succeeded in stealing several items. All the while the Pawnee harassed the whites, they alternated between threatening to attack and seeming to be friendly. Just when it seemed the Indians had decided to attack, Dougherty and his companion returned. Apparently the Pawnee thought that more whites or other Indians were coming, because they fled.[39]

The large number of Pawnee braves had limited the whites' actions to verbal protests because the explorers numbered only thirteen or fourteen men, and only Dougherty's arrival prevented more serious trouble.[40] As it was, they lost their horses and some of their supplies, so they had little recourse but to send several men back to the Kansa village for aid. When those men left, the rest moved their equipment into the bushes and prepared to defend themselves. For the rest of the night the nervous explorers kept each other awake reporting suspicious sounds. By dawn they were exhausted. In the morning, a party of thirty Kansa braves escorted the scientists back to the village, and although courteous, the Indians refused to sell any more horses or supplies. Thomas Say had gotten sick and was too weak to walk all the way to the Platte, so the explorers abandoned plans to finish their assignment. Instead, they rented a pair of horses from a resident trader at the village and set out for Cantonment Martin, where they hoped to meet the steamer.[41]

Exhausted and disappointed, the party arrived at the camp on August 29 to find that they had missed the *Western Engineer*. For once it had gotten ahead of them. Both Say and Augustus Jessup were too sick for more travel by land, so they remained with the soldiers at the camp while the others hurried to overtake the steamer. They found their companions near the mouth of the Wolf River in northeast Kansas, and from there the reunited party traveled north to Fort Lisa, the trading post operated by the Missouri Company. After a brief search they found a suitable mooring place for the steamboat, and there, about one half mile from the fur trading establishment, they halted for the winter.[42]

Although Stephen Long and his companions did not know it, when they stopped near Fort Lisa in September, 1819, their exploring by steamboat was over. The *Western Engineer* had not performed as Long hoped or as Secretary of War Calhoun expected. It had taken the steamer nearly three months to travel approximately 600 miles from St. Louis to Council Bluffs, an average of only six miles each day. Several lengthy stops, not entirely caused by mechanical difficulties, helped to lower the average, but the nearly daily breakdowns and delays resulted from the inadequacies of the steamboat.

Certainly, Long must bear a part of the responsibility for this weak performance. On the other hand, he had worked with experienced steamboat builders at Pittsburgh to design and construct the craft. The difficulties that occurred resulted more from the lack of technical skill and knowledge then available in the United States than because the men who built the experimental craft were incompetent. As an explorer, Stephen Long may be indicted for poor judgment in choosing the relatively untried steamboat as the means to carry his expedition west. Yet several other prominent military and government leaders favored using the same craft. Once Long made the decision to use a steamboat, he worked energetically to carry out his tasks.

Although generally unsatisfactory, the *Western Engineer* achieved some of the goals set for it. It did travel to the vicinity of present Omaha, Nebraska—nearly twice as far up the Missouri as did any of the other five steamers leased by the government that year. In addition, the craft impressed and perhaps even frightened some Indians, as had been intended. According to one resident of Franklin, Missouri, the snake-like features of the boat spread panic among the aborigines who saw it steam up the river. This frontiersman reported that the Indians said, "White man bad man, keep a great spirit chained and build fire under it to make it work a boat."[43] In spite of these modest accomplishments, however, the vessel had failed to carry out its major assignment— transporting the explorers up the Missouri River with reasonable speed and dependability.

Not only had the boat performed badly, but, as a result, Long and his associates failed to complete many of their assignments. Because of mechanical difficulties and other delays at St. Louis, Franklin, Fort Osage, and Cow Island, they lost valuable time. Sickness and injuries also limited their research efforts. Contemporaries were denouncing all aspects of the western troop movements, and the Scientific Expedition received its share of this verbal abuse. Such criticism stemmed from the unrealistic expectations that had been raised during the early stages of the expeditions. For example, the editor of the *Missouri Gazette and Public Advertizer* had claimed that the Yellowstone Expedition, which included Long's group, would improve literature and science, advance geographic knowledge, and increase western emigration—all at the same time.[44] When the soldiers and explorers failed to achieve more than a fraction of these goals, disappointment and criticism followed. Congressmen heard rumors of waste, incompetence, and corruption in the transporting of men and supplies, and amid the general belt-tightening following the Panic of 1819, they slashed the War Department budget. This cut in funds not only ended further troop movements up the Missouri, but also sharply curtailed Long's expedition. Instead of using the *Western Engineer* to travel farther up the Missouri or other western streams, he received orders to return east to Washington, while the craft remained at Council Bluffs for the winter.

[5]

A New Assignment, 1819-1820

When the explorers halted their upriver journey in September, 1819, their first chore was to build suitable winter quarters. Two days after they stopped, Major Long chose a site located on a sharp bend in the river bank about one half mile beyond Fort Lisa. There, a sort of cove in the river offered protection for the *Western Engineer*, and the narrow, tree-covered beach nearby could be used for the camp site. A line of forested bluffs overlooked the beach, blocked the prevailing northwest winds, and provided plenty of building material. Consequently, within a few days the party "had made great progress in cutting timber [and] quarrying stone," and by early October had finished the cabins. Zoologist Thomas Say described the buildings as "snug log houses, amply large, with capacious fire places. . . ." Because there was plenty of fuel nearby, he anticipated that the cabins would be "comfortable winter quarters" for the naturalists. Major Long named the camp Engineer Cantonment.[1]

Once the buildings had been finished, the major prepared for his return east to discuss expedition goals for the coming year with Secretary Calhoun. Among other tasks, Long had to recruit new men to replace those who had resigned. The ailing Dr. Baldwin and two others left the expedition during 1819. Geologist Augustus Jessup apparently had tired of exploring, and he planned to return east with Long in late 1819. Major Thomas Biddle, official journal keeper for the party that year, was the third man to quit. He and Long had quarrelled frequently, and Biddle refused to perform his duties as expedition journalist during the *Western Engineer*'s struggles up the Missouri that summer. Convinced that the steamer was nearly useless for exploration, Biddle denounced the expedition as "chimerical & impossible," at least under Long's command. Although he reported that Long was "an amiable good man and I daresay respectable in his own department," Biddle wrote, "I cannot but believe [that] he is entirely unqualified for an expedition of this sort." When the Pawnee warriors robbed the exploring party near the Kansa village in August, 1819, Biddle claimed to be humiliated by this "defeat." He feared that it would hurt his future advancement in the army, so, when Colonel Henry Atkinson invited him to join his staff a few weeks later, Biddle accepted and resigned from the expedition.[2]

These three vacancies caused Long to realign the duties of the men remaining at Engineer Cantonment. He placed Lieutenant James Graham in command of the camp and told him to report periodically to Colonel Atkinson at St. Louis. Graham was to keep the *Western Engineer* in good repair and to run its engines frequently so that the steamer would be ready for use the next spring. Thomas Say, the one remaining scientist, was to direct nearly all of the information-gathering efforts that winter. Long authorized him to get military help from Lieutenant Graham and ordered Samuel Seymour, Titian Peale, and John Dougherty to help Say "examine the country, visit the neighbouring Indians, procure animals, &c. . . ." The major suggested that the remaining explorers re-read his orders of the previous March, the questions submitted by the American Philosophical Society, Secretary Calhoun's instructions, and even President Jefferson's orders to Lewis and Clark written some sixteen years earlier. Long hoped that during the five months he would be gone "all the gentlemen of the expedition will find ample range for the exercise of their talents. . . ." Then on October 11, 1819, he and Augustus Jessup started downstream for St. Louis.[3]

With their commander absent, the explorers settled into a winter routine. From Colonel Atkinson they got clothing and material for repairing the *Western Engineer*. Lieutenant Graham made a seemingly endless series of minor adjustments and repairs, and he remained optimistic about steamboat travel. On November 20 he reported having completed the repairs, but that same day, the engineer Benjamin Edwards wrote that the craft needed more work, that the river was nearly impossible to navigate, and that he had no idea whether the explorers would use the steamer the next year or not.[4]

While Graham and Edwards tinkered with the balky boat, the rest of the explorers set to work gathering specimens, making sketches, interviewing Indians, and taking notes. In fact, they probably gathered as much scientific data during that winter at Engineer Cantonment as they did on the rest of the expedition. John Dougherty, interpreter for Indian Agent O'Fallon, had orders to assist Say's efforts to study Indian life, and he cooperated fully. He translated the texts of speeches made at the councils held at Council Bluffs; he accompanied the scientists when they visited Omaha, Oto, Missouri, and Iowa villages; and when among the Indians he helped interview many red men. With Say busy asking questions and taking notes, Seymour and Peale painted and sketched for days on end.

Some of their information came from visits to the nearby Indian villages, but much of it the explorers got during the frequent councils held at nearby Cantonment Missouri, a few miles north of their own camp. There Benjamin O'Fallon met with bands of area tribesmen many times that fall. For example, in November, 1819, a group of Sioux arrived and asked to see the *Western Engineer*. One of Long's reasons for designing the craft as he did had been to impress the Indians, so the whites brought their visitors to the boat. At first, several of the tribesmen hesitated to board. They thought that the steamer "was, or that it contained some *great medicine* of the Big-knives that might injure them." Despite their misgivings, the Sioux boarded the vessel, and once they realized that it would not harm them, joked nervously with each other. One much-relaxed warrior boasted that "he hardly thought the Big-knives had any medicine to hurt them.'" While their visitors clambered over the boat, Say recorded their appearance and Dougherty interpreted their comments. Certainly, the scientists used every opportunity to get information and impressions about these people.

Applying their curiosity and persistence, the investigators recorded an amazing variety of data. Few things were too minor to record. One day, while several of the whites chopped wood for fuel, an Omaha brave lounged nearby. After a time he noticed a large knot on one log that he thought would be suitable for carving into a bowl, and he asked the scientists to cut it off the log for him. They, in turn, offered him an ax. He declined, pointing to his hand and indicating that chopping wood would make his palm sore. Instead, he called one of the women, who took the ax and chopped the knot loose. While she worked, several other young Indian men walked past and the whites asked the woman why she had not asked one of them to help her finish the work. Laughing, she shook her head and told them that their idea was amusing.[6] By noting incidents of this type, the party recorded many insights into Indian customs and thought.

When Edwin James compiled the narrative report of the expedition several years later, he included much of the ethnological material gathered during the 1819-20 fall and winter. This contained discussions of nearly all phases of Indian life. Clothing, food, eating habits, housing, hunting techniques, ideas about marriage, child-rearing methods, dances and ceremonies, and methods of leadership and government were studied and noted. Some of this vast collection of data may have been known to western travelers, or perhaps even to a few educated easterners who studied the latest reports of western explorers. The fact is, however, that although the discussion occasionally seems disorganized and rambling, the ethnological data gathered that winter offered a significant batch of new material about the Indians. In particular, the discussion of the Kansa and Omaha tribes provided an authoritative source of ethnological findings unrivaled for decades.

Studying the Indians was only one of the assigned tasks at which the scientists worked that winter. They spent long hours examining the insects, birds, and animals found in profusion along the Missouri. As the expedition zoologist, Thomas Say directed these efforts with considerable success. While he looked, measured, and recorded his findings in bulging notebooks, Titian Peale worked as his assistant. A crack shot with both a rifle and a bow, frequently Peale supplied the party with fresh meat, as well as animals for study. Not only was he an able collector, but he was also an experienced taxidermist who could prepare study skins and preserve specimens for later shipment east. Peale had been trained to make laboratory drawings with a draftsman's care. He filled several notebooks with sketches of birds' eyes and extended wings, with detailed drawings of insects, and with some examples of moles, shrews, and rats seen nearby. Usually he did these sketches in pencil or with an ink-and-wash technique. Occasionally he painted small watercolors of scenes or groups, but these appear less competent than his single-subject drawings.[7]

Peale spent much time trying to capture live animals for study, but he found this considerably more difficult than shooting them. The party wanted to capture and observe a live prairie wolf or coyote, and Peale first tried putting bait under a raised box. The trap, "plentifully baited with offal," attracted the animals, as expected, but failed to catch one. Instead of taking the bait from the stick supporting the box, the animals dug beneath the trap and pulled the bait to safety through the hole. Next, Peale built a cage-like trap with a small, one-way entrance. Again the bait lured coyotes, but they refused to enter the trap to get it. When this device failed, too, the scientists set regular, large, steel traps. These they buried in leaves and then hung bait near and over them, but again the beasts outwitted their would-be captors. The next morning, only the bait hanging directly over each trap remained. Peale claimed to be undaunted "by these futile attempts, many times repeated, and varied in every obvious manner," and eventually he got a coyote, but not a live one. He built what trappers call a deadfall, consisting of a log supported by two small sticks. When the quarry took the bait from one of the supporting sticks, the log fell and killed it.[8]

After Peale caught the coyote, he and Say examined it with interest. They speculated about its relationship to the domesticated Indian dogs that they thought it resembled and then decided, incorrectly, that it had not yet been identified as a separate species. Lewis and Clark had done this in 1804, but their account described the animal as a "small species of wolf about the size of a gray fox," hardly an accurate or scientific representation of a coyote.[9] The fact is that while Lewis and Clark had recognized both the coyote and the gray wolf as new species, their discoveries failed to be included in the existing corpus of knowledge. Therefore, the careful description and detailed measurements of these two animals that Say provided rightly entitled him to have his name attached to each. Later zoologists recognized this, and, as a result, the plains coyote bears the name *Canis latrans latrans* Say, while the gray wolf is listed as *Canis lupus nubilus* (Say).[10]

Such activity may seem routine and basic today, but the rudimentary nature of the natural sciences at the time made these efforts both necessary and significant. In fact, in the early years of the nineteenth century, American science consisted chiefly of discovery and description work. Classification and related work did not become important parts of scientific labor until later in the century. Therefore, although much of the scientific data gathered by this expedition has been overlooked by historians, natural scientists at the time and since realized the significance of the data the explorers collected. In 1826, the botanist John Torrey described the specimens gathered by William Baldwin in 1819 and by Edwin James in 1820 as "exceedingly interesting," and noted that of the 700 items, "not a few are new species." That same year James De Kay told the members of the Lyceum of Natural History of New York that these two expeditions had collected many new and rare specimens for others to study. Similar recognition by other scientists continued throughout the nineteenth century, and in 1873, naturalist Asa Gray also mentioned the importance of these early findings.[11]

While the men at Engineer Cantonment occupied themselves in these ways, Stephen Long traveled east to Washington. He and Augustus Jessup arrived at St. Louis on October 25 and paused there for several days. When asked about the progress of the expedition, Long assured the editor of the *St. Louis Enquirer* that the explorers could have gone several hundred miles farther up the Missouri that year. They had decided to coordinate their movements with those of the Missouri Expedition, however, "until the temper of the Indians was better ascertained."[12] This statement overlooked the fact that the explorers had reached the Council Bluffs late in the season and certainly had at most two or three more weeks to travel farther upriver before having to stop and build a winter camp. Based on the six to eight miles a day that the *Western Engineer* had averaged on the Missouri that summer, another few weeks surely would not have given them time enough to travel hundreds of miles more, as claimed.

At St. Louis, Long wrote a preliminary report to the War Department informing Calhoun that his party had stopped at Council Bluffs, that they would continue their scientific activities there during the winter, and that he was returning to Washington to discuss the expedition and prepare for the next year.[13] Then he traveled to Philadelphia to visit his bride, and from there went on to Washington. In early January, 1820, he reported the activities of the expedition to Secretary Calhoun. His description minimized the difficulties and shows Long's effort to promote continuing frontier exploration. In it he blamed the delays on faulty machinery aboard the *Western Engineer*, on his own inability to hire either an experienced mechanic or steamboat pilot because of insufficient funds, and on navigational difficulties on the Missouri. Ignoring his failure to accomplish more than a fraction of what he proposed the year before, Long emphasized the positive accomplishments of his companions. He mentioned the small collection of botanical specimens gathered for Dr. Baldwin, discussed the contributions of the other scientists, and noted the occasional flashes of speed exhibited by the steamboat.[14]

Although angry congressmen were then investigating the failure of the Missouri Expedition and the enormous War Department expenditures for 1819, Long seems to have been oblivious to, or ignored the danger this activity might pose for his expedition. In fact, it appears that he learned little from his demonstrated shortcomings as an organizer and leader during 1819 because he proposed an even more unmanageable schedule for the next year. The mechanical difficulties that beset the *Western Engineer* did not dim his enthusiasm for using the craft again, and he reported that it would be "highly practicable to ascend with the boat several hundred miles farther, probably to the Falls," the next season. A mere voyage up the Missouri beyond Council Bluffs seems to have lacked much challenge, and he revived several earlier proposals. He wanted to cross the Great Lakes to the western tip of Lake Superior, then descend the St. Croix River to present Minneapolis. From there he would travel north and west to the northern bend of the Missouri River and then descend that stream until he met the rest of the expedition, by this time traveling upstream. The reunited party would then go west, seeking the sources of the Platte, Arkansas, and Red rivers. If Calhoun wanted a side trip to the Pacific, his agreeable subordinate suggested that might be accomplished as well.[15]

This wild-eyed proposal suggests several conclusions. One is that Long had never read the Lewis and Clark journals or studied the maps of their expedition. This seems unlikely, however, because as an army topographer and map maker he would have used such material in his work. Not only that, but the Scientific Expedition carried a copy of the Lewis and Clark narrative and certainly Long had used it. A second conclusion is that the congressional investigation of the Missouri Expedition so unnerved him that he proposed doing what he realized was impossible for a single year, hoping to get a long-range commitment from Secretary Calhoun. Finally, there is the chance that his optimism allowed Long to believe what he suggested actually could be accomplished. His ideas seem not nearly as absurd as was the fact that they received serious consideration by the War Department. Lewis Cass, then governor of Michigan Territory, had asked for an expedition to explore the upper Mississippi region and Calhoun wrote to him that "perhaps Major Long, now here, will be directed to take that route [up the Mississippi and overland to the Missouri]to join the expedition which he commands up the Missouri."[16]

It is difficult to understand why Calhoun considered Long's proposals seriously when the desks of clerks in his department must have overflowed with evidence that the Scientific Expedition of 1819 had achieved few of its major goals. If the explorers could not carry out their duties one year, there seems to have been little reason why Calhoun would expect them to do significantly better the next. Perhaps the harried secretary of war hoped for some brilliant discovery, or at least a demonstration of solid competence by the scientific party in order to divert public and congressional attention from the failures of 1819. Certainly, when Calhoun's former reluctance to fund the scientific efforts of Long's group only a year before and the intense fiscal pressure on his department in 1820 are considered, it is strange that he allowed the scientists to continue their explorations that year.

In a second letter, written the same day as the one that included Long's casual offer to travel west to the Pacific, the major suggested that he recruit replacements for those who had left the expedition, and then, with these new companions, return west. At Council Bluffs, in early May, the reunited party, without the *Western Engineer*, would follow the Platte River to its source. Next, the explorers would move south to the source of the Arkansas River and there divide the party. Half would continue east along the Arkansas, while the rest continued south and west searching for the source of the Red River before turning east to rejoin their companions. All of this, Long claimed, could be done in four months and would cost the War Department no more than $8,000. He also suggested that the government get a license from the Spanish authorities allowing the explorers to traverse what might be Spanish territory.[17]

Five weeks later, Calhoun approved the second, more modest plan for the expedition. He authorized the purchase of horses, but warned that little money was available, so that expenses had to be kept to a minimum. Fearing continuing congressional criticism of the War Department budget, the secretary urged Long to lead his party as far as possible during the coming summer in an effort to make the expedition gather more interesting and significant material than its limited nature would lead the public to expect.[18] Thus, as a result of political and fiscal pressure that forced Calhoun to cut his budget and show some positive results from his administration of the War Department, distance and speed became more important than quality or thoroughness of investigation. The resulting plan forced Long's party to travel hundreds of miles rapidly with few supplies and little equipment. Under these circumstances the explorers lacked time for careful study, and it is not surprising that later the results of their summer work would seem meager. In fact, an expectation of hurried, mediocre effort seems to have been built into the expedition of 1820 by Calhoun's troubles in Washington.

While Long discussed his plans with War Department officials, he had other duties to complete as well. One was the unpleasant task of bringing Dr. Baldwin's notes to his widow and arranging to have the botanist's other effects shipped east. Once that had been done, he turned to recruiting men to replace Baldwin, Biddle, and Jessup. To fill the position of journalist, Calhoun forwarded the application of Captain John R. Bell, then an instructor of tactics at the Military Academy. A native New Yorker, Bell had graduated from West Point and served in the army since 1812. When he learned that the position with Long was open, he wrote to Calhoun asking for a chance to exchange the "dull rounds of garrison duty" for western travel and exploration, and subsequently he was accepted for the expedition.[19]

By February, 1820, Long found the man he considered to be an ideal replacement for both Baldwin and Jessup. He was Dr. Edwin James from Vermont. The twenty-eight-year-old James had graduated from Middlebury College, where he studied botany, geology, and medicine. Then, after completing his studies at Middlebury, James continued his botanical studies informally by corresponding with Dr. John Torrey of New York and Amos Eaton at Albany. At the same time, he studied medicine with his brother John James. By 1820, he had published items on botany and geology.[20] With this experience James could serve as physician for the expedition, as well as doing the work of the botanist and geologist. Apparently, the sharp reduction of available funds made it necessary in 1820 for him to assume the tasks done by both Baldwin and Jessup the preceding year.

Long spent the early months of 1820 working in Washington and Philadelphia to get funds and personnel for the new assignment. Then on March 31, he, James, and Bell left Pittsburgh as passengers on the steamboat *Telegraph*. Their downriver trip took nearly a month, and on April 23 they arrived at St. Louis.[21] There, Long discussed his plans with Colonel Atkinson and asked for cooperation in getting supplies and an escort for the explorers. The War Department had promised that funds for the expedition and additional orders would be sent to Long at St. Louis, but he waited in vain for them to arrive. Earlier, Calhoun had warned that no bills for supplies or equipment could be paid until Congress passed the annual appropriation bill. It was not until April 28, 1820, that the War Department sent a $2,000 draft to Long. Unfortunately, it usually took correspondence between Calhoun in Washington and officers at St. Louis about six weeks to arrive, so that by the time the money came the explorers had traveled hundreds of miles to the west and got no benefit from the funds. In the meantime, Long was "at a loss how to account for the delay. . .[because he mistakenly thought that] the money promised him should have been [there]on his arrival. . . ."[22]

The major had more to do in St. Louis than merely wait for money and new orders, however. After arriving in that city, he had orders to complete a survey of several tracts of public land nearby, but some of the settlers on the land had not yet filled their claims, so he could not finish the job. In the meantime he demonstrated "great zeal, firmness, and resolution" in trying to get a pledge of substantial help from Colonel Atkinson. When neither the expected money nor as much help as the explorers claimed to need was forthcoming, Long decided to leave, anyway. On May 3, 1820, Long, Bell, and James rode out of St. Louis. Just as they got to the outskirts of the city, the major's Indian pony threw him into the street, "rid herself of her equipments & baggage, and took a turn thro' town. . . ."[23] Long reported little about the bruises to his physique or pride, but could not help having been discouraged at the difficulties he was having even before getting to Council Bluffs, starting point for the expedition.

From St. Louis the three men rode to Franklin in five days. There, they halted for nearly a week while Long tried to decide whether he should wait for the money from Washington or proceed without the minimum equipment and supplies he needed.[24] At Franklin the would-be explorers spent several days repairing their saddles and waiting for the heavy, cold spring rain to stop. This pause and the earlier one at St. Louis set back the probable starting date of the expedition by about three weeks. Now the scientists were certain to encounter more hot, dry weather than would have been the case had they gotten started in early May, as planned. Also, the late start reduced the time they had to explore, gather specimens, and paint, and so it affected the completeness and value of the explorers' findings.

When no news or funds came from Washington, Long and his companions set out at mid-morning on May 14 for Council Bluffs. During the next two weeks, personal discomfort and occasional danger seem to have been the rule, rather than the exception. The travelers had no tent, so at night they huddled near the fire, trying to stay reasonably warm and dry, but with limited success. On May 16, according to Edwin James, the party experienced several "disasters," which included getting rain-soaked again, having to track their horses for three miles, and losing a pocket compass. The frequent rain made dry fuel scarce and several times they ate raw bacon with their bread and water because they could not start a fire. At times they supplemented their staples of coffee, bread and bacon with roast squirrels, lamb's-quarters, or wild onions, but on days when they killed no animals or found no edible herbs, they had the same meal again and again.,[25]

On Saturday, May 27, the small party reached Boyer River

in western Iowa. There they built a raft on which Long crossed the river and then rode north another couple of miles to the cantonment. The scientists who had wintered there welcomed him with enthusiasm and then rode to the Boyer and rafted the others across the Missouri.[26] For the first time that year Long's explorers were gathered in one place. Now they had to be equipped, supplied, told about their new assignment, and then led west.

[6]
Exploring the Plains, 1820:
West to the Rockies

History has not been kind to Stephen Long's expedition across the central and southern Plains during the summer of 1820. In 1822, when Edwin James prepared the expedition journals for publication, he apologized that the "travels and researches of the Expedition, have been far less extensive than those contemplated. . . ." Writing some eighty years later, Hiram M. Chittenden claimed that because Congress and the public considered the so-called Yellowstone Expedition of 1819 to have failed, "a small side show was organized for the season of 1820 in the form of an expedition to the Rocky Mountains." Even Long's recent biographer accepted this negative attitude, and he entitled his chapter on the 1820 expedition "Sideshow to the Rockies."[1]

These assessments are partly accurate but obscure the nature and scope of Long's expedition and other federally sponsored exploring efforts taking place at the same time. Certainly, if one compares the 1820 movement across the Plains with the Mississippi, Missouri, and Scientific expeditions, which had moved well over 1,000 men the preceding year, it seems tiny indeed. On the other hand, except that they traveled overland rather than aboard the *Western Engineer*, the explorers' lot was not much different the second year from what it had been during the first. Only two new members—Edwin James and John Bell—joined the party, while the rest of the men traveled west with nearly the same duties as they had performed during 1819. True, the scientists had poorer equipment and fewer supplies while crossing the Plains than they did ascending the Missouri, but that was accidental.

Not only was Long's 1820 expedition not a "sideshow," it was the main attraction as far as government-sponsored exploration that year was concerned. Three other expeditions occurred in 1820. The first and least significant included five army officers and an escort of enlisted men who traveled from Camp Missouri at Council Bluffs to what would become Fort Snelling at the confluence of the St. Peter's and Mississippi rivers. This party had orders to find a usable overland route between the two posts so that a military road might be built.[2]

Michigan Territorial Governor Lewis Cass led the second and largest group of explorers that year. He took other Anglo-Americans, French-Canadian voyageurs, and friendly Indians across Lake Michigan and along the southern shore of Lake Superior. There they examined the copper deposits and then traveled west and south to the Mississippi. Along the way, Cass spent most of his time negotiating with the Indians. Although this was the largest exploring party that year, it collected less scientific data than did the Long party because Secretary Calhoun provided little money and because Cass's associates lacked the collective scientific skill and interest of the Plains explorers.[3]

Geographer Jedediah Morse's assignment to study the Northwest Indian tribes for the War Department was the third effort sponsored by Calhoun that year. Morse traveled as far west as Mackinac and Green Bay on Lake Michigan in the summer of 1820, and two years later published his significant *Report*, which described the northern Indian tribes. Certainly, when seen in the context of this other government-sponsored exploration, it is clear that Stephen Long's expedition on the Plains in 1820 was "an instrument of national policy"—a part of Calhoun's continuing effort to expand American influence in and knowledge about the West by using Indian Office and army personnel.[4] Unfortunately, the political and economic problems of the War Department in 1819-20 forced drastic reductions of funds for exploration and curtailed the contributions of the scientists.

This lack of adequate support became apparent before Long, John Bell, and Edwin James got to Engineer Cantonment in late May, 1820. The funds Calhoun had promised to send west never arrived, and although the army officers nearby tried to cooperate, they had little money or supplies to spare. While still at St. Louis, Long had asked Colonel Atkinson for a twenty-man escort. The Colonel was pleasant but refused. He replied that the garrison at Council Bluffs had been "reduced by deaths and weakened by" the scurvy epidemic the preceding winter and could not spare that many men, but he authorized the commanding officer there to assign a detachment of seven men to escort the explorers. A similar lack of troops caused Indian Agent Benjamin O'Fallon to cancel his proposed expedition to visit some of the Missouri River Indian tribes only a few weeks later. It failed to deter the explorers, although the seven soldiers could offer little more than token protection. At least the men could be of some help with routine camp chores, such as getting water and fuel, pitching tents, and packing and unpacking equipment each day.[5]

While their commander sought supplies, horses, and weapons, the scientists prepared their personal goods. Some bought leather moccasins and leggings for the trip, and others repaired or replaced harnesses and saddles. Those who had spent the winter on the Missouri packed specimens and notes to be sent downstream with the *Western Engineer* later that summer. All of the men checked and cleaned their weapons, gathered, tested, and packed whatever scientific instruments or other tools they needed to take along, and prepared to leave their temporary camp along the river bottom.

Despite their combined efforts, the explorers gathered a meager supply of instruments and equipment for their work. For survey, mapping, and topographic purposes they had one large sextant, one pocket sextant, an artificial horizon, three small compasses, two small thermometers, a measuring tape, and "Pikes map of the upper part of the Platte, Arkansaw & Red rivers. . . ." The naturalists had small packing boxes for carrying skins, plant samples, and insects, as well as tin canisters and packing cloths to keep their papers and samples dry. They also brought paper, blank books, portfolios, and other sketching and painting material.[6]

In addition to their personal scientific or artistic equipment, each explorer carried weapons of some sort. The "hunters, interpreters, and attendants" all had muskets or rifles. The squad of soldiers had rifles, and the officers and naturalists carried either rifles or muskets, as well as a pair of pistols each. If this were not enough, the men also had forage bags for carrying food or specimens, bullet-pouches, and powder horns. Each person had a horse or mule to ride, and the few extra pack animals carried equipment and supplies.

To feed the expedition, Long got rations from the garrison commander at Camp Missouri. These included 450-500 pounds of hard biscuit, 150 pounds of parched cornmeal, 150 pounds of salt pork, 25 pounds of coffee, 30 pounds of sugar, 5 gallons of whiskey, and "a small quantity of salt." Given the size of army rations at the time, this supply provided food for only thirty days and meat for less than two weeks—hardly enough for men who expected to be out on the plains for four months. It is impossible to know why Long received so little food from the local commander. Perhaps the recently ended scurvy epidemic made that officer unwilling to part with supplies he thought were needed for the well-being of his own men. At the time Long was asking for supplies, the Missouri River had just flooded the camp gardens, and this too may have been a part of the decision.[7] No matter what the reason, Long seems to have taken the rations without public complaint. Perhaps he felt confident that the detachment could supplement its meager food supply by hunting and trading. If this were the case, however, it shows how little the soldiers and scientists knew about the region they were about to cross.

Regardless of whether Long was over-optimistic about feeding his men by hunting or was foolhardy and willing to risk their lives on a difficult, perhaps dangerous mission with inadequate supplies, he had little choice. Secretary Calhoun had ordered him to lead the men west that summer and promised funds that had never arrived. If Long had tried to write to Washington yet that summer to get the money or have the orders changed, there would have been no time left to explore. As it was, he found that the nearby garrison commander had few men and little food to spare, and the resident fur traders refused to sell their goods to him on credit. If the major expected to keep his men fed by trading with the Indians, he was mistaken. The inventory the explorers carried with them shows that they were no better supplied with trade goods than with necessities. As a government-sponsored expedition, the group could not carry illegal whiskey into the Indian country for trade. Their stock of other trade goods included 30 pounds of tobacco, 5 pounds of vermillion, 2 pounds of beads, 2 gross of knives, 1 gross of combs, 1 dozen fire steels, 300 flints, 2 gross of hawks bells, 2 dozen moccasin awls, 1 dozen scissors, 6 dozen mirrors, and "a few trinkets."[8] Certainly, the Indians would trade for these items, but the explorers carried too few of them to keep themselves supplied with food for three of the four months they would be on the Plains.

On June 1, Long had issued orders that stated the objectives of the expedition and the duties of each member. He reminded his associates that the War Department had changed their goals. Rather than continuing up the Missouri by steamboat, they would proceed overland up the Platte and then return along the Arkansas and Red rivers. Referring them to his orders in 1819 in which he had stated that the "prime object of the expedition being a Military Survey of the country to be explored, " the major listed the following tasks for each man:

> Stephen Long, commander
> John Bell, journalist
> Edwin James, botanist, geologist, and surgeon
> Titian Peale, assistant naturalist
> Thomas Say, zoologist and ethnologist
> Samuel Seymour, landscape artist
> William Swift, assistant topographer and commander of escort

Seven civilians served as interpreters, guides, hunters, and baggage handlers, while a detachment of seven soldiers completed the party.[9] Instead of accompanying the group, Lieutenant James Graham remained with the *Western Engineer*. Later that summer he was to take the vessel back down the Missouri and Mississippi to Cape Girardeau, Missouri, in order to meet the others when they returned.

At the same time that he clarified the assignments for the expedition personnel, Long described the hardships they were likely to encounter and urged his companions to complete their duties in a "successful and speedy" manner.[10] This emphasis on speed was not new. In fact, his previous frontier assignments had stressed this element rather than the thorough examination of the regions through which he had passed. If he continued to consider the distance traveled as the chief goal, it would be difficult to survey or map the central and southern Plains competently. Certainly, his continuing stress upon distance would hinder careful exploration.

During the week the party planned and packed, they heard tales that must have shaken the confidence of all but a few.

The nearby Indians laughed at the whites' proposed route, warning the naturalists that the Plains had so little grass or water that neither they nor their horses could survive. A resident fur trader cautioned them about the dangers a small group faced from Indian attack. Thomas Say, the zoologist and a veteran of the 1819 expedition, claimed that the local Indians "assured us that the country was covered with hostile Indians, who would not fail to massacre every individual of our small party. . . ." If these warnings were not enough to frighten some of the men, the actions of those who lived or worked at Council Bluffs surely weakened their confidence. When Major Long tried to hire hunters, interpreters, and guides, "many good and useful men" refused to join the expedition because it was too small.[11] Such incidents alone might not have discouraged all the explorers, but the naturalists realized that they lacked even the minimum amount of food to stay alive that summer.

Much of the party's equipment was makeshift or crude, and many items they thought necessary were missing. Their journey was supposed to last four months, and it was already early June. This meant that the party would have to travel during the least favorable part of the summer. Not only that, but the route that Long expected them to follow had not been carefully explored. Certainly, a few traders had crossed parts of the Plains, but there was little cartographic or literary material for the explorers to examine. As far as the scientists were concerned, they were heading into an unknown region, and while this may have been stimulating, it also caused some apprehension.

During the last harried days before the expedition began, the officers at nearby Camp Missouri invited the explorers to a banquet. There, for a few hours, they enjoyed "an excellent dinner" that included most kinds of domestic and wild meats and fowls, and all sorts of garden vegetables washed down with wine, rum, whiskey, and brandy. After dessert of apple and gooseberry pie, the officers and scientists drank, sang, and toasted each other before listening to a concert given by the Sixth Infantry regimental band.[12]

In spite of this pleasant interlude, some of the expedition members remained uneasy about their chances for a successful venture. Edwin James, one of the two new explorers, mentioned the recent flurry of Indian depredations in the Missouri Valley and complained about "the very inadequate outfit" they had for the journey. Thomas Say later recalled having "set out for the Mountains under the most discouraging circumstances."[13] Such fears seem not to have bothered Long, who remained outwardly optimistic. He praised his associates for having performed their duties with "laudable zeal and assiduity" during the preceding months. Despite the delays and shortages now facing them, he claimed that the chances for success seemed "flattering" and that the goals of the expedition could be achieved within four months.[14] Neither Long nor his less enthusiastic associates proved entirely correct, but his prediction overlooked the many serious difficulties that lay ahead.

By June 5 all the last-minute details had been settled, and the next morning the contingent of twenty-one men, twenty-seven horses, and two large hunting dogs rode away west from Engineer Cantonment. While those who remained cheered the explorers with an artillery salute, the column—described by a recent critic as "a curious cavalcade of disgruntled career officers, eccentric scientists, and artist-playboys"—followed Captain Bell and the guide west. Long had organized the soldiers, hunters, and laborers into two squads and these followed Bell, riding single file. The naturalists rode where they pleased as long as they stayed with the party, and the major followed the column to prevent straggling and supervise any repacking or other duties that might become necessary.[15] The column moved slowly that first day because some of the men "were not very expert or skillful" in handling the pack horses and mules. They had loaded the animals carelessly and the resulting "derangement of the packs, [and] the obstinacy of the mules" forced many stops, so that by evening the party had traveled only nine miles. That evening Long assigned a particular man to each pack animal so that they would become used to each other and less time would be needed for loading and packing.[16]

The first day of march Captain Bell got orders to supervise the camp location and organization. He ordered the men to pitch their three large tents in a row with the entrances all facing in the same direction. Then they were to stack their equipment in two piles in front of each tent and cover each pile with bear skins to keep everything dry. In case of Indian attack, each man knew where his equipment was, and, at the same time, the skin-covered piles offered some protection if the explorers had to defend themselves. Each man had two small blankets, and some had greatcoats to spread on the ground for bedding. For pillows they had to use their holsters or valises, certainly uncomfortable substitutes. When they thought Indians might be near, the travelers picketed the animals close to camp, and each night two soldiers stood guard.[17]

Earlier that year Long had hoped to start west by May 1, but it had taken another five weeks to get his party equipped and moving. Their late start and minimal supply of provisions made speed essential, so after the first day the major pushed men and animals to their limits of endurance. Usually the explorers rode twenty miles each day, and occasionally they traveled twenty-five or even thirty miles. Forced to ride all day at this pace, the naturalists had little chance to observe or gather specimens during the day.

Despite the tiring pace, however, the scientists took advantage of frequent stops to do their work. For example, after halting on the evening of June 7, one of the hunters brought a live young antelope back to camp. There, Titian Peale sketched the frightened beast and then released it. Several days later, traveling up the Loup River Valley, the naturalists noted some edible plants, some new grasses, and flowers they had not seen previously. They also identified many species of birds. So even though traveling and gathering and preparing food occupied most of their time, the explorers refused to let these daily chores push aside their scientific duties altogether.[18]

As they rode toward the Pawnee villages, Long's detachment encountered most of the difficulties and obstacles that travelers then faced. Crossing rivers proved more tiring and time-consuming than dangerous but was not easy. Some of the instruments, ammunition, and food had to be ferried across the deeper streams by bull-boat. This consisted of buffalo hides with small holes near the edges stretched over a round willow frame. The travelers passed a rope through the holes, and by drawing the rope tight, pulled the hide into a sack-like shape. They then loaded their goods into this flimsy but usually watertight container and floated it across the river. On July 7, when the explorers first tried this, it took more than an hour.[19] The weather caused inconvenience and, at times, suffering. Frequent showers and occasional storms soaked the tents and clothing. Summer heat often pushed the temperature into the nineties and made both travel and sleep difficult. Dry, continuous wind and hot sun combined to chap and burn the explorers. Within a few days they suffered from burned and peeling skin and from cracked and bleeding lips and ears, all with little medication. Apparently, the expedition members tolerated these discomforts as part of their assignment. Certainly they grumbled, but they diplomatically left such complaints out of their published narratives.

On June 10 the contingent halted about eleven miles from their first objective—the village of the Grand Pawnee. While resting, the group welcomed a party of three French-speaking traders and several half-breeds. These men had left Council Bluffs in order to trade at the Pawnee villages and carried messages and a package for Long. The package contained smallpox vaccine for the explorers to use among the Indians.

Unfortunately, the package had been aboard an army keel-boat that had sunk in the Missouri, and the river water had ruined the vaccine. The traders also brought a runaway horse with them. This animal belonged to John Dougherty, whose brother was working for the explorers. The extra horse was a welcome addition because several of the party's animals were already sick or lame.[20]

Long thanked the traders for the horse and asked them to tell the Pawnee leaders that the explorers would visit their village the next day. In the morning he arranged the men according to rank or position, ordered that the American flag and the expedition banner depicting shaking hands before a crossed sword and peace pipe be flown, and led the whites toward the village. When they reached the Indian camp, the "reception was a little less cordial than we had expected," Edwin James noted. No chiefs or even warriors appeared to greet them, but instead a large group of women and children clustered around Long's men. They led the whites to Chief Long Hair's lodge, gave them some boiled corn, and left. After eating in silence, the explorers learned from a resident fur trader that the village leaders were participating in a medicine feast and would not leave it to welcome their guests.[21]

Later that afternoon, several Pawnee chiefs walked out to Long's camp and apologized for not coming sooner. They explained that they could allow nothing to disturb the ceremony and claimed that they could not have "left their medicine feast, if the village had been on fire." After the ritual of shaking hands and smoking silently, the Indians listened as the explorers described their purposes for crossing the Plains. The Pawnee warned that the journey would take them into dangerous country with little game, grass or water, and which was the home of powerful Indian tribes. "You must have long hearts, to undertake such a journey with so weak a force," one said, "hearts that would reach from the earth to the heavens." Long and his companions assumed that the Pawnee wanted the whites to stay out of the Indians' hunting areas and ignored these warnings.[22]

While talking with these Pawnee leaders, both Dr. James and Long tried to persuade the Indians to have some of their tribe vaccinated. They discussed the dangers of smallpox that the red men had experienced, but the Indians refused to be vaccinated.[23] It is hard to understand why the whites wanted to use this vaccine. They knew that it had been dumped into the Missouri River and ruined and that it was worthless for preventing disease. Had they succeeded in vaccinating some of the tribesmen and the Indians then contracted the disease, the result could have been catastrophic for Pawnee-American relations. The Indians might have thought that they had been tricked and infected by Long's men or, at least, that the medicine was worthless and refused future efforts to vaccinate them. In any case, the ruined medicine could have had only negative results, and suggestions to use it indicate that neither Long nor James had given this matter any serious thought.

The next day the whites moved on to the Pawnee Republicans' village, where the chiefs acted slightly more friendly, but here they declined to offer a feast or otherwise formally welcome their visitors. Discouraged, Long's contingent rode several miles farther to the Pawnee Loup village. There they received a more cordial reception. After shaking hands, the chief had "bowls of corn & guts boiled" given to the whites. Captain Bell reported that "this dish relished well, & we eat heartily of it." Once the eating and smoking was over, Long explained his objectives and assured the Pawnee of continuing American friendship. Here too the Indians warned the explorers of the danger ahead, but the whites did not change their plans.[24]

A personnel crisis arose while the detachment camped near this village. Joseph Bijou, the French-Canadian guide who had led them this far, had agreed to travel only as far as the Loup village, so Long made arrangements to hire a replacement there. At first several men volunteered, but they changed their minds quickly and declined to serve. This left the explorers without guides and about to enter an unmapped region. Long knew that a guide was essential and demanded that the resident traders at the Pawnee villages choose one of their number to help. When they refused, he threatened to write agent Benjamin O'Fallon and have him revoke the trading licenses of every trader there. At a hurried meeting, the traders chose two men, Joseph Bijou (Bijeaux) and Abraham Ledeux, to accompany the expedition. Long's angry threat had worked. He needed at least one competent guide and interpreter and got two men for the job.[25]

As they traveled west during the first two weeks in June, the explorers had learned new skills gradually. By the time they got to the Pawnee villages, they had become accustomed to a standard daily routine. While visiting the Indians, they learned how to "jerk" or dry thin strips of fresh meat over a smoky fire, as well as to use "buffalo chips" or dung for fuel. On June 12 and 13, some of the men bought or traded for brass kettles, while others exchanged their horses and mules for fresh stock from the Indians. All of the travelers laundered dirty clothes and blankets, repaired harnesses, cleaned weapons, and repacked supplies and equipment. Then, on the morning of June 14, the detachment of twenty-two men, thirty-four horses and mules, and two hunting dogs left the Loup village and turned south and west toward the Rockies.[26]

During the next week, the folly of having set out from Engineer Cantonment without enough food became apparent. Long chose to issue partial rations and depend on the skill of the hunters to make up the difference. This did not always work, and by June 15, the explorers had been reduced to eating biscuit and jerked buffalo meat, "and that of a very bad quality," which they had bought from the Indians. That same evening one of the hunters sighted a lone buffalo and four of the men gave chase. All they could do was to wound it with an arrow, so they returned to camp with tired horses, but no meat. In the morning each man got a half pound of biscuit, their ration of food for the day, so when someone later shot two prairie dogs, the explorers ate them with gusto.[27]

The naturalists had some time in early morning or late evening to do their work, but certainly spent most of their time riding and not gathering scientific data. To give them more opportunity and to have enough time for cleaning equipment and resting the horses, Long halted the command each Sunday. For the first weeks of the expedition, these rest days helped keep morale high and also gave Long and Swift a chance to make astronomical observations. While the officers carried out their topographic chores, the naturalists sketched, gathered, took notes, and prepared specimens. As a result, the scientists seem to have had enough time to complete their assigned tasks, despite the long distances traveled each day.[28]

Even with these weekly rest days, frequent halts for hunting and for crossing difficult streams, the expedition moved up the Platte Valley at a steady pace. On June 19 they reached the sand hills and from there west reported less vegetation, poorer forage for the animals, and little game except buffalo. Their dependence upon game for much of their daily ration soon made the explorers connoisseurs of wild meat. They agreed that buffalo was better than other game animals, and whenever they got a fresh supply they threw away any deer or elk meat they had. Not only was buffalo more tasty than other game animals, but, according to Edwin James, "the flesh of the bison is in no degree inferior in delicacy and sweetness to that of the common ox."[29]

The naturalists theorized that this good flavor resulted from the "nutritious" grasses the animals ate. They recognized that Plains grass differed from the "less solid grass" raised in the Eastern United States, and speculated that there must be some relationship between the nutritive qualities of the Plains grass and the poor-quality soil found there. On the other hand, they soon found that the grass that supported the buffalo so well was less satisfactory for horses and mules. Their experience was not an isolated instance, and later explorers, as well as cavalry units, had similar difficulties when they had to depend on the native grasses to feed horses and mules.[30] Some critics have denounced the naturalists for not recognizing the grazing potential of the Plains, particularly after they noted the thousands of buffalo that roamed across the region. Given the difficulty the explorers had in keeping their own horses and mules alive, much less strong and healthy, it seems unreasonable to expect that the party would have considered the Plains a rich grazing area for domestic livestock.

Traveling along the South Platte, the detachment crossed many barren, sandy places. All of the explorers mention these, and the narratives include much grumbling about the "intense reflection of light and heat from the surface of many tracts of naked sand." Edwin James went so far as to describe the Rocky Mountains "as forming the shore of that sea of sand, which is traversed by the Platte. . . ." He was not alone in denouncing the Plains because Bell, Long, and Say all made similar comments. Bell grumbled more than the others that loose sand and gravel slowed the horses, while dust and bright sun reflected off the sand inflamed the eyes of the riders. Swarms of gnats bit the men as they rode, and when they halted, sand fleas continued the persecution. Consequently, the men suffered from swollen, itching hands and faces much of the time.[31]

During the night of June 27-28, the sound of horses running through the camp roused everyone. The men scrambled from their blankets, thinking that Indians had attacked or were trying to steal the horses. To their relief, they soon learned that a nearby herd of buffalo had frightened the animals. As soon as they quieted the horses, the explorers went back to sleep, but not for long. Within a couple of hours a rifle shot brought them out of their beds a second time that night. This was the warning signal, so all hands fumbled for their weapons in the darkness. Once up, they learned—probably to their disgust—that Major Long had ordered a false alarm, just to be sure that everyone knew what to do in case of attack. Then, because the entire command was up, anyway, the major ordered the march to begin early, and the tired travelers rode out of camp at five that morning.[32]

On June 30, the detachment saw the Rocky Mountains for the first time. They could not decide whether what they saw in the distance was a bank of clouds or the mountains, but by late afternoon they "had a distinct view of the summit of a range of mountains." They had sighted what is now Long's Peak in Colorado. The mountains, even though more than a hundred miles away, cheered the travelers who had "been so long confined to the dull uninteresting monotony of prairie country." Hoping to celebrate July 4 in the mountains, they pushed steadily south and west, but the Rockies lay farther than the explorers had guessed, and it took until July 6 to reach them.[33]

The expedition camped near a gorge through which the Platte flowed out of the mountains, and there, on July 7, Long decided to ignore Calhoun's order to seek the sources of that stream. It is not known why he chose to disregard one of his major assignments as a topographer and military engineer. Surely, any map he drew of the region would be more accurate and valuable had he followed his assignment, but he may have decided that the party lacked time and supplies to continue any farther west. Apparently he chose to sacrifice what he thought were insignificant goals in order to accomplish more important ones. Whatever his reasons, few of his companions objected.[34]

For the week or so that the expedition traveled along the Front Range, they experienced many physical problems. Zoologist Thomas Say had been sick on the entire journey, but now others got sick, too. On July 7 they found patches of wild currant bushes, and the ripe fruit was the first they had seen since leaving Engineer Cantonment. Within a few hours after they ate the berries, many of the men suffered from "violent pains in the head, breast, & limbs, in some cases attended with vomiting & surging." All the sick had eaten the wild berries, so the rest of the men avoided the fruit. Two days later, Long gave the command a day to rest. Apparently, some of the men suffered from the higher elevation and they complained of headaches. Others said that they felt as though "the blood in their faces seems almost ready to break thro' the skin. . . ." To cure these discomforts, Dr. James bled his patients, a treatment then in general use, but hardly recommended to conserve strength for more travel.[35]

Unexpected changes in the weather also brought discomfort. On the Plains they had suffered from heat, but near the mountains this changed. On July 10 Captain Bell reported the temperature so low that everyone stood around the fire to get warm. Rain did more than make the travelers uncomfortable. The detachment camped along a small stream and expected to use the "pleasant"-tasting water for drinking and cooking when a sudden storm began. Runoff from the rain caused the stream to overflow and the water became "thick with buffalo dung. . .accompanied with a most intolerable stench. . . ." Despite their obvious lack of enthusiasm, the men had little choice but to use this liquid for their dinner. They dipped it out of the stream in kettles, let it stand long enough for the mud to settle, skimmed off the floating dung, and then poured some of the remainder into other containers carefully. These efforts got the obvious filth out of the water, but the "disagreeable smell remained" to spoil their cornmeal and boiled meat soup.[36]

The continuing food shortage and an often unbalanced diet—even when the group had enough to eat—remained constant difficulties. Long had anticipated finding enough game to keep the men fed easily, but this was not the case.

Few animals were seen on the Plains that summer, and often the naturalists had to halt for a few hours or even all day so that the hunters could get food. Even then, they had either feast or famine. For example, on July 12 they killed a buffalo and four deer. Three days later, however, each man received only one pint of cornmeal, which had to last him four days. To supplement this slender ration, they ate soup with tiny scraps of salted or dried meat.[37] The uncertainty of the food supply frequently disrupted plans and increased the sense of haste that prevailed during much of the expedition.

Nevertheless, Long chose to halt for three days to give his men a chance to climb Pikes Peak. A detachment of seven rode the twenty-five miles to the base of the mountain. There Lieutenant Swift took some highly inaccurate measurements and with one of the men returned to camp. Edwin James and four others hung some of their food in the trees for safety and began the ascent. One of the guides had warned them that piles of loose weathered rock covered large parts of the mountainside, but the climbers struggled through the shale before making camp. They spent a miserable night with little sleep because the slope was so steep that they had to rest behind a log jammed between two trees.[38]

On the morning of July 14, the climbers left their blankets, all but three pounds of meat, and some of their heavier clothing behind and set out for the summit. By noon they reached the timberline and at four that afternoon they stood on top of the mountain. Edwin James described the summit as a level plain of several acres where "scarce a lichen was to be seen." From there the climbers could see the streams feeding into both the Platte and Arkansas rivers, and the only obstacle to their view part of the time was a vast cloud of grasshoppers. By five o'clock the temperature had dropped to forty-two degrees, and the shivering men started back down their trail. They reached the timberline by sunset but soon got lost in the dark and so had to stop for the night.[39]

At sunrise they continued their descent, guided by a "dense

column of smoke" that they guessed correctly came from their campfire the previous day. The blaze had destroyed the clothing and equipment left behind, so they pushed on down the mountain and by noon rejoined the men waiting with the horses. Thus, James and three companions became the first recorded group to climb Pikes Peak. On the theory that climbing the mountain was more noteworthy than discovering it, Major Long renamed it James' peak and thus marked it on his map. The name change was never accepted, however, and eventually a lesser peak was named for James.

Climbing Pikes Peak may appear as time wasted in light of the vast region the explorers still had to cross, but that was not true. During the ascent and while at the summit, James described the river valleys in all four directions, and, in particular, since Long had chosen not to explore the headwaters of the Platte, these observations helped him fill in some gaps in the geographic knowledge of the area. Not only that, but the climbers saw clearly the divide between the Platte and Arkansas basins, more valuable information. Moreover, the small party had done more than just climb. On their way up, James noted animals that resembled prairie dogs—probably marmots. Once above the timberline, he described numerous alpine plants and gathered some specimens on the way up the mountain. The preserved samples and the notes he took on other species proved to be one of the major botanical contributions of the expedition.[40]

On July 15, Dr. James and his companions rejoined the main camp, and the next day Long ordered his men south to the Arkansas River. The expedition was supposed to explore this river to its source, and so the major detailed Captain Bell, Dr. James, and two others to follow it into the mountains. The detachment traveled about thirty miles upstream, to the neighborhood of present Canon City at the lower end of Royal Gorge. There they found numerous salt springs. The next day they continued their ride deeper into the mountains before turning back toward the main camp.

Bell seems to have been disappointed that they could go no farther into the mountains. "I am confident our party has omitted to visit the most interesting spot," he wrote, "where subjects for each department of science is [sic] to be found, that will be met on our whole tour. . . ."[41] By the time Bell and his companions got back to the camp, Long had decided to abandon further efforts to explore the Arkansas. He already had James's report from Pikes Peak, and probably the continuing difficulties with getting food and keeping his party healthy convinced him that it was time to hurry east.

The decision not to explore and map the Arkansas had more significance for the nation at the time than did any of Long's other decisions on this expedition. The Adams-Onis Treaty negotiated between the United States and Spain in 1819 had established a new western boundary for the nation, and in part this line followed the south bank of the Arkansas River to its source before turning north. No existing map depicted the Arkansas that far west, and one of the explorers' goals had been to locate the sources and to trace accurately that river. The major never indicated why he chose to abandon this part of his assignment and instead concentrate his efforts on finding the sources of the Red River. Under the new treaty, the headwaters of that stream lay well within Spanish territory, as Long had anticipated when he urged Secretary Calhoun to get a license for him to cross Spanish territory even before he left Philadelphia the preceding spring. The treaty line followed the Red only as far west as the one hundredth meridian, so there seems to have been no good reason for trying to find the sources of the river, except that the task had not yet been done. Certainly, in 1820, exploring the Arkansas was more important than following the Red, but Long chose to do the latter.

On July 19, he ordered the expedition east and south, away from the mountains and down the Arkansas. Thus, the outward leg of the journey ended. The explorers had traveled from the Missouri River west through the Platte Valley to the

Rockies and then south to the Arkansas. Much of the region they crossed was then unknown, except to a few traders. During the six weeks the party rode west they gathered masses of data, took many samples, and made dozens of sketches and paintings. Considering the difficulties they encountered, their inadequate equipment, and the pace of travel, the naturalists' work was as thorough and competent as their circumstances permitted. As a result, the published reports of Long and Edwin James, the official journal kept by Captain Bell, the letters and later papers written by Thomas Say, the sketches of Titian Peale, and the paintings of Samuel Seymour all contributed much new information about the central Plains. Unfortunately, the problems that had become so annoying on the outward leg of the expedition intensified on the homeward leg and reduced greatly the achievements of the last half of the expedition.

Exploring the Plains, 1820:
East to Fort Smith

From the time Stephen Long's detachment left Council Bluffs in June, 1820, until it arrived at the Rocky Mountains six weeks later, the men had experienced occasional food shortages, lack of good water, and poor forage for their animals. On the return trip these difficulties became more serious. What had been inconvenient and annoying on the ride west grew worse steadily and now became dangerous to the health and perhaps even to the lives of the explorers. By mid-July, when they turned south and east to follow the Arkansas and to find the Red River, both the tired men and the jaded animals needed frequent rest and an improved diet, but neither was available. The explorers' actions during the return trip may be understood best in terms of their unequal struggle with the inhospitable environment. Increasingly, the effort to get food, water, and fuel forced the naturalists to reduce some of their scientific investigations and even to abandon others. More significantly, however, their increasing hardships affected the explorers' interpretation of their experiences and the data they gathered on the Plains that summer. Certainly, the unanimous labeling of that region as desert came from their difficulties with heat, sand, lack of vegetation, and a shortage of food and water.

On July 19, 1820, Long and his companions turned their backs on the Rockies, abandoned the significant geographic objective of exploring the Arkansas River to its source, and instead began their descent of that stream. Although eager to return east, the prospect of having to recross "a dusty plain of sand and gravel, barren as the deserts of Arabia. . .," dimmed their enthusiasm. At the mountains the naturalists had found many plants and animals to study. Now they could only look forward to the "one thousand miles of dreary and monotonous plain" that lay between them and "civilization."[1] Clearly, by this time the explorers considered much of the high Plains as desert, and their experiences during the rest of the summer would only reinforce this belief.

Two days later, the explorers met an Indian couple, Buffalo Calf and his wife, riding west toward the mountains. These Indians told the whites that fifteen days earlier they had left an encampment of "the greater part of six nations of Indians," which included many of the large tribes of the southern Plains. This news explained why the travelers had ridden through the Indian country for more than six weeks without meeting any tribesmen. According to Buffalo Calf, just a few weeks ago, the Indians had gathered south of the Arkansas River in order to attack the Spanish.[2]

Major Long hoped that this Indian couple might have other useful information and convinced them to travel with the explorers for a few days. Buffalo Calf and his wife led a "beautiful bay horse," in addition to the animals they rode, and Captain Bell bought the extra mount. This gave the detachment another usable animal, which they certainly needed, but caused some trouble for Bell later in the summer. Indians on the southern Plains appear to have known this animal well, and on several occasions other tribesmen claimed to own the horse. Buffalo Calf showed the explorers a suitable place to ford the Arkansas and answered Long's questions about the location of the Red River. His information was of little help. Either he failed to understand what the whites wanted to know or he lied to them, because his directions proved wrong.[3]

For several days the expedition remained encamped at the Arkansas because the major had decided to divide the detachment. He would lead some of the explorers south and east looking for the Red River, while Captain Bell would take the others and follow the Arkansas east to Fort Smith. Considering that both men and animals were no longer in top physical condition and that the journey back to the settlements was likely to prove more difficult than what they had just completed, it is surprising that Long continued to follow his orders when he had already broken them twice earlier. Perhaps he wanted to enter Spanish territory, as had Zebulon Pike during the winter of 1806-7. Certainly, he realized that finding the Red would take him into Spanish-held areas because he had asked for permission to do so before leaving Philadelphia the preceding winter. Or he may have thought that locating the Red would be a significant geographic discovery and would divert attention from his failure to explore either the Platte or the Arkansas valleys, as ordered. Long left no record to explain his choice, so one can only speculate why he risked possible arrest by Spanish authorities, attack by hostile Indians, and disease or even possible death among his men because they lacked essential food and medical supplies.

While the hunters killed game and some of the men butchered the animals and jerked the meat, Long and Bell made their final plans. The major chose Dr. James, Titian Peale, and seven others to accompany him beyond the Arkansas. The remaining eleven men he assigned to Captain Bell. The two leaders divided the animals, with Long taking the strongest horses and mules because he expected to travel farther than Bell. The captain's group had fourteen animals to carry most of the camp equipment and the naturalists' specimens, but many of these horses "were worn out with fatigue & sore back,'' so they could not be used. From Bell's inventory, the inadequacy of the explorers' supplies is evident. His group took only nine pints of corn, three pecks of cornmeal, twelve pounds of biscuit, three-quarters of a pound of coffee, one-half a pound of sugar, one ounce of tea, five pints of whiskey, and four bottles of lemon acid.[4] The ride down the Arkansas or the Red would include no variation in diet for the expedition.

On Monday, July 24, Stephen Long and his men rode out of camp and crossed the Arkansas River. At the far bank they paused to give three cheers, which their comrades with Bell answered. Then Long's detachment turned south and east on a route at nearly a right angle from the Arkansas toward what they called the ''First Fork,'' probably the Purgatory. They rode twenty-seven miles that day, across a ''sterile and Sandy'' trace, and saw no water except that standing in stagnant pools left by recent rains. At noon, their thermometer registered an even 100 degrees in the shade of the tent. There was little vegetation except near the small water pools, and there were usually no trees or substantial bushes, either. In fact, Edwin James commented later that after leaving the Arkansas they saw barely enough wood to have supplied them for a single night. Buffalo chips provided their only fuel.[5] Thus a pattern emerged: little game, grass, wood, or drinking water, accompanied by high temperatures, numerous insects, and later sickness and potential danger from the Indians. These difficulties made the trip both uncomfortable and hazardous and limited sharply the amount of scientific investigation either detachment could do.

Even the most elementary activities became difficult for the explorers. For example, sleeping arrangements were awkward. With ten men and only a single tent, there was not room for everyone. Long decided that all of the men needed some protection from the weather, so at night they lay down with their heads toward the center of the tent and their legs and feet protruding out in all directions. Although this protected the head and upper body of each person, it meant that from the waist down the men lay exposed to insects, rain, or dew.[6]

Food gathering continued to be a difficult task. On the evening of July 27, several of the hunters wounded a young buffalo bull, but he ran off with a pack of wolves in pursuit. The hungry hunters returned to camp, got more men and some horses, and set out after the bull. They found him trying to fend off the wolves, drove the predators away, and killed the buffalo. By moonlight they dressed the meat, returning with it late that same night. The men were all so hungry that they sat up much of the night eating the fresh meat and talking.[7]

Frequent summer storms made travel difficult, too. Late the next afternoon the explorers arrived at a small stream that they thought was one of the sources of the North Canadian River. This, however, was more probably the Cimarron, which heads near the Canadian in the Raton Mountains. After fording the stream, they stopped to camp because of heavy rain. At midday on July 29, they encountered another, more violent storm that soaked them and made it nearly impossible to find any dry fuel. Although they got some and cooked their noon meal, the storm raged for another two hours. The dripping travelers huddled over their sputtering fire until the rain abated. Then they rode on, only to be overtaken by more rain with cold wind and hail. The second storm was so fierce that the horses refused to walk except with the wind, so the cold, wet explorers sat huddled on their horses with their backs to the storm. Once the hail passed, they continued with "water pouring in streams from our mockasins and every part of our dress." The rain continued until dark and the tired men pitched their tent and went to bed supperless. During the night the temperature dropped from seventy to only forty-seven degrees, so they huddled together, unsuccessfully trying to keep warm. Sometime during that "cheerless night," Titian Peale suffered an attack of cramps that he treated with "the free use of opium and whiskey."[8]

The next morning, stiff, hungry, and still wet, the men hurried from the "comfortless camp" and started across a wide plain. By noon they reached a small creek, which, like the others they had crossed since leaving the Arkansas, flowed through a deep gully lined with rocks and partially choked with underbrush. This made getting up and down the banks difficult for both men and animals. Numerous sharp rocks hurt the horses and mules; some became lame, and all were "much exhausted and weakened."[9] These problems, when added to Long's lack of any accurate map and the inexperience of his guides with this part of the Plains, must have convinced the men that their hopes of locating and exploring the Red were slim.

Under these conditions it is not surprising that the members of the detachment hoped that the dry stream bed near which they camped the evening of July 30 was one of the sources of the Red. Actually, it proved to be a tributary of the Canadian. Edwin James blamed the mistake on the faulty directions that Buffalo Calf had given them almost two weeks earlier, claiming that the warrior had tried to deceive them. Sometime later, however, he noted that the "sufferings from the want of provisions, and from the late storm, had given us a little distaste for prolonging farther than was necessary our journey towards the southeast."[10] Whatever their reasons for choosing to follow this stream, it was probably all that the explorers could have done. Their food supplies were gone and both men and animals had been weakened by continuing exposure, hard travel, and poor diet. It is unlikely that they had either the strength or the desire to continue to the Red, even had they realized their mistake.

In failing to find the sources of the Red River, Long's expedition became the third group sent out by the United States government to miss this objective. In the summer of 1806, Captain Richard Sparks and Thomas Freeman had tried to ascend that stream, only to be turned back by units of Spanish cavalry. That same year, Zebulon M. Pike traveled west up the Arkansas, but before locating the Red he was arrested by Spanish troops.[11] Unlike these earlier explorers who had failed to locate the Red River, Long did not encounter foreign troops. His failure was not the result of Spanish intervention, but was the consequence of inadequacies in planning and support of the explorers.

The party resumed its journey on July 31, but found the terrain more difficult than ever. In places stones so obstructed the valley that the travelers climbed up onto the plain. This was nearly as bad, however, because each time they came to a stream they had to clamber down the high, steep bluffs, often as much as 400 feet down, to the stream bed below, then cross it, and again ascend the opposite bank to the plain. This rough travel caused more of the horses to go lame, and again Long halted the detachment for a rest.[12]

The continuing efforts put into travel and getting food not only used most of the time and energy the explorers had but affected what little scientific observation they did, too. For example, the hunters had sighted what they called black-tailed or mule deer, and the naturalists wanted a specimen to study and perhaps bring east with them. Worried that they might leave the area without one of the animals, they offered the hunters a fifty-dollar reward if they would bring a full-grown male to camp. On August 1, Joseph Verplank killed a deer close enough to the camp so that it could be carried there whole, rather than being butchered and dressed where it had been shot. The hunters returned with their prize just after dark but were so hungry that they refused to wait until morning for Titian Peale to measure and sketch the beast. Instead, several of the men built a large fire to furnish light, and Peale took the measurements and made his drawings by firelight so that the hunters could eat before going to sleep.[13]

At sunrise the next morning, the party left their camp and continued downstream. By noon, the water in the creek had disappeared, and when they halted for lunch at a stagnant pool, the water was so bitter that not even their thirst could overcome its taste. After lunching on roast venison "without bread, salt, water, or any thing else," they followed the river valley all afternoon without finding a trace of water. Along the route they passed a few scrubby willows, but when they encamped after sunset at another pool of water, there was neither wood nor buffalo dung nearby for fuel. One of the hunters had shot a badger that afternoon, but they could not roast it. Instead of badger meat, each man got one-quarter of a sea biscuit, which he was to divide between the evening meal and breakfast in the morning. To make matters worse, the travelers had to eat this paltry fare dry because the water was undrinkable.[14]

The next morning they hurried from camp to find water, but were without success. By this time, it had been more than twenty-four hours since they had seen either water or wood, and they rode all afternoon through a hot, dusty wind that seemed "almost suffocating." At evening they found a muddy pool of brackish water and some wood nearby, so they roasted their day-old badger and a young owl one of the men had shot.[15]

Somewhat refreshed and certainly in better spirits, Long and his men crossed more "barren and desolate" country the following day. Again, they saw no game, wood, or water until late in the afternoon, when the river water rose to the surface of the sandy bottom for the first time in over 100 miles. Here the brackish water contained so much red silt and sand that the explorers described it as "the colour of florid blood." This coloration may have convinced Long and his companions that this was a part of the long-sought Red River. At this point the stream still flowed to the southeast, the correct direction for the Red or its tributaries. When they saw a well-worn Indian trail paralleling the river, the men guessed that the trail connected the Pawnee Pict village on the Red with Santa Fe.[16]

That evening Verplank again brought in a young deer and the group ate its first full meal in several days. After eating, the men noticed a wild horse nearby, and several of them tried to catch it. They staked their own animals under a large cottonwood tree, and one man climbed into the tree with a long, noosed, rope. He sat there for hours waiting for the horse to pass under him, but it did not. Early in the morning another hunter saw the horse standing under a nearby tree, apparently asleep, and shot him. If any of the party had been squeamish about eating horsemeat, such ideas now vanished. "Instead of questioning whether we should eat the flesh of a horse," James noted, "we congratulated ourselves on the acquisition of so seasonable a supply." Although several of the travelers felt sorry that such a beautiful animal had been killed, their "scruples yielded to the loud admonitions of hunger."[17]

Throughout the difficulties of this ill-planned expedition, the naturalists continued their efforts to gather, study, and record what they saw. Titian Peale was one of the best marksmen in the group and often shot animals and birds for study and sketching. The burrowing owls that shared the prairie dog villages with the rodents fascinated the explorers. Some of the men were certain that the birds must feed on their four-footed neighbors, but it took until August 7 before Peale could shoot one of the birds. The owl fell into one of the burrows, but the eager naturalist reached in and dragged his prize to the surface. When he and James opened the bird's intestines, they found many insects but no evidence of bone or flesh from the prairie dogs. Late that same day, one of the men captured a "formidable centipede." The creature was dark brown, about eight inches long, and "bit at everything which came within its reach."[18] The narratives of the return trip include some discussion of similar scientific observations, but on a scale reduced from the westward trip. The struggle for survival certainly was a significant reason for this.

At mid-afternoon, August 10, Long's detachment saw a

large party of Indians approaching. Except for their brief visit with Buffalo Calf, the travelers had seen no other Indians since leaving the Pawnee villages in mid-June. When all of the Indians stopped, Chief Red Mouse approached and shook hands with each of the explorers. Talking through an old man who spoke Spanish, the chief told Long that the band was a part of the Bad Heart or Comanche tribe and that they expected to meet Spanish traders near the source of the river. When Long asked Red Mouse if the river they were following was the Red, the chief replied that it was. He claimed that if the whites followed the stream, in another ten days they would come to the Pawnee Pict village. This information was incorrect and yet may not have been a deliberate falsehood, either. Several rivers in the Southwest carried red silt, and the Spanish usually called them Rio Colorado. The Canadian was so known at the time, and the Indians could have borrowed the Spanish name for that stream.[19]

When the chief finished answering Long's questions, he in turn asked the travelers who they were, why they were on the Plains, and where they were going. Red Mouse accepted the explorers' answers at first, but later acted as though he thought they were traders. He asked the whites to accompany his band and to camp with them that evening, and although Long would have preferred not to do this, he hesitated to antagonize the Indians. Recognizing that this was a hunting, rather than a war party, the major wanted to avoid trouble, and the whites followed the Indians reluctantly. At the campsite the tribesmen stopped and "in perfect silence and good order" erected their tepees before their fascinated visitors. Then they put up a lodge for the explorers.[20]

Long's men unloaded their baggage, put it in the tent, and began negotiating for fresh horses, food, and clothing. When the whites spread out their few trade articles for the Indians, Red Mouse assumed that some of the best articles had been held back. He insisted that the Americans open more of their packs, but they refused. Still not satisfied, he called to several braves who tried to open the packs. This brought the whites running, while Indian women and children fled in all directions. The soldiers' determined resistance impressed the tribesmen, and those who stayed in the lodge asked Long not to be angry. Apparently, the 250 Comanches had hoped that their numerical superiority would frighten the visitors, but Long's 10 heavily armed men showed that this was not the case. Actually, none of the warriors had any firearms and only 22 of them had bows or lances. The explorers reacted to the Comanches in the same way that the Lewis and Clark party had in their 1804 meeting with the Teton Sioux. By refusing to be intimidated, they kept an uneasy peace with the tribesmen.[21]

When the abortive trading session ended, the whites waited in vain for the Comanche to offer them the usual courtesies of welcome. The explorers had been on short rations for days, so when it became obvious that their Indian hosts had no intention of offering them any food, they asked for some. It took several requests before the chief's wife brought a "little half-boiled bison meat," from which she took the best chunks for her children while the travelers watched in hungry silence. Long and his men ate the meat quickly and when they asked for more, the squaw brought a little jerked meat "with such an ill grace" that they asked no more. Several requested water, but to their dismay, their hosts brought it in "paunch of bison." The buffalo stomachs held water well, but because they had not been cleaned, the liquid smelled and tasted like buffalo entrails.[22]

That same evening, Red Mouse and other band leaders held a closed meeting. Long knew that his hosts had already stolen some camp equipment from the scientific party and he feared that they planned to seize more. Hoping to prevent this, he ordered his men to keep their horses under guard that night, but when the soldiers went to get their mounts, they could find only a few. Early the next morning, the explorers awoke to the shouting of orders and the scurry of women packing as the Indians prepared to leave. Alarmed that their hosts had taken the horses, Long got the old Indian interpreter and asked Red Mouse to order the return of the missing equipment and animals. The chief claimed that the horses had strayed and that he had already sent men to search for them, but Long thought this was only a delaying tactic to give the women more time to get the camp ready to travel. In order to prevent the Indians from leaving his party stranded on the Plains, the major ordered his soldiers to seize an equal amount of Indian property. This brought an immediate crisis. The Indians surrounded their visitors and the twenty-two armed warriors held their weapons ready, but the whites' superior weapons and refusal to yield convinced the Comanche not to fight. Much to the explorers' relief, the tribesmen found the missing horses and all but a few ropes and halters of the equipment they had taken. Then the whites and Indians parted.[23]

The next day, Titian Peale and one of the soldiers left the rest of the detachment to hunt. When they reached a nearby wooded area and dismounted to shoot turkeys, the rifleman's mule fled. Peale rode after the beast, and although the mule found the trail of the main party, the naturalist got lost. By evening he hurried along the river, firing his pistol every few hundred yards to attract attention. His companions built a large fire, hoping that he would see it during the night, but he had passed beyond them and was searching in the wrong direction. At nightfall Peale stopped to rest, but had an uncomfortable night because of the mosquitoes. Early the next morning, he rode upstream until he saw the campfire smoke from the main camp, and soon rejoined the others.[24]

Beginning on August 15, the hunters saw more frequent signs of game, and within a few days the travelers had enough meat and water. This did not stop unexpected difficulties, however. Great swarms of blowflies were everywhere, and when the men did not eat the game the same day they killed it, the flies ruined the surplus. In fact, when the explorers sat on the ground to eat, the insects covered everything and left the food "white with the eggs [they] deposited. . . ." Soon the men learned to cook and eat with only one hand, using the other to brush away flies. When this failed, the travelers turned to making soup. That way they could keep their meat submerged until they ate it.[25]

The explorers stopped briefly at the falls of the Canadian, surprised that so little water passed over them. They concluded that despite the rain and spring water that flowed down the stream, evaporation consumed most of the water. The falls, Edwin James noted, would prevent further travel upstream by boat. Even if they did not, he assumed that few people would venture farther along that river because nothing but "sandy wastes and thirsty inhospitable steppes" lay beyond. Below the falls the explorers found a small canoe, and because their pack horses were "reduced by long fatigue," they loaded their heavy baggage in the craft and assigned two men to get it downstream.[26]

On September 9, Long took observations to get an idea of their approximate latitude. To his surprise and dismay, his calculations showed the detachment farther north than anticipated, and north of the suspected sources of the Red. Several of the explorers expressed "unpleasant fears" that the river they had followed was a tributary of the Arkansas and not the Red. Any doubt about their location ended the next day when the party reached the Arkansas.[27] Thus, after weeks of toil, danger, and the most primitive living conditions, the tired men learned that they had failed to achieve the last of their major objectives. They had not explored the sources of the Platte, the Arkansas, or the Red. Surely they felt keen disappointment now.

In explaining this mistake, the explorers offered several reasons. They had, wrote James, been misled by the vague maps of that region. Moreover, both Buffalo Calf and Red Mouse had given information that was either incorrect or false. Realizing that some confusion over the river names existed, the explorers had asked Red Mouse specifically if the stream they were on led to the Pawnee Pict villages. The Indian replied that it did, but the uncertainties of translation may have obscured the whites' question or the chief's reply. The Picts may have had a hunting camp along the stream, or Red Mouse may have been mistaken. In any case, Long's command missed the Red.[28]

Two days later, the explorers met some whites who told them that Captain Bell's detachment had arrived at Fort Smith a few days earlier. With this welcome news to spur them on, the party reached that post on September 13, 1820. Officers came out to meet Long's men and escorted them to the fort after they crossed the river ferry. There, post commander William Bradford invited the travelers to dinner but warned them to be careful about what and how much they tried to eat. In spite of his friendly warning, the men ate such long-forgotten items as bread, sweet potatoes, and vegetables. As the major predicted, most of his guests got sick from eating foods to which their bodies were no longer accustomed.[29]

Captain Bell's detachment, in their descent of the Arkansas, had experienced many of the same difficulties as Long's men. Mr. Say and the captain both wrote accounts of their travels and between them provided more detail than Long and James did about their half of the expedition. The chief difference in the experiences of the two groups occurred about half-way down the Arkansas when three of the soldiers in Bell's party deserted. No disaster in itself, this became one when the deserters took three of the best horses, much of the baggage, and most of the scientific and narrative journals being kept by the explorers. For example, Thomas Say alone lost five notebooks filled with data and narrative. The theft of these documents reduced drastically the amount of information that the naturalists brought back that summer.

Bell's party of twelve began their downriver trek on July 24, the same morning that Long had crossed the Arkansas to look for the Red. That first afternoon, during one of the frequent thunderstorms that plagued both detachments, Julian the interpreter was "electrified" by a bolt of lightning that struck the ground near him. Apparently, he was more frightened than hurt, because he continued his duties.[30]

The command following the Arkansas met many more Indians than did Long's men, and these red men were friendly or at least not openly hostile most of the time. For example, on the third day of the march the explorers met a party of Indians encamped along the river. Traveling single file and with Bell leading their small column, the whites rode toward the Indian camp. When the Indians noticed them, some of the warriors and several chiefs rode from camp to greet their visitors. Bell learned that this was a Kiowa band, and his men put up their camp near the Indian lodges. Soon many of the tribesmen walked to the whites' camp. Some Indians poked the equipment, while others examined the shoes on the Captain's horse. They crowded around the beast, lifting its front feet to look at the shoes. At dark the curious visitors left.

In the morning, Bell and the scientists met with chiefs of the Kiowa, Comanche, Cheyenne, and Arapahoe tribes who had camped nearby. Translating the talks proved difficult. The explorers could not understand the language of any of the assembled tribes, and the Indians knew no English. Soon they discovered that one of the Indians spoke Pawnee, as did Abraham Ledeux, and so it was possible to work out a cumbersome but apparently effective system. Captain Bell spoke in English. Julian the interpreter, translated his remarks into French, whereupon Ledeux repeated the comments in Pawnee for the Indian, who repeated it to the chiefs in their languages. The multiple translations made the meeting a long one, but no one seemed to have complained. Bell told the chiefs that the explorers were Americans and that they were examining the country. He apologized that he lacked authority to conclude any treaty with them and also

KIOWA ENCAMPMENT by Samuel Seymour. *Courtesy Yale University Libraries.*

for his shortage of good presents. After the talks the parties exchanged gifts, and Bell and his companions got horses, mules, and other items worth far more than the paltry trinkets that they had for the tribesmen.[31]

Later, Bell told the Indian leaders that his men wanted to trade for food, and soon a noisy, quarreling group of squaws came. In exchange for an awl, a comb, a small mirror, or a bit of vermillion paint, the women cheerfully traded packets of six to eight pounds of jerked buffalo meat. The explorers also got animal skins and leather strips for tying and packing their baggage. Several chiefs supervised the noisy trading session to make sure that all would be satisfied. Some Indians complained about the small gifts and the lack of variety among the trade goods of the whites, but when Bell explained for a second time that his men were not traders, the tribesmen seemed content.[32]

While Indians came and went, Mr. Say and one of the interpreters visited several Indian lodges to observe and take notes. It is not certain how he communicated with his hosts when previously it had taken two interpreters to translate Bell's speech, but within a few hours he had compiled word lists and was busily trying to outline a grammar. These Indians had several habits that the whites disliked. The women were ugly and were continually hunting lice on each other. "In the rear of our tent a squaw who had become possessed of a wooden small-toothed comb, was occupied in removing from her head a population as numerous, as. . . well fed," Say noted. "[A] female companion. . .alternately crunched the oily vermin between her teeth, and conversed with the most rapid and pleasant loquacity. . . ." At evening some Indian men brought their wives to the travelers, hoping to get presents in return for bed partners. Captain Bell had some trouble convincing the Indians that his men did not want to spend the night with the women. In fact, Arapahoe chief Bear Tooth became so insistent that the explorers take his wife that Bell ordered the sentry to remove the chief and to keep him away.[33]

On July 28 the Indian bands moved on, but within a few days the explorers met a second, smaller group of Indians. This small band had been part of a larger group that had ridden north to steal horses from the Pawnee without much success. The same evening one of the men tried to take Captain Bell's horse, claiming to have lost it two years earlier. The captain rejected the brave's claim and finally stopped him at gun point. From this band the explorers got a sort of Plains variety of pemmican consisting of crushed wild cherries mixed with buffalo fat. When eaten with dried or pounded buffalo meat, the explorers pronounced it "quite delicious."[34]

Only a day after the two parties separated, Bell's men saw a lone Indian on top of a nearby sand hill. They unfurled the flag and sent Julian the interpreter forward. Just then, the rest of the Indians, members of a Cheyenne war party, appeared. Carrying lances, bows and arrows, the forty braves presented a formidable force as they hollered and galloped toward the explorers. They met briefly with the whites, but seemed to fear pursuit by the Pawnee and indicated that they wanted to continue south. After an exchange of handshakes and hugs, the chief ordered the party to mount, and the Indians rode off in one direction, while Bell's command continued in another. Apparently the explorers had feared an attack because the war party was large, so they left the Indians with considerable relief at the peaceful meeting.[35]

Bell's hunters enjoyed more success than did their counterparts on the Canadian, although even they went empty-handed occasionally. For example, on August 3, the hunters chased four buffalo, shooting three of the lumbering beasts three times each. "Yet they moved off as if nothing had disturbed them," Bell wrote. He thought that wet powder explained this failure, but poor marksmanship may have been a second factor. The next day their luck changed. The hunters had no difficulty killing three buffalo cows, and the command spent the rest of the day jerking meat.[36]

On August 7, the interpreters Bijou and Ledeux, who had been forced to accompany the expedition west from the Pawnee villages near the Platte, were allowed to return north to their homes. Bell and his companions felt some regret when the two Frenchmen left. They had served well, both as hunters and interpreters. Bijou dictated a memoir to Thomas Say that discussed his wanderings through the Plains region and while traveling with hunting and trading parties. He also gave Say much information "concerning the manners and habits of these mountain Indians, their history, affinities, and migrations." Ledeux also worked with Say in compiling a Pawnee vocabulary, as well as providing much ethnological information about the Pawnee. Unfortunately, these items disappeared when the three soldiers deserted, and the manuscripts were either lost or destroyed.[37]

Nearly a week later, on August 12, the explorers met yet another Indian band. This included thirty men and five women fleeing from a defeat several days earlier. The Comanche told Bell that two days before enemies had attacked them during the night. The attackers killed three, wounded six more, and escaped with fifty-six of their horses. As a result, this seems to have been the most ragged group of Indians either detachment of explorers met that summer. Most of them had no robes, leggings, or even moccasins. The relatives of the dead warriors had mutilated themselves and allowed the blood to dry, giving them "a most distressing appearance of dispair & sorrow."[38]

The Indians begged the explorers to camp with them for mutual protection from pursuing Oto warriors, but Bell refused. He guessed that the Comanche wanted his horses, and the Indians' actions confirmed this suspicion. Even before the leaders of the two parties had begun talking, one of the braves seized the rifle of an enlisted man. Surprised, the soldier jerked his weapon free and rejoined his companions. During the pipe-smoking ceremony, the chiefs tried to stall by hiding the pipe. Then, one of the warriors tried to take Bell's controversial horse, and when the chief ignored the captain's objections, Bell shouted at the warrior. He may not have understood the words, but Bell's tone was clear and he stopped grabbing the horse. When the talk ended, the whites gave their visitors a few presents and prepared to leave. As Julian the interpreter mounted his horse, the Indians tried to pull him off. At that, several soldiers leveled their rifles while the Indians drew arrows, but the Indian leader motioned to his men, who lowered their weapons, and the whites rode away.[39]

During their journey along the Arkansas, the travelers experienced difficulties similar to those of Long's command.

Both parties suffered from inadequate diet, and by early August the two large hunting dogs, Caesar and Buck, had both died, in spite of the care Bell's men lavished on them. For weeks, all the explorers had eaten was half a cup of cornmeal and whatever game the hunters brought in each day. By mid-August even the cornmeal was gone and they had only a "small quantity of mouldy crumbs" left. On August 20 the hunters saw no game, so all they had to eat for lunch was soup made from the crumbs "with the nutritious addition of some grease." That evening the men killed a skunk, which they threw eagerly into the soup pot. Day after day, the explorers fasted or had reduced rations. By August 25 they were so hungry and weak that they chose one of the weakest horses to be slaughtered if they could not get other food. Although the famished men considered the horse very lean, they could not resist "an occasional wishful glance" at it as they plodded along the river.[40]

It is hardly surprising, under such conditions, that some of the soldiers deserted. When the company awoke on August 31, they noticed that three of the best horses were gone. Horses strayed every day, so at first there was little concern. After checking, however, Bell realized that three of the enlisted men had deserted, robbed their companions of food and equipment, and fled with the best horses and some of the scientific specimens and journals. A heavy dew obscured the fugitives' trail, so the rest of the detachment chose not to pursue the deserters. The thefts left the party with only the clothes on their backs, no Indian trade goods, and without many of the papers and much of the data that the naturalists had gathered that summer. Of more immediate significance, the travelers were so weakened by shortages of food that Bell claimed they grew weaker and lost weight daily. Some of the men could barely walk and when they dismounted wanted only to "sit or lay down" because exercise caused "a trembling and pain in the knees & legs." To make matters worse, that day the hunters saw no game, and the discouraged men had only a few grapes and unripe persimmons to eat.[41]

Fortunately, the next morning the exhausted whites met a large Osage hunting party that gave them food. The deserters were at the Indian village only fifteen miles away at the time, but before Bell's command learned of this from their hosts, they had fled again—this time escaping for good. From the Osage encampment it took the explorers only a few more days to reach Fort Smith, where they arrived on September 9, 1820.[42]

For the next few days the tired explorers worked on their reports and maps, while waiting for Major Long's detachment. It arrived on September 13, and the next day both Long and Captain Bell wrote brief reports of their activities to Secretary of War Calhoun. Within a week after the men had gathered at Fort Smith, they separated again. On September 19, the first of three contingents left the post, traveling east toward Cape Girardeau, Missouri. By October 12 they reassembled there and met Lieutenant Graham, who had been left to tend the *Western Engineer*. He brought the steamer to Cape Girardeau, but few of the explorers chose to accompany it east. Long and Bell left first, traveling overland to Washington. Shortly after that, Say, Peale, Seymour, and Graham traveled south to New Orleans, and then east. Edwin James set out overland alone, but later traveled part of the way up to the Ohio River with Lieutenant Swift, who now commanded the *Western Engineer*. Thus, the expedition ended. The soldiers and naturalists scattered, each to his former activity, while the public showed little interest in the explorations of that summer.[43]

In many ways, the 1820 expedition resembled John C. Fremont's 1848 attempt to explore the Rockies. Both were under-financed, headed west at a difficult time of year, and received warnings of danger before starting. Neither group had competent guides when it started, and both employed men who lacked knowledge of the region into which they traveled. Long and Fremont were determined to travel west in spite of the obvious difficulties they could see, and neither was as careful or well-prepared as he should have been.

Here the similarities end; the results of the two expeditions differed widely. Long's men lost only horses and dogs to the summer heat and drought, while those accompanying Fremont actually starved and froze to death. Later, some of Fremont's men denounced his leadership bitterly, while most of the scientists with Long readily agreed to accompany him on another expedition three years later.[44] Clearly, Long's leadership received a vote of confidence from his associates, while that of Fremont did not.

[8]
The Explorers Report to the Nation, 1821-1823

No aspect of Stephen Long's forty-nine-year military career has received more attention or been less understood than the scientific expeditions of 1819 and 1820. From contemporary expectations, which soared far beyond any hope of fulfillment, to modern historical discussions that denounce the expeditions, participants, and results, all commentators have given inadequate, if not incorrect, descriptions of what occurred. Few historians examined the contemporary responses to the explorers' work, and fewer still considered carefully the scientific contributions of these investigators. A brief look at western history textbooks leads the reader from simple factual errors to misunderstandings of the explorers' goals, and from there to an unwillingness or inability to recognize positive contributions. Such accounts concentrate on Long's failure to locate the sources of the Red River and on his designation of the high Plains as the Great American Desert. By doing so, they obscure the genuine contributions to such fields as botany, zoology, entomology, geology, cartography, and ethnology that Long and his associates made during their travels up the Missouri and across the Plains.

When the explorers left Cape Girardeau, they chose divergent paths east. Long and Captain Bell rode to Washington in November, 1820, and there the major reported to the secretary of war. Calhoun directed him to prepare a comprehensive report of the expedition and to draw a map showing the region through which he had traveled. Captain Bell and Lieutenants Swift and Graham were to assist him. Working at his home in Philadelphia, Long completed a tentative report in January, 1821, and after he submitted it the War Department ordered his fellow officers to return to their former units. The major urged unsuccessfully that the others be allowed to help him complete the cartographic work and write a narrative manuscript of the expedition.[1]

Despite this setback, Long gathered the expedition's civilian scientists and artists in Philadelphia so that they might complete their reports. He persuaded Secretary Calhoun to continue their per diem pay and rations while the naturalists prepared specimens or did other chores related to the expedition. Once the scientists finished their studies, their plant, animal, and insect specimens were to be deposited in the Philadelphia Museum, a private organization operated by Titian Peale's father. Because the War Department had no particular interest in keeping these items, and the government wished to avoid the cost of preserving and displaying the specimens, their donation to the museum would still make them available to the public, as well as to interested scholars.[2]

While Long cajoled his reluctant superiors to continue their financial support of the expeditions' scientific activity, his colleagues straggled east to complete their project duties. Edwin James, expedition botanist and geologist, certainly had the most difficulty getting from Missouri to Philadelphia. In November, 1820, he left Cape Girardeau and traveled as far as Smithland, Kentucky, where he stopped for the winter. James suffered recurring attacks of malaria that made his "first and last winter in Kentucky" one of sickness and despondency. Nevertheless, he did prepare scientific reports on geology and botany that he sent east to Long by mid-1821. From Smithland, James traveled up the

Ohio with the *Western Engineer* to Shippingport, near Louisville. There, the craft stopped for repairs and he was stranded because he had run out of money. Fortunately, a local judge provided him with enough cash to continue east, but even then his trials continued. Some weeks later, while in Haggerstown, Maryland, thieves took his trunk with all his money and notes from the expedition. He recovered the trunk and notes but not the cash, and again had to borrow money to complete his trip.[3]

Other members of the expedition got back to Philadelphia months before James. Thomas Say and Titian Peale had arrived by January, 1821, and in mid-February the specimens came by ship from New Orleans. Within a couple of months, Peale had started working on the specimens at his father's Philadelphia Museum. Now he used his skill as a taxidermist and also as a draftsman. Stuffing and mounting birds and animals took time, but not nearly as much as did Peale's effort to complete his drawings. Working from rough sketches and field notes, he frequently took weeks to complete a single drawing. In March, 1821, when Titian deposited his art work from the expeditions in the museum, the collection included 124 drawings, sketches, and paintings. While Titian worked on his drawings, Thomas Say continued his duties with the vast insect collection.[4]

Their work went slowly because of other duties and because nearly all of the explorers had contracted malaria during their western travels. Edwin James had two attacks of fever while traveling east, both Titian Peale and Thomas Say suffered from the disease when still in Missouri, and Long was sick much of 1821. Although a mild strain that proved more of a nuisance than a menace, the sickness certainly disrupted the travel and work of the explorers. In fact, when James finally got back to Philadelphia in the early autumn of 1821, he and Long had no chance to discuss their publication plans and unfinished responsibilities to the government because the major was sick with the fever again.[5]

By autumn, 1821, Stephen Long proposed that he draw a general map of the United States, incorporating his findings during the preceding four years. He also reported that the explorers could edit and publish a popular account of their travels at no expense to the government if negotiations with Henry Carey, the Philadelphia publisher, would be acceptable to the War Department. Secretary Calhoun agreed to both requests and ordered the quartermaster general to furnish an office for the scientists until they completed the project. At the same time, however, Calhoun warned that the War Department would buy only a dozen copies of the completed book, and he reminded the major that James's notes and plant collection remained government property.[6]

Calhoun's limited enthusiasm paralleled the reception the explorers had received since their return. In contrast to the widespread and optimistic newspaper discussions prior to their departure, the press gave the returning scientists little coverage. In November, 1820, Captain Bell had an interview with a reporter for the *National Intelligencer* in Washington, and at least one other eastern paper printed extracts from that report, but certainly the travelers received no heroes' welcome. What little response there was seems to have been negative. In fact, six months after most of the party had returned east, Edwin James complained from Kentucky that "little is said here as far as I know or anywhere else, about the past performances of our party." What news he got from friends in New York indicated that "those who speak. . .at all there speak with little respect" about the expedition.[7]

Despite the lack of encouragement, the explorers set to work. Long, James, and Say got a small office with government funds but had to pay from their own pockets the cost of candles, stationery, wood, and other similar items. The major asked Samuel Seymour to finish his sketches so that they might be used for illustrations. Long continued work on his two maps—a small one of the Arkansas region to be included in the published report, as well as the larger map that he had proposed to Calhoun earlier. Thomas Say had numerous duties. He described the Indian tribes and bands the expedition had met and prepared vocabularies of several Indian languages. Say also had "to describe the new Quadripeds [sic], birds & reptiles" that they had seen and to arrange the meteorological observations he and Lieutenant Swift had taken. To Edwin James fell the task of putting the various reports, notes, and tables into some kind of finished product. The published book does not indicate how much of the actual prose James wrote and how much of it was the work of Say or Long. However, James did note that both of his colleagues remained "constantly attentive to the work, both to the preparation of the manuscript and its revision for the press."[8]

Most of the explorers struggled with the difficult assignment of turning information from notes, animal skins, boxes of insects, and half-finished drawings into a manuscript ready for publication. Samuel Seymour, expedition artist, seemed to be the only exception. In January, 1822, the major reported that he was not working on his drawings, but six months later Seymour had completed 60 of his 150 drawings. Ironically, despite Long's apparent eagerness to use the artist's work, only a few of the paintings appeared in the book. This was a substantial loss because Seymour was the first American artist to visit the Rocky Mountains, and much of his work has since been lost or destroyed. While urging his companions to complete their labors, Long drew two vertical geological sections and completed his small map. The latter he finished before the manuscript was ready, and Henry Carey, the Philadelphia publisher who would print the expedition report, included Long's map in his 1822 atlas. Finally, in mid-June, 1822, after six months of work, the explorers finished their manuscript. They still had to get it to the publisher and the inevitable last-minute delays remained to bedevil them, but the bulk of the work was done. Edwin James left Philadelphia for a vacation, and Long took charge of the manuscript during the last steps toward publication.[9]

As is so often true, having a completed manuscript was no assurance of rapid publication. Long's superiors in the Corps of Engineers wanted him to prepare reports, and he objected, grumbling that he was still serving on detached duty and therefore was responsible to the secretary of war and not the Engineer Department. In addition, his wife and children became sick and the major had to manage the household affairs for some weeks. Even the publisher Henry Carey had difficulties. He promised Long that he would print eighty pages each week, but completed less than half that much. When the major complained, Carey responded that he did not have enough paper and that similar paper could not be purchased on short notice. What seemed like an unending series of delays and unmet deadlines "almost exhausted" Long's patience, but he assured his superiors that he had used "every means in my power to expedite the business in question." By early December he noted that all but fifty pages of tables had been completed, and later that month he sent a copy of the finished report to Secretary Calhoun.[10]

The published narrative appeared as Edwin James, *Account of an Expedition from Pittsburgh to the Rocky Mountains. . .Under the Command of Maj. S. H. Long. . . .* Why James edited and authored the narrative is not known, but certainly Long did not anticipate having to prepare the final version of the manuscript himself. Both the 1819 and 1820 expeditions included officers who served as official journalists, so it is logical to assume that he expected these men to do the writing. Repeated clashes with both officers made this impossible. Major Biddle became so unhappy serving under Long that he refused to keep any narrative of the 1819 expedition. At least Captain Bell had completed his tasks during the 1820 journey. Neither officer, however, was willing or available to undertake the editorial work. One scholar claimed that Long had "judiciously faded into the background, allowing Edwin James to be the official

chronicler of their collective misadventures." This is mere
conjecture and ignores the fact that Long's name and rank
both appear in the book title. Not only that, but the major
obviously did not consider the 1820 expedition a failure since
he submitted plans and cost estimates for more exploration
the next year.[11]

That each of the participants expected to prepare his own
report is clear from a comment by Edwin James. As early as
December, 1820, he mentioned that he would have to write a
"memoir on the Geology of the Country. . . .I should be de-
lighted with my present situation," he grumbled, "if it were
not for the necessity of telling my story to the publick
[*sic*]. . . ." Less than a year later, the reluctant author went
to Philadelphia to conclude his responsibilities as a member
of the 1820 expedition. Instead of ending them, however, he
learned that Major Long "wished and expected that a part of
our materials should be published in the form of a popular
journal. . . ."[12]

The duty of compiling the report fell to Long, Thomas
Say, and Edwin James. Early in November, 1821, the three
discussed the project and their duties. Long had his continuing work as an army engineer, which occupied at least
some of his time. Say, on the other hand, had been appointed
curator of the American Philosophical Society that year and
also continued working on his multi-volume study on insects.
This left James as the one with the fewest responsibilities and
the most time. Apparently, his colleagues persuaded him to
undertake the assignment, but only after he proposed "certain conditions" to them. What these were is not entirely
clear, but he did get a small salary, an office allowance, and
assurances that both Say and Long would continue their
help.[13]

This they did and the Philadelphia edition of James's
narrative contained appendices by Say including Indian sign
language, Indian speeches, and partial vocabularies for six
Indian tribes. Astronomical and meteorological records pre-

pared by Say, Long, and Swift, as well as extracts from Long's 1821 report to Secretary Calhoun, extracts from James's reports on minerals and geological formations, and a volume of maps and illustrations completed the three volumes. That same year, a London publisher brought out a second three-volume edition that included some items the American version had omitted, while dropping items from the Philadelphia edition. The net result was that although the two versions differed, the basic narrative text remained the same, with alterations in the appended material.[14]

No matter which version one chose, the James narrative offered scientifically inclined readers a wealth of fascinating new data. James organized the body of the text as a day-by-day journal account of where the explorers went, what they did, and what they saw. Occasionally the narrative thread all but disappeared behind a screen of scientific discussion and detailed, complex footnotes. For the general public this surely inhibited enthusiastic reading; yet the explorers had gone west to gather scientific material, so it would have been surprising had they not included much of it in this final report.

After the *Account* reached booksellers' shelves in 1823, reviewers and scholars began commenting on it. Probably the most favorable notice appeared with a brief portion of the narrative in the *Baltimore Niles Register*. The "two handsome volumes. . .accompanied by a beautiful atlas," the editor claimed, was "a very valuable work." Because it was "superior to the usual works of its nature," the reviewer predicted that James's book would "be extensively read." Other reviewers had more mixed reactions. Edward Everett, writing in the *North American Review*, seems to have been unable to evaluate the book consistently. At the beginning of his twenty-five-page review article, he claimed that the "public will not be disappointed" with the work. Later, however, he complained that in spite of the "considerable accession" of new material, the explorers had accomplished less than had been anticipated. This he blamed on the "detestable parsimony" of the federal government. His judgment of the prose shows a similar uncertainty. He grumbled that the explorers had cluttered their writing with an "affectation of scientific language," but, in spite of this, described the "literary execution" of the project as "highly respectable."[15]

Several years later, when reviewing the narrative of Long's 1823 expedition, the historian Jared Sparks praised the major and the "distinguished naturalists" who had carried out the 1820 expedition "with so much credit to the persons employed, and advantage to the cause of science." In a review of a related book, Henry R. Schoolcraft, himself an explorer and ethnologist, praised James's earlier work for its "geological and botanical observations." The 1823 British edition received less favorable comments, at least from the London *Quarterly Review*. The journal noted that parts of the books were long and of little interest to English readers, particularly the ethnological material gathered during the winter of 1819-20 at Council Bluffs.[16]

While contemporaries offered moderate praise and criticism of James's *Account*, historians have been less generous. Both the written record and the expedition itself have received much criticism. In 1902, Hiram M. Chittenden denounced the expedition as a fiasco and claimed that the public response to it was one of disappointment. One of the more recent damning treatments is given by Ray A. Billington. He attacks Long for his "false designation" of the Plains as desert, for failure to "unlock the secrets" of the region, and for erecting a "psychological barrier" that prevented others "from disproving his falsehoods." Although the most negative, this discussion reflects accurately what numerous scholars have said about the expedition for the past six decades.[17]

When the explorers described the southern Plains as inhospitable desert, they gave modern critics, armed with hindsight, much to denounce. In what must be the most frequently quoted paragraph in American literature describing the Plains, Long wrote:

> In regard to this extensive section of country, I do not hesitate in giving the opinion that it is almost wholly unfit for cultivation, and of course uninhabitable by a people depending upon agriculture for their subsistence. Although tracts of fertile land considerably extensive are occasionally to be met with, yet the scarcity of wood and water, almost uniformly prevalent, will prove an insuperable obstacle in the way of settling the country.

Then, to compound his guilt, Long traced the words "Great American Desert" boldly across the southern Plains.[18]

From that day to this, Long has been attacked erroneously for creating the myth of the Great American Desert. There is no doubt that he first used the term on his maps of 1822 and 1823, or that for the next several decades other cartographers copied his maps freely and also used the desert term. Yet, except for coining the phrase, he offered no new assessment of the region. Zebulon Pike had reported virtually the same description of the southern Plains more than a decade before Long set foot in the area, and other travelers before and after the 1820 expedition reacted to the Plains in much the same manner. In fact, almost no one came forward to dispute the desert characterization for decades.[19]

Given the experiences of the explorers during the summer of 1820, it would have been surprising had they described the Plains as anything but desert. The two surviving narratives written by members of the exploring party both record vast areas of sand and gravel, areas with little water or game and less vegetation. For example, James likened the region between the falls of the Canadian River and the base of the Rockies as "sandy wastes and thirsty inhospitable steppes." In fact, he remarked, "we have little apprehension of giving too unfavorable an account of this portion of the country." Captain John Bell, official journalist for the expedition, mentioned traveling "over a dusty plain of sand and gravel, barren as the deserts of Arabia. . . ." Even the mild-mannered Thomas Say, who seemed to get along easily with everyone, complained that the region within 500 miles of the Rocky Mountains was "destitute of timber and miserably poor. . .totally unfit for the tillage of civilized man. . . ."[20] Clearly, this idea was unanimous among the explorers and not Stephen Long's single-minded or perverse view.

There may be other reasons why the scientists reported negative views of the Plains, but generally these fail to stand under close scrutiny. One recent study describes several variables that affected the exploratory process. It concluded that subjectivity existed in all levels of exploring—both in recording and interpreting the data.[21] For example, men often recorded items that fit preconceived ideas of a region, in spite of contrary data. The 1820 explorers had access to conflicting accounts by Lewis and Clark and by Zebulon Pike, so it is difficult to determine their view of the Plains prior to crossing them. On the other hand, there is no evidence that Long's men altered or ignored data they gathered to present their gloomy report.

Obviously, the desire for personal fame and advancement might color a scientist's report, but there is no reason to think that any of the men describing the Plains as a desert after the 1820 expedition had anything positive to gain from such action. It is possible that Long might have considered stressing the problems his men faced that summer in order to draw attention away from his failure to complete several assigned tasks, but even this possibility seems remote. Had he tried to do so, it was likely that Captain John Bell would have denounced the effort. The two officers had quarreled frequently during the expedition, and Bell's narrative would hardly have agreed with those of Long and James unless he, too, thought the region inhospitable. One other idea also needs consideration. With War Department spokesmen talking of expansion, there was little to be gained by Long in telling his superiors facts they would not welcome hearing. Certainly, the tone of the 1820 descriptions was not the result of conscious efforts to please Washington officials or to becloud the issue. Although other subjective factors undoubtedly played a minor role, their trek across the Plains in the summer of 1820 persuaded the explorers that the region presented formidable barriers to settlement.

Some critics asked how men of science could have misjudged or ignored the grazing potential of the Plains. Surely the vast herds of buffalo demonstrated to all but the most obtuse that livestock would flourish there. These same herds of buffalo, however, would trample crops and eat the grass needed for domestic animals. Predators, then far more numerous than now, would have caused enormous losses for would-be herdsmen. Whether the explorers considered such arguments is unknown, but they wrote with their summer ordeal still fresh in their minds. Certainly the shortage of water would preclude large-scale livestock raising. If this did not, the experience of having their own horses and mules weaken and almost die convinced the explorers that the Plains grasses lacked sufficient nutrients for domesticated animals. Stephen Long had recognized the treeless Illinois prairies as excellent grazing and farming land in 1816—before many pioneer farmers accepted the idea—so there is little likelihood that he and his companions failed to discuss this possibility for the Plains during their travels.[22]

In spite of the anguish the Great American Desert idea seems to have caused some scholars and the bitter objections that some western chambers of commerce still make to any such idea, the scientists who participated in the 1820 expedition judged the high Plains correctly in terms of their own day. As Walter Webb has noted, the science and technology of the 1820s remained too immature for successful agriculture on most of the Plains. American farmers depended heavily on wood for fencing, building, and fuel. This dependency was so much so, in fact, that when young Abraham Lincoln began to run for public office in Illinois years later, he used the rail-splitter image to gain rapport with his rural constituents. Moreover, strains of drought-resistant grain, dry farming techniques, and irrigation all remained many years in the future. When Stephen Long and his associates labeled the Plains as unfit for agriculture during the early 1820s, they hurt almost no one. While it is true that recent scholarship shows that James Fenimore Cooper based his descriptions of the West in *The Prairie* on the 1823 James *Account*, there seems little reason to think that Cooper's writing slowed migration to the Plains. In fact, a historical geographer considering the matter concluded that although writings such as Cooper's might have influenced educated Easterners, most would-be pioneers held a folk view that differed from the elite views of Cooper's audience. In view of this, it is unlikely that pioneers accepted the idea of a western desert, or that the desert concept played a significant role in slowing western settlement.[23]

Attacks on the explorers and upon the published *Account* went beyond the desert issue. A second point for criticism was the failure to locate the sources of the Red River. A recent discussion of that topic concludes that "once again an American expedition had failed in its primary mission"—finding the Red. This view, merely a current echo of frequently voiced complaints, misses the point. Locating the headwaters of this stream was less important than finding those of the Arkansas, a task included in Long's 1820 orders. Both of these streams were part of the new southwestern boundary between the United States and Spanish territory in North America under the Adams-Onis Treaty concluded in 1819. Only the central portion of the Red, however, was part of the border, which moved west and north along the south bank of the Arkansas to its headwaters before turning west to the Pacific. Thus, exploring and mapping the upper reaches of the Arkansas, not the Red, was the most significant geographic task.[24] This Long and his companions chose not to do, and for that omission they deserve censure.

Certainly Long's party hoped to find the Red and trace its course eastward across the Plains, but critical historians seem to have overlooked one difficulty. How were the explorers to distinguish the Red from other streams of a similar size flowing in the same direction? Following the river upstream from its mouth might have been arduous, but there would have been no question about being on the wrong stream. Obviously, starting in the middle of the river course and traveling either east or west was more uncertain. To help choose the correct stream, the explorers carried Zebulon Pike's map of his explorations fifteen years earlier. However, since he had failed to locate the Red, his map had limited value. Not only that, but the explorers' guides had lived and traded among the Pawnee in eastern Nebraska and had never been in most of the region, so these men could offer little help, either. Thus, Long's party had to rely upon information they got from the Indians while using questionable interpretation techniques. Under these circumstances, it is hardly surprising that they chose the wrong stream.

Nevertheless, Long's leadership of the exploring party left much to be desired. He chose not to take them to the headwaters of the Platte and west into the mountains. Where the Arkansas flowed out of the Rockies he sent only a small party to make a hasty examination of the region and again disregarded his orders to make a military survey of the area. Finally, when his half of the expedition reached what they thought was the Red River, they headed downstream instead of in the other direction. Neither Long nor his companions comment on the reasons for these decisions, so there is no way to assess blame. Critics who denounce the explorers for "cursory," "incomplete," and "halfhearted" efforts on this portion of the expedition have a valid point.[25]

On the other hand, these critics have overlooked the fact

that Calhoun's orders to the explorers made their assignment open-ended by stating that "the farther you can extend your route to the West *with safety* [emphasis added]," the better it would be.[26] Thus, although the naturalists were to explore the headwaters of the Platte, Arkansas, and Red, their own discretion concerning personal safety is stated clearly in the orders. By the time the detachment had traveled west to the Rockies, it had become obvious that without the funds Calhoun had promised Long for equipment and supplies, long-term, careful exploration was impossible. Instead, the party hurried along the Front Range and then back across the Plains because they lacked food, water, pack animals, and trade goods that might have bought the items they needed. These shortages and the resulting lack of time were the major factors in the decisions to abandon some of the expedition goals.

The most unjustified censures of the 1819 and 1820 expeditions are those claiming that they produced "negligible" scientific accomplishments and that the explorers "added almost nothing to the knowledge of the region." Such generalizations are incorrect. Rather than gathering almost no new data about the American West, these two expeditions provided contemporary scholars and scientists with a wealth of significant material. Edwin James's three-volume *Account* was merely the most visible wave in a veritable flood of information the explorers gathered and disseminated throughout the intellectual community of that day. In 1823, the same year that the Philadelphia edition of the James work appeared, the London publishing house of Longman, Hurst, Orme, and Brown printed a second three-volume edition. Between 1820 and 1828, books, articles, scholarly papers, and maps based upon data gathered on the two expeditions came from the pens of Long and his associates. These included Long's two maps, as well as articles on geology, botany, and entomology. Almost all of these first appeared as scholarly papers read before such groups as the American Philosophical Society, the Lyceum of Natural History of New York, and the Philadelphia Academy of Natural Sciences. A second multi-volume book, *American Entomology* by Thomas Say, included many of the insects gathered in 1819 and 1820.[27]

However, this mere noting of papers, articles, and books gives no idea of the real scientific impact Long and his companions had on the scholars of their day. As noted previously, the men chosen to conduct the scientific exploration of the West were young but also usually able and experienced. Equally important, they knew most of the other leading scholars and naturalists, often through close personal relationships, memberships in local scientific societies, or at least because of correspondence. Therefore, when the naturalists returned east and began telling their story to friends and associates, they spread knowledge and information to scientists throughout the country.

A fact easily overlooked by twentieth century historians is that during this early period the natural sciences were concerned largely with description and classification. Therefore, the first step in expanding knowledge had to be the effort to describe the particular qualities of an element or mineral, a plant, or animal and to name each one. Certainly, the naturalists of Long's party did this. Although descriptions of their collections vary, the following items can be verified as having been collected during the two years in the West: Titian Peale—124 drawings of animals, birds, insects, plants, fishes, snakes, lizards, and shells; artist Samuel Seymour—150 pictures of scenery, geographic features, wildlife, and Indians. Of these, Seymour completed 60 in time for some of them to be included in volume three of James's *Account*. This vast collection of sketches, drawings, and pictures included illustrations of plants and animals never seen by eastern naturalists and afforded scholars in Philadelphia an opportunity to enlarge their knowledge without having to travel west.[28]

Thomas Say, the most accomplished naturalist among the explorers, added much zoological data. Primarily an entomologist, he gathered "several thousand insects, of which many hundreds were new" to American science. In addition, Say had done much more than preserve insects. Together, he and Titian Peale spent hours trapping, dissecting, and examining animals and birds of the Plains. Even a brief glance at the scientific names of common wild animals reveals that zoologists have credited Say with identifying numerous species. Such western predators as the coyote, gray wolf, and kit fox are all credited to him, as are various ground squirrels, shrews, rats, and bats.[29]

Perhaps here the immediate scientific impact of the Long expeditions may be most clearly understood. In his excellent study of Lewis and Clark as naturalists, Paul Cutright demonstrates the wide range of scientific discoveries made by these explorers. For example, he proves beyond any reasonable doubt that Lewis and Clark—not Thomas Say—first identified both the coyote and the gray wolf as new species. What he overlooks, however, is the fact that the Lewis and Clark findings were not quickly or competently published. Therefore, they made little impact upon contemporary scholars. In fact, few scientists knew of their contributions until eighty years after the famous expedition. Consequently, their discoveries were of little immediate value and many remained outside the existing body of knowledge—unlike the findings of Long's men. For this reason, Say—rather than Lewis and Clark—was credited with the first identification of several new species, the coyote being just one example.[30] The significant point is that much information from the 1819 and 1820 expeditions moved into the mainstream of scientific knowledge within less than a decade.

The findings of Long's explorations provided a major boost for the development of American botany. In 1826, John Torrey, a New York botanist, obtained the sketches and specimens gathered by William Baldwin and Edwin James.

He reported that they numbered "about 700. Many of these," he noted, "are exceedingly interesting, & not a few are new species." These plants had more significance than just being new species, according to several botanical scholars. One called Edwin James's climb up Pikes Peak "the most notable day" for the expedition botanist because on it he gathered the first collection of American alpine plants. These herb samples provided other botanists "an introduction to the rich and beautiful alpine flora of the central Rocky Mountains" and provided the opportunity for a major breakthrough in botanical development. Torrey used the expedition's collection as the basis for a controversial paper discussing the plants according to the "natural system" of plant classification. Certainly, the large number of plant specimens, the new species, and the use that Torrey made of them in suggesting a more satisfactory classification system must be considered as major contributions to the rapid development of botanical studies.[31]

The 1820s saw vast new amounts of ethnological material being collected, with Long's companions gathering much of this information. Together with the efforts of Henry R. Schoolcraft and Jedediah Morse, James's *Account* provided Easterners and the government with specific information about northern and western tribes. Much of the data came from the labors of Thomas Say and Titian Peale. During the two expeditions, Say attempted to gather word lists from the Indians. With an interpreter he would visit the tribesmen and ask the names of objects he pointed out. The interpreters also provided much information, even though it was secondhand and not always reliable. Along with Peale and Seymour, Say observed carefully and kept voluminous notes. Despite the loss of some of his material when three of the soldiers deserted in 1820, his data on the Missouri Valley tribes provided an accurate picture of numerous aspects of Indian life.[32]

Although the explorers failed to add as much to geologic

knowledge as they did to some other sciences, they did make some contributions. Perhaps the shortage of geologic data resulted from the change in geologists in late 1819, when the naturalists halted at Council Bluffs. Augustus Jessup left the expedition and Edwin James took over his duties the next summer. Thus, during the months when Say, Peale, and Seymour got most of their material about plants, animals, and Indians, no geologist was on hand to examine nearby minerals and rock formations. Nevertheless, James's *Account* included "numerous references to the geology of the region, which are of interest considering the time at which they were made. . . ." Geologic knowledge was so rudimentary at the time that most basic techniques for geologic study had not been developed. For example, in 1818 Thomas Say had proposed that stratigraphic correlation through the use of fossils might be used, but this idea was "only partially accepted" ten years later when another scholar repeated the suggestion. With little knowledge and few scientific techniques, the party's geologists could do little more than describe rock formations, locations of mineral deposits, and soil types. Beyond that, they could only guess about major geological questions. This the two geologists did in four scholarly papers that were published. Some years later, Amos Eaton included some of their findings in his *Geological Textbook*, so what little knowledge they did contribute was eventually used.[33]

Although Long has received much condemnation for his maps showing the Plains as desert, even the critics admit that his cartographic efforts added new knowledge of the central and southern Plains. By discovering and mapping the source of the Canadian River, Long changed geographers' ideas about the river systems of the southern Plains. Prior to this expedition, it was thought that the upper branches of the Canadian were part of the Red River system. Now it became clear that the rivers of the area were more complex than had been thought, and that the sources of the Red lay farther to the south and east. There were other cartographic benefits, too. Even though the explorers failed to follow the South Platte to its headwaters, Long's men saw several branches of that stream flowing through the eastern Rockies. Bijou, one of their guides, told them that the North and South Platte had their sources within 120 miles of each other and that small creeks flowing down from North Park in Colorado formed the headwaters of the former. For the first time, the "easterly front wall of the Rockies was now correctly mapped from Long's Peak to the Spanish Peaks. . . ." Other minor contributions included using the name "Wisconsan" for the region west of Lake Michigan, thus giving that area its eventual name, and showing the Black Hills of Dakota as running north and south. According to Carl Wheat's exhaustive cartographic study, "Long's map, in several forms, represented a distinct step forward," and served as one of "the progenitors of an entire class of maps of the American trans-Mississippi West."[34]

These contributions notwithstanding, Long's map had errors and flaws. It failed to trace the sources of the Arkansas or Red. In fact, because Captain Bell's detachment had traveled down the Arkansas and yet somehow missed recording the mouth of the Cimarron, that stream does not appear on the map. Other errors include showing the Rio Grande flowing west of Pikes Peak and, in that same region, sketching in a westerly flowing stream that the major labeled the Lewis Fork of the Columbia River. Because it was actually the Colorado, this and the other errors compounded earlier ones and consequently led an entire generation of cartographers afield.[35]

Despite these contributions and errors, however, the item that drew most attention and abuse is the label "Great American Desert," which appeared on the small map of the Arkansas region. On his larger map, Long limited himself to "Great Desert." Describing the region as desert was not new, but his term caught the imagination of other cartographers, and the myth of the desert spread to maps and atlases for the next half century. A careful study of Long's published maps shows that he limited the desert label to the region beyond the ninety-eighth meridian, or the high Plains. Even a casual glance at a modern landform map shows much of the area between the South Platte and the Canadian as sand hills, sand, sand land, and gypsum hills.[36] This is not to say that the region is indeed desert, but given the amount of sand and gravel there, it is not difficult to understand why the thirsty and tired explorers compared the region to one.

Historians have denounced the explorers for calling the area a desert and for temporarily blocking America's westward advance. None of them, however, has provided examples of how this idea actually inhibited population movement. They merely assume that this was the case. However, there was one way in which the desert idea may well have done its pernicious work. The Indian removal policy, although informally in operation since the early days of the government, became a formal part of United States Indian policy during the mid-1820s. For years historians assumed that the "discovery" of the West as desert had stimulated removal, but Francis P. Prucha showed that this was not the case. Instead, the government expected the nomadic tribes of the Plains to remain in their dusty homeland, while the eastern tribes would move to the more fertile eastern fringes of the Plains. Yet in one important way, the knowledge of a western desert indeed may have affected removal. Throughout the rhetoric supporting the policy ran the theme that the tribesmen needed to remain isolated from the corrupting influence of frontier whites. By placing the eastern tribes on good land near the edge of the desert, reformers and humanitarians who supported the policy could relax. Frontiersmen could no longer surround the Indians because only the desert lay beyond to the west.[37]

A last—but usually overlooked—contribution to science came from the astronomic observations and weather data that the explorers gathered. The expedition of 1820 made the first recorded American effort to determine altitude above sea level by using a barometer, although the technique was already well known in Europe. Unfortunately, the instruments soon were damaged and Long and Swift were unable to make further accurate measurements. Their partial findings appeared in a table appended to the Philadelphia edition of the *Account.* Of more potential interest was the meteorological register that the explorers kept during both 1819 and 1820. This included weather information such as morning, noon, and evening temperatures; wind direction, with an estimate of wind velocity, although they had no instruments for measuring it; notice of precipitation and storms; barometer readings, until these instruments were damaged; and types and movement of the clouds. Some of this information was incomplete, some even incorrect, yet the record the explorers compiled included the most extensive and scientific weather data gathered by Americans to that time. When combined with similar data then being collected by the Surgeon General's Office, these weather records provide the first basis in historical sources for comparative studies of weather and climate.[38]

Contemporary scholars recognized the significance of the 1819 and 1820 expeditions for the American scientific community. Dr. John Torrey's comments on the importance of Edwin James's botanical collections have been mentioned, as have examples of the use textbook authors made of data from these expeditions. Speaking to the New York Lyceum of Natural History in 1826, James De Kay reminded his listeners that the collections from the expeditions had been "numerous and important." Furthermore, he noted, "more than sixty new or rare animals, and several hundred insects were added to the Fauna, and many interesting plants to the Flora" of the nation.[39]

The scientific community showed its immediate and enthusiastic response to the expedition findings in another manner, that of honoring the participants. Botanists named new species of plants for William Baldwin and Edwin James, while zoologists attached Thomas Say's name to numerous species of animals that he described. Other honors followed. Say, already widely known in scientific circles, became the curator of the American Philosophical Society in 1821, and the next year, the University of Pennsylvania appointed him professor of natural history and geology. For Edwin James, participation in the 1820 expedition also brought added experience and scholarly recognition. The Philadelphia Academy of Natural Sciences elected him a corresponding member in 1823, and that same year he became a member of the Albany Lyceum of Natural History in New York. The following year, the American Geological Society offered him membership.[40]

While American scholars praised the explorers' work, Paul Wilhelm, Duke of Wurtemberg, used the *Account* as his travel guide up the Missouri River in 1823-24. He noted the explorers' solid accomplishments in cartography, archaeology, and comparative linguistics.[41] Clearly, contemporary scientists thought that Long and his companions had performed well and had aided substantially the cause of science. That the explorers blundered, failed to achieve some goals, and disappointed people is true. Nevertheless, in light of obvious contemporary acceptance and praise for most of their work, it is time for historians to reconsider their assessments of the expeditions of 1819 and 1820 on a scope broader than whether or not they found the Red River. Perhaps a recent description of Edwin James's *Account of an Expedition* that labels it "a landmark in the literature of American exploration" should help turn scholarly thinking toward the positive contributions of those expeditions.[42]

Exploring in the North, 1823

Stephen Long's last assignment as an explorer came shortly after the James *Account*—which described his expedition to the Rocky Mountains—had been completed. In early 1823, Colonel Alexander Macomb, the new chief of engineers, wrote that the War Department hoped Long would lead another expedition. Rather than moving west as he had done in 1820, Macomb wanted his subordinate to travel north up the Mississippi, Minnesota, and Red rivers to the 49th parallel, and then east along the international boundary to Lake Superior.[1] This would lead into the area the United States had acquired from Great Britain through the Convention of 1818, a region in which little exploring had been done. There, Long and his group would gather specimens and study the area.

It is not known if Colonel Macomb's request was related to Long's 1817 proposal to explore the Great Lakes and the major western streams, but examining this region was clearly part of the national policy to strengthen American influence —if not outright control—in remote frontier areas. The Convention of 1818 had established the international boundary as a line drawn from the northwestern point of Lake of the Woods south to the 49th parallel.[2] Following that agreement, the Monroe administration set into motion several expeditions to explore and locate American troops there. In 1819, Colonel Henry Leavenworth led the Mississippi Expedition up that river to establish what became Fort Snelling at the site of present Minneapolis-St. Paul.[3]

Later that same year, Secretary of War Calhoun decided that the region west of Lake Superior should also be explored. He authorized Lewis Cass, then governor of Michigan Territory, to examine the area between Lake Superior and the Mississippi. Cass had urged such a move for some time in order to extinguish Indian title to land there, locate the copper deposits on Lake Superior, and, as usual, to reduce British influence with the Indians. The Cass expedition traveled from northern Michigan across Lake Superior and then overland to the Mississippi. It included civilian scientists as well as government and army personnel, and gathered considerable information in 1820.[4]

In late 1820, Major Long proposed another expedition to explore the Red River, Plains, and Rocky Mountains during the next year. On its return, the detachment could follow either the Missouri or St. Peter's rivers to the Mississippi. A lack of funds ended discussion of his idea, and it was not until two years later that he again broached the subject of frontier exploration. On February 1, 1823, he suggested a national astronomical survey to locate all the major towns, cities, rivers, and other points of interest. During this he could gather an "account of the Topography, soil and productions of the country." Now, only a few weeks later, the federal government decided that it needed more data about the region west of Lake Superior and Stephen Long seemed to be the logical choice to conduct such a scientific investigation. William Keating, one of the participants of the 1823 expedition, later claimed that the project resulted from "the success which attended the expedition" of 1820 across the Plains. Long and his companions gathered such "important information" on that journey that Keating claimed their success had "induced the government. . .to continue its endeavours to explore the unknown wilds" within the nation.[5] The muted reception that government officials had given members of the 1820 expedition, however, would seem to negate this contention. Nevertheless, Major Long had been up the Mississippi previously in 1817, had just completed a recent assignment, and was known to enjoy exploring.

When Colonel Macomb's request arrived, Long seemed to hesitate briefly. He had been disappointed at the lukewarm response to his 1819 and 1820 expeditions. More important, the financial strain of a growing but sickly family and his desire to remain closer to home had induced him to apply for a position as civil engineer for the state of Virginia. Therefore, when he replied to Macomb, the major asked for time to consider the assignment and to await news about his application to Virginia. At the same time, he sent Macomb a list of men he hoped might be persuaded to accompany him as scientists and army officers. Once Macomb responded favorably to Long's request for more time, the major turned his attention to gathering equipment and writing associates about the new assignment.[6]

It is not known when Stephen Long decided that the Virginia authorities were unlikely to act on his application, but within a few weeks after Macomb's first letter, the major had thrown himself into planning the expedition with enthusiasm. By mid-April, 1823, he outlined his proposal, and by return mail the secretary of war confirmed it. The explorers would start at Philadelphia and travel west via Wheeling, Fort Wayne, Chicago, and Fort Armstrong on the Mississippi. From there they would move up that stream to the St. Peter's River (now the Minnesota), follow it to the Red River of the North, and then go down the Red to the 49th parallel. From there they were to move east along the border to Lake Superior, and then return via the Great Lakes. The war department orders called for the party to make a topographical description of the area, gather scientific data about the plants, animals, and minerals they found, and record information about any Indians they met.

Secretary Calhoun assured Long that his previous experience on the frontier "renders it now unnecessary to be more particular in these instructions. . . ." and expressed "great confidence" in the skills possessed by the explorers. A few days later, the Adjutant General's Office sent specific orders about the route, personnel, and funds available for the expedition.[7]

As he had done earlier, Long asked for permission to take both civilian scientists and army officers as members of the exploring party. This was approved. Some of the men he wanted as companions could not participate; nevertheless, the group he assembled was a competent one. As had been the case previously, Long's acquaintances within the Philadelphia scientific community predominated. Both Thomas Say and Samuel Seymour, veterans of the 1819 and 1920 expeditions, also joined this trip.

A third Philadelphian, William H. Keating, was a new recruit. Born at Wilmington, Delaware, in 1779, he spent most of his early life in Philadelphia. In 1816 he received a B.A. from the University of Pennsylvania and then traveled to Europe. There he studied geology, mineralogy, and mining at technical schools in France, Germany, Switzerland, Holland, and England. As a result, when young Keating returned to the United States in 1820, he possessed an exceptional technical education. In fact, one writer claims that he was "perhaps the nation's one and only professional mining engineer."[8] Keating helped establish the Franklin Institute in Philadelphia, and in 1821 published a book on mining. Within a year he was an active member of the Philadelphia Academy of Natural Sciences, serving on several committees and presenting papers at the frequent meetings of that group. In 1822, the University of Pennsylvania appointed him to an unpaid position as professor of mineralogy and chemistry. Clearly, although only twenty-four years old at the time of the expedition, Keating stood among the leaders of American science.[9]

James Colhoun, the one non-Philadelphian in the group, apparently was assigned to the expedition by his cousin, Secretary of War Calhoun. Major Long had asked for a second engineer to assist him with the survey and cartographic work, but the man he wanted could not participate. Instead, Colhoun, a navy midshipman, received the assignment. He had served in the navy since 1816 and during that time had traveled widely. Apparently, he had learned some navigation and astronomy because he served as the assistant topographer and astronomer for the explorers.[10]

As the exploring party prepared to leave Philadelphia in April, 1823, it included only four men. Long served as the commander, Keating as mineralogist, Say as zoologist and antiquary, and Seymour as landscape painter and designer. In addition, Keating and Say shared duties as literary journalists and ethnologists. James Colhoun met the others as they traveled through Ohio, and he helped Long with astronomical observations and cartographic duties. Later, guides, interpreters, and a military escort were added, but Long and his five companions had the responsibility for the scientific and exploratory activity. The major had asked Dr. Edwin James to serve as expedition physician and botanist, but slow mail service prevented the doctor from learning of his assignment until it was too late for him to overtake the others. When Long realized that James could not participate, he asked Thomas Say also to gather botanical specimens. Say did collect some, but the explorers recognized his lack of knowledge about plants. William Keating remarked that the absence of a skilled botanist "was much to be regretted."[11] With this exception, the expedition included competent men, although the group was not "the first government endeavor of its kind which boasted scientists of such ability. . . .," as one scholar has claimed.[12] That distinction belongs to the Scientific Expedition of 1819, which had included several of the same men.

Having received their orders, the explorers left Philadelphia on April 30, 1823. Their journey to Fort Dearborn at Chicago went badly from the start. Riding horseback and occasionally in light wagons, they struggled west over the mud-clogged National Road. Through Ohio, Indiana, and Illinois conditions improved little, and most of the time they contended with muddy roads, poor lodgings, and lame or worn-out horses. These miserable conditions could hardly have cheered the travelers. In fact, they had to stop often to repack their wet belongings, to make sure that books and instruments had not been damaged by the dampness, and to trade their wagons for fresh horses.[13]

On the evening of June 5, the bespattered scientists rode up to Fort Dearborn, where they stopped to rest and exchange their "overdone" horses. The fort and small settlement of Chicago offered "few features upon which the eye of the traveler can dwell with pleasure," according to Keating. The village, he grumbled, included only a few huts "inhabited by a miserable race of men," the mixed-blood citizens.[14] Despite such feelings, Long hired an old French and Indian trapper as a guide, and on June 11 the party left Chicago.[15] Traveling north and west, they stopped to visit a mixed village of Sacs, Foxes, Winnebagoes, and Menomonies. By the time they had reached this Indian camp, Long decided that his new guide knew little about the region, so he hired a Sac named Wanebea to accompany them as far as Prairie du Chien.[16]

While they rested at the Indian village, the explorers tested the accuracy of a Winnebago vocabulary that Long had compiled on his 1817 expedition up the Mississippi. To do this they had to work through several interpreters, a cumbersome process that increased the chances for misunderstanding and error. One of the men read the words from the list to an Indian. He, in turn, told the French guide the meaning in Sac because the Frenchman did not understand Winnebago. The guide repeated what the Indian had said in French, and another man translated this into English. Despite this awkward arrangement, the Winnebago brave understood

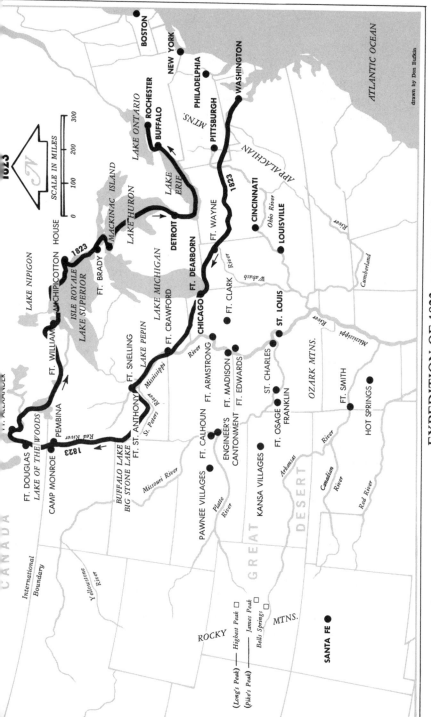

EXPEDITION OF 1823

about one-third of the words as the whites pronounced them. He recognized a second third when they were repeated in Sac by the interpreter. Keating thought that differences in pronunciation from local dialects caused more of the difficulties than any inaccuracies in the list Long had compiled from the earlier Indian informants.[17]

Leaving the Indian village, the explorers continued their northwesterly path across thinly wooded and prairie areas between the Mississippi and Rock rivers. Each day the naturalists took notes on birds, vegetation, rock formations, and mineral deposits they saw along the route. They kept thorough descriptions of the Indians they met and questioned their Sac guide closely about past battles and legends. In addition, the whites scrutinized their red companion's skills as a woodsman. He knew many of the landmarks, and, while the expedition followed the river valleys or he could see nearby hills, he knew their location. On overcast days, however, the guide seemed unsure of the route much of the time.[18]

The party reached the Wisconsin River on June 19. They built a small raft and sent the lone enlisted man of the party ahead to Fort Crawford. About sunset Lieutenant Colonel Willoughby Morgan arrived with men and boats, ready to help the explorers across the river and to the post. After the Colonel shared a bottle of wine with them, Long's companions crossed the river and rode to the fort.[19]

There the party rested while the major obtained a troop escort and additional supplies and equipment. The naturalists used some of the time to gather more specimens, make sketches, and study their findings. Working through the interpreters, Thomas Say interviewed several Indians, and from Wanebea, their guide, he learned much about the Sac and Fox tribes.[20] Colonel Morgan proved most cooperative. He provided a detachment of one officer and ten soldiers for an escort, some fresh horses, and a sturdy mackinaw boat for moving both men and equipment. Because they were entering an area inhabited by Sioux and Chippewa tribesmen and therefore needed new interpreters and another guide, Long hired men for those duties.[21]

For the next part of the journey, the major divided his companions. He led one group overland along the river. The remainder of the men comprised what he called the river party. This included the explorers Say, Keating, and Seymour, one interpreter, and the troop escort. Both groups were to stay close together and would reunite at Fort St. Anthony.[22] The rationale for having two parties seems clear. They would gather different information, and by combining two accounts a more complete record could be obtained than if all the men traveled by either water or land. What is less clear is why Long assigned all the naturalists to the river party. Certainly, he knew that several earlier expeditions had ascended the Mississippi, and therefore it was unlikely that his men would find significant new information to report. On the other hand, few Americans had ridden overland through the region, so that mode of travel would have seemed to offer the best opportunity for exploration. Here Long erred. He should have put some of the scientists in each party. Putting all of the escort aboard the boat made little sense, either, unless he lacked horses for the soldiers to use.

On June 24, 1823, the expedition left Fort Crawford. The explorers crossed to the west side of the Mississippi, where the major and his small land party separated from the others. Long expected to reach Fort St. Anthony in six days, but traveling proved more difficult than anticipated. The explorers rode a few miles west of the river to escape the tangled growth along the stream banks, but had little success. There was no trail to follow, and even more annoying was the need to cross numerous small tributaries flowing into the Mississippi. Many of these passed through deep, steep-sided valleys, and often the weary travelers had to detour for miles until they found a path down to the valley floor. Once there they encountered clouds of mosquitoes and frequent bogs that tired the horses, irritated the men, and slowed travel.[23]

During their first week in Minnesota, the overland detachment visited several Indian camps. On June 30 the explorers stopped at the Sioux village of Shakea, or Red Wing. There Long decided to wait until their waterborne comrades arrived so that he could get extra food for his men. When the others reached Red Wing's village the next morning, the chief invited his guests to dinner. Red Wing received the visitors with the usual handshakes, pipe smoking, and speechmaking. From time to time, the assembled warriors showed their approval of their leader's words with strong, nasal "ah hahs," which reminded Colhoun of the "Amens" pronounced by many "of the Baptists & Methodists" of his native South Carolina.[24] In his response to the chief, Long explained the purposes of his expedition and assured the Indians of American friendship. When he gave presents of tobacco, lead, and powder to his hosts, the chief asked for whiskey to "comfort them in their afflictions," but the major replied that he had none.[25]

That same afternoon, the overland party left the village and late on July 2 they arrived at Fort St. Anthony. Their comrades, meanwhile, had worked their way upriver in what Keating described as an "eight-oared barge," using their tent fly as a supplementary sail. They had more difficulty traveling than the land party did, right from the start. On the first day, immediately after leaving Fort Crawford, trouble began. While Long conferred with Lieutenant Martin Scott, commander of the troop escort, and the naturalists walked along the river bank, the guard detail broke into a keg of whiskey and got drunk. When Scott and the scientists came aboard, the soldiers took the craft out into the river and then refused to row or obey orders. Immediately, Scott loaded his pistols in front of the intoxicated men and threatened to shoot them if they tried to mutiny. Then he ordered the craft beached until the crew became sober, and so it was evening before the party resumed its journey.[26]

On the evening of June 26, after they stopped to camp for the night, Thomas Say scratched his thumb while examining the head of a dead rattlesnake. Later, he opened one of the reptile's poison sacs and got some of the liquid into the scratch. Although certain that only a small amount of poison had entered the wound, Say suffered considerable pain and numbness in his hand. Later that same evening, the mosquitoes became so bothersome that at eleven o'clock the explorers decided sleep was impossible. They broke camp, loaded the boat, and set off upstream—only to encounter heavy winds and then pelting rain later that night. After that, the party traveled upriver without problem. They left the Red Wing village shortly after the land detachment had, and on July 2 entered the St. Peter's River.[27]

When the explorers visited it in 1823, Fort St. Anthony was already the largest and most permanent of the northern frontier posts. As Long had recommended after his 1817 expedition, the partially completed fort stood at the confluence of the St. Peter's and Mississippi rivers. Colonel Josiah Snelling, the garrison commander, cooperated fully with the scientists. During the week they remained at the fort, he provided a dozen horses, some saddles, and other equipment. From the post commissary the explorers got 420 pounds of bread biscuit, 350 pounds of pork, 100 pounds of sugar, 15 pounds of coffee, and 6 pounds of tea. Finally, the Colonel assigned a detachment of one officer and twenty-one men to assist the explorers.[28]

The next portion of the expedition crossed a region largely unexplored by representatives of the United States, so Long prepared carefully for his meetings with the Indians there. He hired two new interpreters, both of whom seem to have been highly competent. Of the two, Joseph Renville was the more well known. A mixed-blood Sioux, he had served with the British during the War of 1812, worked for the Hudson's Bay Company, and then helped to organize the Columbia Fur Company within the United States. It is not known why

Renville chose to accompany the expedition, but certainly he knew the Indians of the region. To interpret for any Chippewa the party might encounter, Long hired Louis Pellais, another mixed-blood. Then, just before the expedition left the fort, Lawrence Taliaferro, Indian agent for the St. Peter's region, traveled into the wilderness to explain the whites' presence to tribesmen living near the line of march.[29]

At Fort St. Anthony, the explorers met Giacomo Beltrami, an Italian traveler who hoped to find the source of the Mississippi River. The Italian had been at the fort since May 10, and, recognizing a chance of getting into the wilderness with Long's party, asked permission to accompany the detachment. At first Long tried to dissuade him, but then gave his assent. This proved to be a mistake, because the two men clashed repeatedly—even before leaving the fort. Their troubles stemmed from abrasive personalities and perhaps from professional jealousy as well. Both men were exploring the northern frontier and eventually would prepare popular accounts of their travels.

From the start Long considered Beltrami a troublesome and difficult companion, and the Italian's role in the expedition remains clouded in official silence. Long listed him as an "Italian gentleman" and "amateur traveler." Colhoun's diary adds nothing, and the first edition of Keating's published account ignored Beltrami altogether. In the 1824 London edition, however, the Italian was mentioned in a brief footnote. When Beltrami's book *La Decouverte des Sources du Mississippi* appeared, William Keating described it as containing "fictions and misrepresentations" and suggested that the Italian had left the expedition on something other than the best of terms.[30]

Beltrami, on the other hand, felt abused by Long and most of his companions. He claimed to have asked Major Long's permission to accompany the scientists "simply in the character of a wanderer who had come thus far to see Indian lands and Indian people." When Major Long finally agreed to let the Italian join his party, it was with such ill grace that Beltrami assumed that Long wanted to keep him out of the northern forests. Beltrami described the difficulties between the two men later and complained that "Major Long did not cut a very noble figure in the affair; I foresaw all the disgusts and vexations I should have to experience." Nevertheless, he was so determined to find the sources of the Mississippi that he accepted acts of "littleness and jealousy" from Long and his companions to achieve his goal.[31]

Despite the antagonism between the two men, when Long prepared to lead the expedition from Fort St. Anthony he included Beltrami in his plans. Again, the major divided his personnel in order to explore both the river and the terrain a few miles away from it. This time he commanded the water-borne party, accompanied by Keating, Seymour, Renville, and thirteen soldiers. Perhaps to keep Beltrami under observation, Long ordered him to stay with the river party. They took most of the baggage and supplies and moved upstream with five small boats. The land detachment included Colhoun, Say, Louis Pellais, and the other ten soldiers. Anticipating possible trouble with the Indians, the expedition members carried plenty of weapons. Each of the "gentlemen"—the explorers and army officers—carried either a rifle or a double-barreled gun, while the soldiers had rifles or muskets and bayonets. As a final precaution, Long ordered both detachments to remain near each other, and, whenever possible, he wanted them to camp together each evening.[32]

On July 9 the expedition left Fort St. Anthony on the last part of its northward journey to the Canadian border. They traveled up the St. Peter's Valley, but not without difficulty. Both land and water detachments encountered swarms of mosquitoes, a continuing shortage of game animals, and strenuous travel. Those following the river contended with rapids, and by the third day had to walk along the riverbank, towing their boats. On July 13 one of the canoes overturned, dumping "all the tobacco intended for presents to the Indians, & ten pounds of our best powder" into the river. No sooner had the explorers halted to make camp and dry their wet belongings when a violent storm hit. Heavy rains soaked the remaining food supplies and powder that they had so carefully packed into one of the canoes and ruined part of their bread, coffee, tea, and sugar. All the men could do was to huddle in their wet tents while thunder roared, lightning crashed into the nearby forest, and rain descended all night.[33]

The next morning Long led his dispirited companions a few miles upriver before halting to dry their damaged goods and to repack. There, the explorers decided that river travel had become too slow—they had gone only 130 miles during the first six days. Their pace of just over twenty miles each day seems fast enough, particularly considering the time needed by the naturalists to gather specimens, take notes, and make sketches, but Long remained dissatisfied. Either his continuing urge to travel vast distances undermined his willingness to allow enough time for careful observation or there was little new for the scientists to study. In any case, he decided that river travel was too slow and that it endangered the food and other supplies. Therefore, when the water party joined their comrades, they abandoned their boats and traveled overland.[34]

Long had expected to visit the Sisseton Sioux village west of the line of march at the confluence of the Blue Earth and St. Peter's rivers, but a report that this tribe had not returned from its annual hunt changed his plans. At the time, American authorities considered these Indians as potentially dangerous because one of the tribe had been arrested for murder and taken to St. Louis by federal officers. The large troop escort had been thought necessary for dealing with the Sisseton, but now the expedition would not even see them. At the same time, the continuing lack of game animals and birds forced the command to depend on its limited food supply, so

Major Long decided to reduce the size of his escort and sent ten men back to Fort St. Anthony.[35]

When the expedition moved ahead again on July 15, each of the nine "officers and gentlemen" had a horse to ride, but the soldiers walked. The party also had ten pack horses for the supplies, notes, and specimens. For several days they trekked across monotonous prairies that seemed virtually destitute of animal life. In fact, the explorers commented repeatedly about how few birds or animals they saw. On the other hand, geologist William Keating described the terrain has having "such a confusion and diversity in the nature of the primitive blocks, as well as such signs of friction, as satisfied us that these were out of place. . . ."[36] This was an astute observation because geologists at the time had not accepted massive glaciation as the cause of natural features in America. Long himself had made a similar suggestion while traveling up the Mississippi in 1817, and perhaps the two men discussed their ideas during the expedition.

Travel conditions remained difficult since the explorers suffered from daytime temperatures in the nineties, innumerable mosquitoes, and shortages of water, game, and wood for fuel. The insects bothered them so much that the men slept with all their clothing and even their boots on for protection. By the evening of July 19, the tired explorers met some Indian hunters who invited them to share some buffalo meat, and the whites accepted gladly. After pitching their tents, the soldiers joined the Indians, but the meal proved disappointing. Instead of fresh, tasty buffalo, their hosts served jerked or sun-dried strips of meat boiled in plain water. Long's men had a tough, tasteless dinner.[37]

Three days later, on July 22, the detachment reached Big Stone Lake, which was really only a broadening of the river. Here, according to Keating, the St. Peter's River "may, in fact, be said to commence," although a small creek that entered the lake retained the St. Peter's River name. That stream and its tributaries extended west another twenty-five miles to Polecat Lake, where the river actually began.[38] It is not known why the explorers listed Big Stone Lake as the source of the St. Peter's when they knew that the stream extended farther west, unless it was to justify their not following it any farther. Nevertheless, the expedition gathered the most complete information in existence about the river valley. Keating offered reasonably accurate estimates of the overland distance and actual length of the river from its mouth to Big Stone Lake, noted the inaccuracies of earlier distance reports, and suggested that much of the river could never be navigable unless the government spent vast sums to dig channels and build locks, at an expense he thought "far exceeding the importance of the object."[39]

Near Big Stone Lake the explorers met a large band of Sioux encamped nearby. When they discovered the whites, the Indians rushed over to welcome them, and men, women, and children came to shake hands, trade, and gawk. According to James Colhoun, the Sioux women had small hands and feet, but otherwise he thought they looked clumsy. He described them as thick-waisted and broad-hipped, and when they walked he quipped that they reminded him of the song "My Love walks about like a goose."[40] Regardless of the Indians' appearance, the whites enjoyed their visit with the Sioux and busily asked questions, took notes, and gathered whatever information they could about tribal customs. The Indian camp included thirty skin lodges or tepees, and the headman welcomed Long and his companions to his lodge. There he served the whites bowls of pounded buffalo meat covered with bone marrow. The explorers responded "with great delight" because this was the first fresh meat they had eaten since leaving Fort St. Anthony two weeks earlier. Just as the naturalists finished their meal and prepared to leave the camp, their hosts told them of a second feast that had been prepared for them. So they trooped into another lodge where the women gave them dishes of cooked roots similar to turnips. Then, to the guests' dismay, the Sioux insisted that their over-full visitors participate in a dog feast. By this time Long's impatience showed, but he agreed to wait for another hour while the women killed and cooked the dog. When the time passed with the dog yet uncooked, he took his men back to their own camp.[41]

Later that same day, after stopping briefly at an American Fur Company trading post on Lake Traverse to get fresh supplies and horses, the explorers moved into the Red River Valley. Here, the party experienced its only real danger from Indians. On July 28 they sighted a large herd of elk, and six of the men set out after the animals. They killed one but had chased it so far that they became separated from their comrades. While Long and the others continued along the trail, they heard a shot and then saw about fifteen Indian warriors armed and apparently prepared for battle. The braves belonged to a band of Sioux or Assiniboin, which, Keating claimed, even the other Indians considered untrustworthy. At first they seemed friendly, but when their numbers swelled to thirty or forty, they outnumbered the explorers and became insulting and demanding. The Indians told the whites to follow them and meet their chiefs, but Long refused because the missing hunters had not returned.[42]

While they talked, the warriors infiltrated the detachment so that several Indians stood near each of Long's men. The braves seem to have wanted the whites' horses, and when Joseph Snelling heard the Indians talking about the animals, he warned the major immediately. At that, Long mounted his horse and ordered his men forward along the trail. For a few moments the Indians made no move to interfere, but then more braves arrived. When the whites resumed their march a second time, armed warriors began firing their rifles across the line of march and quickly formed a large crescent in front of the explorers. By this time, nearly seventy armed Indians confronted the twenty-five whites, and it was clear that the warriors coveted the horses. Neither group wanted to start fighting because casualties would be heavy for both, and the whites guessed that the Indians would wait for nightfall before taking any more overt action.[43]

Meanwhile, Long feared that the few men still out hunting might stumble into the Indian camp on their way back to the main party, so he ordered his command to continue another five miles beyond where the Indians had demanded they stop. When the expedition moved forward again, one of the braves rode up to the first man in line and cocked his rifle. At that, one of the soldiers did the same thing, pointing his weapon at the warrior while Long rode to the head of the column. Seeing that the whites were determined to march off or fight, the Indians let them go across the prairie. That evening, the explorers hobbled their horses with short ropes, kept a vigilant guard, and built a large fire so that the hunting party might find them if they came that way. Much to Long's relief, the missing hunters returned with fresh elk meat later that evening.[44]

The Indians continued to make themselves disagreeable by loitering around the camp. Some begged for tobacco, but Long announced that there was none. Others wanted whiskey, and when told that the whites had none of that, either, one old man asked, "what then can you give me?" When William Keating took a drink from his canteen, another warrior was sure that it contained whiskey and tried to grab it. Once all of the explorers had eaten, Long ordered the fire extinguished, hoping that the Indians would then leave, which they did. The major assumed that any Indian attack or effort to steal the horses would come just before dawn, so at midnight he ordered his men to load their gear and march away by moonlight. Despite every effort to slip away unnoticed, noise from loading the horses awakened one old warrior and he ran off to the Indian camp. Then Long led his party away. The Indians made no further effort to interfere and the explorers pushed on for Pembina, arriving there on August 5 with no other incidents.[45]

The journey from Lake Traverse to Pembina, near the international border, took eleven days over an estimated 256 miles, or about 23 miles each day. Most of the trip was dull indeed, and Keating noted that except for sighting a buffalo herd and meeting the troublesome band of Indians "we should scarcely have experienced on that part of our journey any thing to which we could look back with interest."[46] Certainly, the Indians must have provided more than enough danger and excitement to have satisfied everyone. Had the detachment not been well armed and acted so determinedly, there might have been a fight over the horses. Any battle with an armed party of Indians three times the size of their group would have been a disaster for the explorers. That the whites avoided a fight and retained their horses and equipment was in part the result of Long's forceful leadership and shows that he had learned much about leading men during his eight years as an explorer.

[10]
Completing the Expedition,
1823-1824

When they reached Pembina on the Red River, the explorers paused. There, they had only one task—to decide whether the village lay north or south of the 49th parallel. Once they had done that they would begin their journey back to the eastern states. The return trip would take them along the virtually uninhabited north shore of Lake Superior and then south across the Great Lakes, a region that offered them little scientific challenge. In fact, rather than examining animals and plants along their route of march, the naturalists found their chief task to be getting themselves and their equipment back to civilization before the early northern winter blocked travel. This they succeeded in doing. Yet, they encountered so little of interest or significance that the last half of the expedition proved anti-climactic for them.

On August 5, 1823, the explorers rode into Pembina and found the settlement virtually deserted. Most of the villagers had left on their annual buffalo hunt nearly seven weeks earlier and had not yet returned. The next day, the hideous screeching of 115 wooden carts loaded with fresh buffalo meat announced the villagers' return as 300 men, women, and children marched into town, shouting and singing. They had good reason for joy. Each of the wagons carried some

800 pounds of buffalo meat, enough to last for the winter. For a community with almost no domesticated animals, the annual hunt was a matter of grim necessity and this had been a good hunt.[1]

The happy townsfolk straggled into their rude community, which consisted of about sixty log cabins strung out along the banks of the river for nearly five miles. A Hudson's Bay Company trading post had operated there until earlier that same summer, when company officials guessed that the settlement lay within the United States. Now the building stood empty. By August 8, Long and Colhoun completed their survey and astronomical observations and decided that the village did indeed lie south of the 49th parallel. Accordingly, on that day the major had an oak post placed in the ground at the border. On the south side of the pole he put the letters *U.S.*, while *G.B.* faced to the north. At noon the troops raised the American flag and fired a salute. Then, in the presence of the villagers, Long proclaimed that "by virtue of the authority vested in him by the President. . .the country situated upon Red River, above that point. . .was within the territory of the United States."[2]

This simple ceremony completed the explorers' last specific assignment, and all that remained was their return trip. Long's orders called for the detachment to follow the 49th parallel east, but the settlers urged him not to try that route. They described the entire region between the Red River and Lake Superior as a maze of marshes, small lakes, and boulder-filled streams—all virtually impenetrable by a party as large as Long's. Instead, they claimed that the only practical way to travel east was by canoe via the larger streams. This advice convinced the major to use his discretion, as Secretary of War Calhoun had suggested, and he chose to proceed north into Canada before turning east.[3] Accordingly, the party prepared for the last part of their journey.

The brief stay at Pembina precipitated several bitter

quarrels within the detachment, and, as a result, Mr. Beltrami quit the expedition. Long noted that the mercurial Italian, "having taken offense at the party generally, and being highly provoked at my objecting to his turning an Indian out of our lodge, left the party in a very hasty and angry manner."[4] The Italian had proved a troublesome companion, and few of the other explorers expressed any regret when he left. James Colhoun claimed that the Indians said that one of the explorers "must be a foreigner, because he wanted the mild expression of countenance, which they said is universal with Americans. Their judgment was correct," he concluded. When the argument ended, Beltrami bought a horse from Long, and with a single companion rode south to find the source of the Mississippi. They failed to do so, but did find and name Lake Julia.[5]

Just before the Italian departed, Joseph Snelling and three of the guides announced that they had gone far enough and asked for permission to return to Fort St. Anthony. There is uncertainty about why the men chose this moment to leave the expedition, even though Long claimed that they had not intended to go farther. He noted that Snelling and the others, "having proceeded as far as was contemplated when they joined the Expedition, were to return hence. . . ." Snelling, however, was one of the few men in the party who remained on friendly terms with Beltrami, and the latter claimed that the parting between Long and Snelling was "not without violent altercation."[6] No matter which version is correct, the expedition lost six members while at Pembina.

When the explorers chose to travel north into Canada, they did so with the assurance that authorities there would receive them kindly. Before leaving Philadelphia the preceding spring, Long had gotten a letter of introduction from Stratford Canning, British Minister to the United States. The document stated that the expedition was for "purely scientific" purposes and asked British officials and officers of the Hudson's Bay Company to offer the explorers whatever assistance they could.[7] Armed with this letter, on August 9 the detachment started north into Canada.

Guided by two Canadians, Long and a single private rode ahead to Fort Douglas, a village at the site of present Winnipeg. While the rest of the party followed by boat, they hired new interpreters, guides, and boatmen. Once they had enough men to finish the trip, the explorers traded their horses for three large canoes. Each of these was about 30 feet long, 4 feet wide, and 2½ feet deep, and with them it would be possible to move the men and their supplies across the water-laced countryside.[8] At noon on August 17, the party pushed away from the riverbank at Fort Douglas and continued its northward movement down the Red River. Late the next day they reached Lake Winnipeg and then crossed it to Winnipeg River, which led south and east. During the next few days they struggled down that stream, which at times resembled a series of small lakes connected by rapids, more than a river. After numerous portages, they came to Lake of the Woods on August 25 and halted there for a brief rest.[9]

Three days later, they began ascending Rainy River and on August 31 reached the falls of the river, a short distance from Rainy Lake. By this time the explorers had eaten much of their food, and the jerked buffalo meat and fresh pemmican they had bought at the Red River settlements had started to spoil. Hoping to get fresh meat, Long ordered a halt at the fur company trading posts near the falls. Both the American Fur Company and their rival, the Hudson's Bay Company, had facilities within sight of each other, but all the hungry scientists could get from either trader was some wheat flour and potatoes.[10] Long had expected to feed his men partially by hunting, but was "very much deceived in this calculation, the whole of the game being taken being no more than was necessary for. . .a single week."[11]

While resting at the falls of Rainy River, the explorers met John Tanner, a white man who had been captured by the Indians when he was a boy of nine. According to Tanner, his captors had taken him to Mackinac about 1790, and there an Ottawa woman bought him. Subsequently, she took him to the Red River country, where he grew to manhood among the Indians. As an adult he learned his identity and that his family was still searching for him, so he returned to white society for a time. His experiences there, however, convinced him that he needed to remain near the frontier, so he settled at Mackinac with several of his children. When Long's party met him, he had been trying unsuccessfully to get two of his daughters to leave the Red River country and settle with him in Michigan. In fact, men at the trading post convinced the young women to remain in the Northwest, and Tanner had been shot, although not fatally. Some years later, Dr. Edwin James, a former colleague in the 1820 expedition, edited and published Tanner's story. It became a classic among nineteenth-century tales of Indian captivity and is particularly important for its narrative of the difficulties Indian captives experienced when they tried to reenter American society after years in the wilderness.[12]

From the trading posts, the expedition moved east across Rainy Lake and over a series of lakes, streams, and rapids through a beautiful but desolate country. They saw no game animals—only a few birds—and noted that even the Indians who lived here had little success hunting. Keating reported that the Chippewa subsisted chiefly on wild rice and fish, supplemented by an occasional bear they killed. There were few moose, the area was too wet for deer, and Indian trappers had destroyed the native beaver many years earlier. The only animal signs that the naturalists saw were those of timber wolves.[13]

On September 13, the scientists arrived at Fort William, a fur trading post near Lake Superior. The journey from Pembina to the fort had gone well. According to their record, they had traveled 823 miles in twenty-seven days. Along the route they had made more than eighty portages, which had even slowed their pace. Despite their speed of travel, each afternoon when the party halted, Samuel Seymour sketched or painted scenes, and at other times they hesitated while the scientists examined and collected specimens.[14] Nevertheless, the naturalists gathered few new items for their collections on this leg of the journey.

Once the journey through the lake country ended, Long's voyageurs and interpreters wanted to return home, so he gave them one of the large canoes for the trip. Four of the men, however, decided to continue with the exploring party until it reached Sault St. Marie. At the shore of Lake Superior, Long decided that the lightweight canoes had to be replaced by something more substantial, so he appropriated a "very old and crazy" boat abandoned by the American boundary commissioners. Into this thirty-foot craft he jammed all twenty-two men, and on September 15 they set out along the north shore of the lake. To the northeast they saw Isle Royal—a faint blue streak on the horizon—which they soon left behind.[15]

Their journey along the north shore of the big lake added little scientific information to what they had already gathered. In fact, they almost lost some specimens on September 21, when Private Daniel Brown deserted. As well as his own things, he took property from the other soldiers and several of the scientists. Fortunately, his thefts included none of the notes, journals, sketches, or specimens so painstakingly collected that summer. Brown's desertion caught Long and the others by surprise. The major noted that his enlistment was nearly expired, that he had been promised a discharge when they reached Mackinac, and that the army owed him salary for several months. This desertion suggests that Long had been too lax about posting guards. His losses through desertions on the 1820 expedition should have made him aware of this problem, but he thought that there was no danger of the men voluntarily leaving the expedition in such a desolate region, more than 100 miles from the nearest settlement.[16]

Although Brown took no scientific matter, his thefts reduced the explorers' already meager food supply. Since traveling around Lake Superior, the hunters had killed only one small rabbit, one pheasant, and six red squirrels—not much food for twenty-two hungry men. One of the men claimed that it was possible to survive by eating moss and lichens, which the fur traders called *tripe de roche*. So the enterprising explorers gathered and boiled some lichens, but the new food proved "the most unpalatable" they had ever eaten. Actually, the young, tender plants could be cooked into a thin paste or jelly, but the travelers had been in a hurry and gathered the largest chunks they could find. As a result, they got tough, mature plants that, instead of cooking into an edible mush, "left a black matter floating in the liquid, and imparting to it as unsightly an appearance as its taste was disagreeable." Even large doses of red and black pepper did little to make the rock tripe edible, so the men remained hungry.[17]

Heavy wind, frequent rain, and occasional snow all made travel dangerous and uncomfortable. On September 26 the hungry men arrived at a Hudson's Bay Company trading post on Michipocten Bay. Here they watched company employees and Indians net hundreds of whitefish, lake trout, and perch. The clerk directing the post welcomed the explorers, entertained and fed them, and provided new supplies. Then, despite heavy wind and high waves, Long ordered his men back onto the lake on September 27, and three days later they arrived at Sault St. Marie, where they stopped at Fort Brady.[18] There, the tired men rested while Long and the scientists visited with Henry Schoolcraft, the resident Indian agent. Schoolcraft had traveled through part of the same region with Governor Lewis Cass in 1820, so they had much to discuss. The naturalists compared ideas about mineral deposits in the area, and Schoolcraft showed Long's companions ore samples he had gathered three years earlier. In particular, the agent exchanged information and ideas about the northern Indian tribes with Thomas Say and traded topographic sketches and notes with Long. Thus, his findings and those of the exploring party became joined, and both received more attention than they might have alone.[19]

THOMAS SAY by Rembrandt Peale. *Courtesy Academy of Natural Sciences, Philadelphia.*

On October 3 the explorers left Fort Brady and headed toward Mackinac. There, the expedition ended. The military escort left and the scientists boarded a ship for Detroit. Again, Long expected war department funds to be on deposit for him, but they were not. After a short delay, the travelers continued east to Buffalo aboard a lake steamer. At Buffalo, Long paused to write a brief report to Colonel Macomb. Then he and the others took a stagecoach to Rochester and a canalboat to Albany. At New York City they parted. Say, Colhoun, and Seymour stopped, while Long and Keating continued to Philadelphia, arriving on October 27, after having traveled some 4,500 miles in six months.[20]

Unlike his arrival in Philadelphia in 1820, this homecoming brought Stephen Long and his colleagues immediate and favorable public attention. Colonel Macomb congratulated them for completing the assignment, and Secretary of War Calhoun wrote a note of thanks. The *Democratic Press* noted that "the long hazardous expedition. . .greatly redounds to the credit of the distinguished scientific officer [Long]. . .as well as to his intelligent brother officers and companions."[21] Although Stephen Long did not know it, his career as an active explorer had ended. For the next forty-one years, he labored as an engineer officer on railroads, bridges, and river improvements, but because the government, for the next fifteen years, lost interest in Frontier exploration, Long never again received an exploration assignment.

Once home in Philadelphia, Long asked Colonel Macomb for authorization to complete and publish "some account of our researches in a popular form." As he had done several years earlier, Long convinced his superiors to pay for office space, fuel, writing materials, and two dollars a day salary for whoever compiled the expedition account.[22] Once funds had been promised, work began. William Keating, Thomas Say, Samuel Seymour, and Long all lived in or near Philadelphia, so the compilation was done there. How the four decided who was to actually prepare the manuscript for publication is not known, but sometime during the winter of 1823-24, William Keating emerged as the literary spokesman for the expedition, although the other three all cooperated in the project.[23]

Each man worked over his own notes or journals. Seymour completed half-drawn sketches and paintings. Long began a large map and conferred with Keating while the latter prepared the first three chapters. Say pored over his notes, sketches, and specimens of fish, animals, insects, mollusks, and plants. He had agreed to gather plant specimens at the last minute when no botanist could join the expedition, but made no claim of scientific competence in this area. In fact, Say doubted the overall accomplishments of the expedition. "We passed over that immense country in six months," he wrote a friend, and "we had not leisure to make very abundant collections; nevertheless I obtained some insects that are of some interest."[24] He did get some plant samples and sent them downriver for later classification while still on the expedition. Unfortunately, the soldiers and others who took the scientific collections back to frontier army posts proved careless; many items were lost.

When he returned east, Say made no effort to classify the small collection of plants that had survived the journey, but instead turned to other scientists for help. Thomas Nuttall, himself a veteran of frontier exploration, had agreed to classify and describe the specimens, but left for Europe before completing the task. Lewis D. von Schweinitz finally drew up a catalogue of the plants Say and his companions gathered. He described 11 of the 130 species as new to science, and some years later Frederick Brendel noted that the so-called new plants were "mostly riddles not yet solved." Brendel thought Say's botanical contributions small, which, unfortunately, they seem to have been.[25]

Among the lost items were all of Say's collections made between Fort Wayne, Indiana, and Fort St. Anthony at Minneapolis. These included "the skins of many birds, quadrupeds, and fish. . . ," as well as most of the shells Say had gathered. Without these losses, Keating claimed that "the amount of new species described would have been much greater."[26] There is no way to determine how many items disappeared or how significant they might have been, but Say's skill and enthusiasm as a collector stands unquestioned, and it is certain that losing many specimens reduced the explorers' scientific contributions.

Despite the lost material, Say still gathered an impressive number and variety of specimens for other scientists to examine and classify. His collections of insects and mollusks provided material that he published later in his multi-volume books *American Entomology* and *American Conchology*. In fact, his contributions as a pioneer naturalist were so widely respected in scientific circles that within a little more than thirty years, other scholars had gathered and reprinted many of his early papers, including items published as a result of the 1823 expedition.[27]

While Say worked on his reports, Keating struggled to integrate the notes kept by five men into a coherent narrative. Samuel Seymour completed many of the unfinished paintings and sketches he had drawn during the expedition. Stephen Long took much of the 1823-24 winter drawing a map of the region through which the expedition had passed. By spring, 1824, his superiors became impatient, asking when the literary project would be completed. When he could give no satisfactory answer, in late May, 1824, Colonel Macomb ordered Long to join army crews removing sandbars from the Ohio River. This project kept him out of Philadelphia until November, and when he returned the writing stood nearly complete.[28]

In December, 1824, Keating's work appeared. In some ways, the two-volume *Narrative of an Expedition to the Source of St. Peter's River, Lake Winnepeek, Lake of the Woods, &c. . .*, resembled the Edwin James *Account* of the 1819 and 1820 expeditions. Keating's hurriedly prepared manuscript included twelve narrative chapters that described the expedition and what the explorers saw. Appendices included Long's topographical report, Say's discussions of zoological items, a catalogue of plants described by Lewis D.

von Schweinitz, Colhoun's astronomical findings, some meteorological tables, and several Indian vocabularies. Seymour's illustrations and Long's map completed the volumes. Since compiler Keating was the expedition's geologist, discussions of rocks, minerals, and geographic items consequently received much attention. Nevertheless, he gave other topics adequate space, too. In fact, the ethnological material gathered by Say, Keating, and Colhoun probably constituted the most important part of the explorers' findings. Drawings, vocabularies, and general material relating to the Sioux and Chippewa, when coupled with the data Henry Schoolcraft gathered in 1820, provided a vast resource of information.

Stephen Long's map and report also offered much new data about the region. Although he described the entire route of travel, from Philadelphia west to Chicago, north into Canada, and then south and east into the United States, his report concentrated on the St. Peter's and Red River valleys in Minnesota and the Dakotas. First, he traced the course of the St. Peter's, as well as its source and tributaries. Then he noted the abundant timber and water and suggested that the region had good soil. Farther north and west the Red River Valley stretched nearly 350 miles from Lake Traverse to Lake Winnipeg. The valley consisted of "verdant prairie, spreading beyond the utmost extent of vision. . . ." The major expressed mixed views about soil fertility there. He claimed that in the upper or southern part of the valley the soil was light and thin, and dwarf vegetation there demonstrated an infertile soil. On the other hand, he noted that in many places "the soil appears rich, supporting a dense and luxuriant growth of grass." When the party moved northward, downriver, they found the soil deeper and richer. By the time they reached Pembina and Fort Douglas, Long reported the successful cultivation of wheat, barley, millet, potatoes, and "other culinary roots."[29]

The last area Long described lay between Lake Winnipeg and Lake Superior. The major had little positive to say about this region. The country was "literally a wilderness of lakes, islands, and peninsulas," he complained. "A mazy waste, so inhospitable and irreclaimable, as to mock the art and enterprise of man. . . ." There, the thin soil bore only "stinted [*sic*]" growth and "dwarfish" vegetation.[30] The rigorous climate and rugged terrain convinced him that "no part of this country can ever admit of a dense population, if we except, perhaps, the valley of the Rainy River. . . ." He noted that where agriculture had been tried it had succeeded, if only slightly. Despite his negative reaction to the country, Long commented on its variety and great beauty.[31]

In some ways his conclusions parallel those voiced about the Plains after the 1820 expedition. In fact, he claimed that the northern regions resembled the "great American Desert" in that they served as a buffer, guarding the more settled parts of the United States from potential enemies. The river and lake country afforded a better defensive barrier than "any *cordon* of posts," he wrote.[32] Thus, according to Stephen Long, the Plains on the south and west and this impassable barrier to the north combined to protect the nation. Even had the British wanted to invade, he pointed out that the Hudson's Bay Company fur trading interests would be in direct conflict with any plan to move a large population into the nearly deserted border region.[33]

Long's harsh judgment of this northern country came years before technological innovations made more extensive settlement there possible. It would be unreasonable to blame Long and his companions for not anticipating the agricultural developments leading to the "Bonanza Farms" of the Red River Valley later. On the other hand, the explorers ignored the region's lumbering potential, and geologist William Keating badly misjudged the future pace of mining development near Lake Superior. He noted the widespread evidence of copper, yet doubted that "any other advantage would result from it, at least for a century to come, than the mere addition in books of science of a new locality of this metal."[34]

Clearly, Keating was wrong because large-scale copper and iron mining brought many people into the upper peninsula of Michigan, northern Wisconsin, and northern Minnesota during the nineteenth century. His mistake came in part from the willingness of early explorers to discuss regions they had not examined personally. If the expedition had passed through one of the major iron- or copper-bearing areas, the geologist might well have concluded differently.

Keating's *Narrative* bears an 1824 date of publication and probably appeared that December. The next year, a London publisher brought out an English edition and in 1828 produced yet a third. In 1826, the book appeared in a German translation published at Jena.[35] Thus, within only five years, scholars in the United States, Great Britain, and western Europe had the explorers' findings available for study.

The book reviewers received Keating's literary effort with mixed comments. In January, 1825, an unnamed reviewer writing for Poulson's *American Daily Advertizer* described the book as "a credible performance" by the contributors, editor, and publishers. Claiming that many of the details were "new and entertaining," the writer assured his readers that the *Narrative* made "a valuable contribution to the scanty stock of trustworthy" travel accounts for the region.[36] In the *North American Review*, noted historian Jared Sparks offered mostly favorable comments in his critique. He wrote that Long and his associates proved that some authors of earlier travel accounts had "enjoyed an unmerited degree of confidence and reputation."[37] Sparks concluded, "Mr. Keating has accomplished his task, as historiographer to the expedition, with much good judgment, and with full measure of industry. . . ."[38]

After the 1825 English edition appeared, the (London) *Monthly Review* included a critique of Keating's volumes. Less generous than American commentators, the unsigned reviewer devoted a full thirteen pages to his discussion.

Keating's penchant for cluttering the narrative with long discussions of rocks, minerals, and geological formations drew the most fire. In fact, the reviewer criticized his geological skills sharply and noted that the expedition geologist "appears much better qualified to examine mineral specimens in a cabinet, than to explore the geological character of an extensive region."[39] Despite this attack, most reviews gave Keating's work more credit than it deserved, at least as a literary work.

Unlike their activity immediately after the 1820 expedition, the participants of the 1823 journey published few papers or books based on their summer experiences. Thomas Say was the only notable exception. During 1824 he read and published three papers, while the next year he offered scientific colleagues eleven more. Clearly, Say made the most significant contributions to natural science at the time, and scholars at home and abroad recognized this. In 1824, the Philomathique Society of Paris made him a correspondent and the Linnaean Society of London elected him a foreign member five years later. As Say's reputation grew, so did interest in his work abroad, and by 1845 both *American Entomology* and *American Conchology* had been translated into French and published in Paris.[40] In addition, during the 1850s, two American scholars collected, edited, and republished Say's earlier writings about shells and insects. The twentieth century brought no lessening of his recognition. One scholar wrote admiringly that "he described and discovered more species of shells than any one else in the history of conchology. . . .As for our insects," the same author continued, "there is no guessing at the number that go to Say's credit."[41]

Other members of the exploring party remained active, but in a less conspicuous manner. Long's map, when taken with that published in 1822, corrected some errors on distances and rivers and filled some blanks on earlier maps. His untiring efforts to expand scientific knowledge persuaded the

American Philosophical Society to elect him to membership in late 1823, just before the explorers got back to Philadelphia.[42]

William Keating continued to lecture at the University of Pennsylvania and remained an active member of scholarly groups in and around Philadelphia. With Thomas Say and Long, he had collected valuable information about the Indians of the northern frontier. Henry Schoolcraft, himself recognized as an expert on Indians of that area, complimented the explorers for their new information about the Sioux and Chippewa. On the other hand, he did criticize their heavy dependence upon interpreters and guides for their ideas. And more than fifty years later, a bibliographer praised the ethnological material in Keating's *Narrative*. According to him, "nothing escaped the attention or record" of the explorers, and "their statements respecting the Sioux and Chippeway tribes are among the most valuable we have."[43]

In geology, the contributions were less significant. One scholar dismissed the 1823 expedition as offering little of major significance. On the other hand, he conceded that the *Narrative* had many "references, which at the time they were written, were of value." This overlooks one important idea that both Keating and Long considered. To them it seemed likely that much of the region they had crossed had been under water sometime in the past. Long noted this while traveling up the Mississippi in 1817, and during the 1823 expedition Keating also mentioned it. Therefore, these two men must have been among the earliest to consider the existence of what geographers call Glacial Lake Agassiz today.[44] Although neither Keating nor Long had any conception of glaciation as a natural force, the geologist noted the moraines, or ridges of glacial debris, left during the retreat of past glaciers. Beyond that, he certainly offered no startling discoveries of new minerals, no careful analysis of regional soil types, or even positive comments on potential ore bodies for mining. Despite its shortcomings, however, Keating's *Narrative* remained the standard geological description of the region for the next three decades.[45]

By the time Keating's *Narrative* had been completed and was on sale, Stephen Long's work as an explorer was over. In some ways his later activity as an army engineer aided the westward movement of pioneers as much or more than did his early explorations. Working with railroads, canals, river channels, and bridges in the East helped to develop transportation facilities over which the westering flow of people moved. His efforts to remove sandbars and snags in midwestern and western rivers helped as well. In fact, the growing technological skills that Americans developed during the middle years of the nineteenth century proved Long and his companions poor prophets. It became possible for later pioneers to cross and even settle the regions that the explorers had dismissed as useless to the nation except as barriers to protect it from foreign invasion.

[11]
Stephen Long as an Explorer

Historians and geographers have analyzed the exploratory process with care, and for clarity in assessing Stephen Long's expeditions it is necessary to consider some of their ideas. In William Goetzmann's discussion of exploration and discovery mentioned earlier, he presents the two tasks as distinct yet related. Both the discoverer and the explorer travel into unknown or unsettled regions. Both offer a report of where they have been and what they saw. There, however, the similarity ends. Often the discoverer finds things he is not looking for—more by chance than by design. The explorer, on the other hand, searches for particular objects in an organized, planned manner.[1] Using these definitions, Stephen Long and his companions present a classic early-nineteenth-century example of the Goetzmann explorers who also did a little discovery work. They were not the only explorers, or even the first. There had been others: Lewis and Clark, Zebulon Pike, Dunbar and Hunter, and the Freeman party. Nevertheless, it was not until 1819, when Long left Pittsburgh aboard the *Western Engineer*, that a group of soldiers and scientists set out to explore a part of the American frontier in a systematic, organized fashion.

Beginning in 1819 and continuing to the present, Long's expeditions have received more than their share of criticism. Yet nearly all of the negative evaluations focus on his failure to discover the headwaters of the Red River or on his negative descriptions of the Plains. In doing so, the critics have failed to distinguish between the tasks of discovery and those of exploration. Long and his companions made only modest contributions in the former category and certainly failed to achieve some of their assigned goals. Here the critics are right. As explorers, however, the participants of the 1819, 1820, and 1823 expeditions gathered a wealth of scientific data. This information entered the mainstream of American scientific thought almost immediately because of the hundreds of specimens and drawings they gathered and drew, as well as their books, articles, scholarly papers, and correspondence with other learned men across the nation. It seems clear that Long's expeditions made a large and immediate contribution to the rapid growth of American science in the early nineteenth century and that they provided a prototype for the explorations of Charles Wilkes in the late 1830s, as well as for those of John C. Fremont in the 1840s.

In an analysis of the explorations of Lewis and Clark, geographer John Allen describes three degrees of knowledge about the frontier. First—and most accurate—is information gathered by direct exploration. Less reliable, but still usable, are ideas from travelers and their written accounts. The third and least valuable data are those taken from rumors and conjecture, often to fill gaps in knowledge or blank spaces on maps.[2] Applying these criteria to Long's expeditions suggests that his work was indeed successful. The Scientific Expedition of 1819 added much to what was known about the Missouri Valley Indians and the plants and animals of the area during the winter of 1819-20, when the naturalists remained at Council Bluffs. They gathered ethnological data from personal observation, as well as from interviews with Indians, interpreters, fur traders, and government agents. At the same time they worked steadily to gather, describe, and classify hundreds of plants, animals, and insects that they found along the river and on the nearby bluffs.

The 1820 expedition across the Plains moved into an area

about which even the fur traders knew little. The naturalists started west with essentially third-degree information—rumors from traders and Indians. Once beyond the Pawnee villages in east-central Nebraska, however, they moved into what for them was still virgin territory. In the process they obtained first-degree knowledge through their field work that summer. This proved somewhat less true of the 1823 venture into the North. There, fur traders and Indian agents had moved up the Mississippi to Fort St. Anthony for some years. Most knowledge of the region west and north of the fort, however, was either second or third degree. Therefore, here, too, Long's expedition filled scientific gaps and corrected geographic errors by careful measurement and observation.

In all of his frontier rambling, Long was careful to read what previous travelers said about his intended destinations. He also got ideas that varied greatly in value from guides, interpreters, frontier whites, and Indians he met while traveling. While the information that came from others affected his thinking, there is no doubt that when first-hand observation proved his earlier informants unreliable or wrong, Stephen Long admitted it quickly. Much of the data that his three major expeditions obtained then became what Allen describes as first-degree knowledge—that collected by active field work and observation on the frontier.

Another geographer, John K. Wright, proposed two general categories into which the exploratory process might be divided. The first was "the urge to open up the unknown for exploitation or trade, conquest or settlement, or for the satisfaction of curiosity, idle or scientific." The second was traveling between two established "centers of civilization" through unsettled regions.[3] This latter category has no relevance for Long's work, but the former certainly does. The government policy of extending military control and economic dominance over western and northern frontier regions surely qualifies as an effort for trade and conquest.

Such activities provided an opportunity to examine frontier areas and by so doing satisfy "scientific curiosity" at the same time. Stephen Long's three major expeditions achieved some degree of success in all three of these goals.

Having said this, the suspicion remains that the trips of 1819, 1820, and 1823 could have yielded more information had they been better organized, equipped, and led. Several factors inhibited success, and Stephen Long himself was one of these. There is little evidence upon which to base an examination of his personality or character traits, and this study makes no claim to having done so. Yet his experience as a farm boy, cooper, and surveyor gave him a practical, down-to-earth quality. His college education apparently sparked a natural curiosity, and he developed a wide range of interests. Assignments that brought him into the Mississippi Valley stimulated an enthusiasm for travel and exploration that he retained for decades.

Associates generally agreed that Long was pleasant, intelligent, and able, while his superiors demonstrated their confidence in him many times. On the other hand, some of those who participated in his expeditions considered him as unqualified. At least one individual on each expedition—Major Thomas Biddle in 1819, Captain John Bell in 1820, and Giacomo Beltrami in 1823—quarreled violently with him. It is not known what Long thought about these men, but certainly he must have found them difficult comrades. Once, during the 1820 expedition, Captain Bell refused to obey an order from Long, stating, "We are out of the U.S., enforce your orders if you can."[4] Whether such clashes came from personality differences, disagreements over tactics, mismanagement or rigidity on Long's part, or because of the discomfort and danger that the explorers encountered matters little. The arguments happened, and on each expedition. Obviously, Long's leadership brought criticism from some of his companions.

His optimism or what might have been lack of judgment

hurt each expedition, too. Long tended to overestimate the distance that might be traveled each day, while at the same time he understated the food and equipment his men would need. This reduced time for the scientists to do their work and limited their accomplishments. And because time and food ran short, Long was forced to omit assigned tasks, such as tracing the upper reaches of the Platte and Arkansas rivers. Occasionally, he demonstrated a laxity that hurt the expeditions. Twice, men deserted, taking with them badly needed food and equipment. Although in 1820 the desertions were not his fault, they nevertheless resulted in the loss of sketches, specimens, and travel journals and greatly reduced the scientists' contributions. In 1823, however, the desertion was indeed Long's responsibility. Nevertheless, when danger threatened the explorers, he proved equal to the test, as his actions toward the Indians indicated.

Inadequate transportation and communication facilities proved a second factor that reduced the explorers' positive accomplishments. In 1819, dependence upon the relatively untried steamboat badly slowed the expedition. The desperate shortage of food during the summer of 1820 might have been avoided had Long been able to communicate with Secretary of War Calhoun about money for food and equipment. Certainly, had there been any safe way to have sent specimens and notebooks east in early 1820, the explorers would not have risked damaging or losing them on the Plains. This also would have prevented the loss of several cases of specimens and some notes sent east by Thomas Say during the 1823 journey. Such difficulties did limit the scientific achievements of Long's associates, and, after considering the valuable contributions they made despite such problems, one cannot help wonder what the material they lost would have shown.

The third inhibiting factor was using the army to direct the expeditions. There seems to have been no other group willing or able to finance such activity, yet using the military for exploring had several negative effects. Often Congress subjected War Department appropriations to more rigorous annual scrutiny than other parts of the federal budget. This certainly proved true after the Panic of 1819 caused major retrenchments in federal expenditures. Working for Secretary of War John Calhoun must have been stimulating, yet when Calhoun became embroiled in a bitter fight with Congress over his administration of the War Department, Long and his companions suffered from the repercussions. Their ordeal on the Plains in 1820 shows this clearly. Finally, some officers within the army viewed exploring as a minor sideline that tended to disrupt its more regular duties. Generals Andrew Jackson and Alexander Macomb both demonstrated this attitude on occasion. Such official disfavor must have helped Long develop his habit of overestimating potential achievements while underestimating potential costs. Despite these criticisms, it seems unlikely that any exploration would have been tried had the government not used soldiers to lead the expeditions.

Although Major Long's military status may have limited his scientific achievements, it allowed him to function as a promoter for scientific exploration. Between 1817 and 1820 he made at least ten written reports and proposals to his superiors, calling for expeditions into the West. He wrote to his department commander General Smith, to Chief of Engineers General Swift, to Secretary of War Calhoun, and even to President James Monroe. On at least three occasions he pleaded his case in person at St. Louis and Washington, stressing the need to gather scientific as well as strategic information. In this respect he served as his own lobbyist, submitting and resubmitting his calls for exploration. Thus, Long kept the issue before government officials until they responded favorably to his calls for action.

At the same time, he corresponded with naturalists and other civilians interested in scientific matters, getting support from them in his efforts to stimulate government action.

Much like John Fremont and John Wesley Powell years later, Stephen Long focused attention on scientific exploration. His efforts as a promoter came at an opportune time, fit into national policies of expansion, and coincided with a growing desire to learn more about the resources of frontier regions. Certainly, Long's promotion of scientific exploration by itself did not shape federal actions in this sphere, but his repeated urgings made the decision to include it as a part of national policy an easy one for an expansionist government. For this he deserves credit.

Stephen Long's explorations took him across the middle of the present-day United States several times. Alone, and later with small detachments of troops and scientists, he criss-crossed portions of the frontier from Philadelphia to the Rocky Mountains and from modern New Mexico to Minnesota. From 1816 to 1823, he and his companions traveled thousands of miles, crossed plains, climbed mountains, followed rivers, and trekked through forests. They gathered much data about physical and natural resources, as well as about the Indians living in those regions. Their efforts proved a boon to science and set the pattern for later, better-financed expeditions into the West. The work of John Fremont, the Boundary Commission, the Pacific Railroad Surveys, and John Wesley Powell was built upon the foundations Long laid. While his expeditions failed to do all that was expected of them at the time, they accomplished much that has since been overlooked. They deserve recognition for having made significant contributions to American science and cartography, and for committing the government to a policy of sponsoring scientific exploration.

Appendix

The following items indicate the extensive contributions that Stephen Long and his exploring companions made during and following his expeditions. The papers, articles, and books include material gathered during Long's explorations, as well as later items that seem to have used some earlier findings or that built upon the knowledge and experience gained on the frontier expeditions. The list does not include foreign language translations, most reprintings, or the uses by other scholars of the explorers' findings.

1818   Long, Stephen H. "A Description of the Hot Springs, near the River Washitaw, and of the physical geography of the adjacent country." *American Monthly Magazine and Critical Review* 3:85-87.

———. "Extract from a report [respecting the practicability of uniting by a canal the water of the Illinois River, and those of Lake Michigan]." Report to John C. Calhoun, U.S., Congress, *House Executive Document No. 17*, 16th Cong., 1 sess., 1819, serial 32.

1819   Say, Thomas. "Notes on Herpetology." *American Journal of Science and Arts* 1:256-65.

———. "Observations on Some Species of Zoophytes, Shells, etc., Principally Fossil." *American Journal of Science and Arts* 1:381-87.

1820 Jessup, Augustus E. "Fetid Fluor Spar." *American Journal of Science and Arts* 2:176.

Say, Thomas. "Observations of Some Species of Zoophytes, Shells, etc., Principally Fossil." *American Journal of Science and Arts* 2:34-45.

1821 Say, Thomas. "An Account of the Arachnides of the United States." *Journal of the Academy of Natural Sciences of Philadelphia* 2:59-82.

———. "Descriptions of the Myriapodae of the United States." *Journal of the Academy of Natural Sciences of Philadelphia* 2:102-14.

———. "Descriptions of the Thysanourae of the United States." *Journal of the Academy of Natural Sciences of Philadelphia* 2:11-14.

———. "Descriptions of univalve shells of the United States." *Journal of the Academy of Natural Sciences of Philadelphia* 2:149-79.

1822 James, Edwin. "Geological Sketches of the Mississippi Valley." *Journal of the Academy of Natural Sciences of Philadelphia* 2:326-29.

Say, Thomas. "An Account of Some of the Marine Shells of the United States." *Journal of the Academy of Natural Sciences of Philadelphia* 2:221-48, 257-76, 302-25.

———. "Description of univalve terrestrial and fluviate Shells of the United States." *Journal of the Academy of Natural Sciences of Philadelphia* 2:370-81.

———. "On a Quadruped belonging to the order Rodentia." *Journal of the Academy of Natural Sciences of Philadelphia* 2:330-43.

1823 James, Edwin. *Account of an expedition from Pittsburgh to the Rocky Mountains, performed in the* years 1819 and '20, by order of the Hon. J.C. Calhoun, Sec'y of War; under the command of Major Stephen H. Long, from the notes of Major Long, Mr. T. Say, and other gentlemen of the exploring party; compiled by Edwin James, botanist and geologist for the expedition. 2 vols. and atlas. Philadelphia, Pa.: H. C. Carey and I. Lea, 1823.

———. Ibid. 3 vols. London: Longman, Hurst, Rees, Orme, and Brown, 1823.

Say, Thomas. "A Description of Some New Species of Hymenopterous Insects." The Western Quarterly Reporter of Medical, Surgical, and Natural Science 2:71-82.

———. "Descriptions of Coleopterous Insects, collected in the late expedition to the Rocky Mountains." Journal of the Academy of Natural Sciences of Philadelphia 3:139-216, 238-82, 298-331, 403-62; 4:83-99.

———. "Descriptions of the Dipterous Insects of the United States." Journal of the Academy of Natural Sciences of Philadelphia 3:9-54, 73-103.

———. "Descriptions of Insects Belonging to the Order Neuropters, Lin. Lati., Collected by the Expedition Authorized by J.C. Calhoun, Sec. of War, Under Command of S.H. Long." The Western Quarterly Reporter of Medical, Surgical, and Natural Science 2:160-65.

1824 James, Edwin. "On the identity of the supposed Pumice of the Missouri, and a variety of Amygdaloid found near the Rocky Mountains." Annals of the Lyceum of Natural History of New York 1:21-23.

Keating, William H. Narrative of an expedition to the source of St. Peter's River, Lake Winnepeek, Lake of the Woods, etc., Performed in the year 1823, By Order of the Hon. J.C. Calhoun, Secretary of War. Under the Command of Major Stephen H. Long, U.S.T.E.* 2 vols. Philadelphia, Pa.: H. C. Carey and I. Lea, 1824.

Say, Thomas. *American Entomology, or Descriptions of the Insects of North America.* 3 vols. Philadelphia, Pa.: S. A. Mitchell, 1817-28.

Schweinitz, Lewis David von. "A catalogue of the plants collected in the northwestern territory by Mr. Thomas Say, in the year 1823." In William H. Keating, *Narrative of an Expedition to the Source of St. Peter's River, Lake Winnepeek, Lake of the Woods, &c. Performed in the Year 1823, By Order of the Hon. J.C. Calhoun, Secretary of War, Under the Command of Stephen H. Long, U.S.T.E.* 2 vols. Philadelphia, Pa.: H. C. Carey and I. Lea, 1824.

Torrey, John. "Descriptions of some new Grasses collected by Dr. E. James, in the expedition of Major Long to the Rocky Mountains, in 1819-1820." *Annals of the Lyceum of Natural History of New York* 1:148-56.

Torrey, John. "Descriptions of some new or rare Plants from the Rocky Mountains, collected in July, 1820, by Dr. Edwin James." *Annals of the Lyceum of Natural History of New York* 1:30-36.

1825 Bonaparte, Charles L. and Titian R. Peale. *American Ornithology; or the natural history of birds inhabiting the United States, not given by Wilson, with figures drawn and engraved from nature.* 4 vols. Philadelphia, Pa.: H. C. Carey and I. Lea, 1825-33. Peale illustrated vol. 1, 1825, and vol. 4, 1833.

James, Edwin. "Catalogue of Plants Collected during

a Journey to and from the Rocky Mountains during the summer of 1820." *American Philosophical Society Transactions, New Series* 2:172-89.

————. "Remarks on the Sandstone and Floetz Trap Formations of the Western Part of the Valley of the Mississippi." *American Philosophical Society Transactions, New Series* 2:191-215.

Keating, William H. *Narrative of an expedition to the Source of St. Peter's River, Lake Winnepeek, Lake of the Woods, &c. Performed in the Year 1823, By Order of the Hon. J. C. Calhoun, Secretary of War, Under the Command of Stephen H. Long, U.S.T.E.* 2 vols. London: Geo. B. Whittaker, 1825.

————. "Descriptions of Marine Shells Recently Discovered on the Coast of the United States." *Journal of the Academy of Natural Sciences of Philadelphia* 5:207-21.

Say, Thomas. "Description of Univalve Terrestrial and Fluviatile Shells of the United States." *Journal of the Academy of Natural Sciences of Philadelphia* 4:370-81.

————. "Descriptions of New American Species of the Genera Buprestis, Trachys, and Elater." *Annals of the Lyceum of Natural History of New York* 1:249-68.

————. "Descriptions of new Hemipterous insects collected in the Expedition to the Rocky Mountains." *Journal of the Academy of Natural Sciences of Philadelphia* 4:306-45.

————. "Descriptions of new species of Coleopterous Insects Inhabiting the United States." *Journal of the Academy of Natural Sciences of Philadelphia* 5:160-204, 237-84, 293-304.

————. "Descriptions of new species of Hister and

Hololepsta, inhabiting the United States." *Journal of the Academy of Natural Sciences of Philadelphia* 5:32-47.

————. "Descriptions of some new species of Fresh Water and Land Shells of the United States." *Journal of the Academy of Natural Sciences of Philadelphia* 5:119-31.

————. "Descriptions of three new Species of Coluber, inhabiting the United States." *Journal of the Academy of Natural Sciences of Philadelphia* 4: 237-41.

————. *A Glossary to Say's Entomology; or, An explanation of terms used in entomology.* Philadelphia, Pa.: S. A. Mitchell, 1825.

————. "On a New Species of Modiola (opifex)." *Journal of the Academy of Natural Sciences of Philadelphia* 4:368-70.

————. "On the fresh water and land Tortoises of the United States." *Journal of the Academy of Natural Sciences of Philadelphia* 4:203-19.

————. "On the Species of the Linnaean Genus Asterias, Inhabiting the Coast of the United States." *Journal of the Academy of Natural Sciences of Philadelphia* 5:141-54.

————. "On Two Genera and Several Species of Crinoidea." *Journal of the Academy of Natural Sciences of Philadelphia* 4:289-96.

Say, Thomas and George Ord. "A New Genus of Mammalia Proposed and Description of the Species Upon Which it is Founded." *Journal of the Academy of Natural Sciences of Philadelphia* 4:345-49, 352-55.

1826 Long, Stephen H. "On the Rocky Mountain Sheep." *Philadelphia Society for Promoting Agriculture, Memoirs* 5:193-95.

Say, Thomas. "On the Species of the Linnaean Genus Echinus, Inhabiting the Coast of the United States." *Journal of the Academy of Natural Sciences of Philadelphia* 5:225-29.

Torrey, John. "Some Account of a Collection of Plants Made during a journey to and from the Rocky Mountains in the summer of 1820 by E.P. James, M.D." *Annals of the Lyceum of Natural History of New York* 2:161-254.

1827   James, Edwin. "Remarks on the Limestones of the Mississippi Lead Mines." *Journal of the Academy of Natural Sciences of Philadelphia* 5:376-80.

1829   Say, Thomas. "Descriptions of New Species of Hymenoptera of the United States." *Contributions of the Maclurian Lyceum of Philadelphia* 1:67-83.

———. "Descriptions of North American Dipterous Insects." *Journal of the Academy of Natural Sciences of Philadelphia* 6:149-78; (1830) 6:183-88.

———. "Descriptions of some new terrestrial and Fluviatile Shells of North America." *New Harmony Disseminator for Useful Knowledge* (1829, 1830, 1831): 244-46, 259-61, 275-77, 291-93, 308-10, 323-25, 339-41, 355-56.

1830   Peale, Titian R. and Jacob Green. "Description of two New Species of the Linnaean Genus Lacerta (Agama torquata and Scincus Ventralis)." *Journal of the Academy of Natural Sciences of Philadelphia* 6:231-34.

Say, Thomas. *American Conchology; or Descriptions of the Shells of North America.* 6 parts. New Harmony, Ind.: Printed by the School Press, 1830-34.

————. "Descriptions of new North American Hemipterous Insects, belonging to the first family of the section Homptera of Latreille." *Journal of the Academy of Natural Sciences of Philadelphia* 6:235-44; (1831) 6:299-314.

1831 Long, Stephen H. "Fossil Remains of a Mastodon found in Tennessee." *The Monthly American Journal of Geology and Science* 1:565-66.

Say, Thomas. "Descriptions of Several New Species of Shells and of a New Species of Lumbricus." *Transylvania Journal of Medicine and the Associate Sciences* 4:149-60.

1832 Say, Thomas. "Descriptions of New North American Insects and Observations on Some Already Mentioned." *American Philosophical Society Transactions, New Series* 4:409-70.

————. *A Glossary to Say's Conchology.* New Harmony, Ind.: Printed by R. Beck & J. Bennett.

1833 Peale, Titian R. *Lepidoptera Americana; or Original figures of the moths and butterflies of North America, in their various stages of existence, and the plants on which they feed.* Philadelphia, Pa.: W. Gibbons, 1833.

1834 Peale, Titian R. "Black-tailed or mule deer, Cervus macrotis." *Advocate of Science and Annals of Natural History* 1:11-13.

1835 Say, Thomas. "Descriptions of new North American Coleopterous insects, and observations on some already described." *Boston Journal of Natural History* 1:151-203.

1836 Long, Stephen H. "Report on a Reconnaissance of Maine to Quebec." *Senate Document 9,* 16th legislature, State of Maine.

Say, Thomas. "Descriptions of New North American Insects and Observations on Some Already Mentioned." *American Philosophical Society Transactions, New Series* 6:155-90.

———. "Descriptions of new species of North American Hymenoptera and observations on some already described." *Boston Journal of Natural History* 1:209-305; (1837) 1:361-416.

1840 Say, Thomas. *Descriptions of some new terrestrial and Fluviatile Shells of North America, 1829, 1830, 1831*. Reprinting of earlier items from the *New Harmony Disseminator of Useful Knowledge*. New Harmony, Ind., 1840.

1858 Say, Thomas. "Descriptions of new species of the heteropterous Hemiptera of North America." *Transactions of the New York State Agricultural Society* 17:754-812. Reprint of a rare earlier item from New Harmony.

1860-67 Long, Stephen H. "Voyage in a Six-Oared Skiff to the Falls of Saint Anthony in 1817." *Minnesota Historical Society Collections* 2:8-88.

1862 Peale, Titian R. "The Ancient Mounds at St. Louis, Missouri, in 1819." Washington, D.C.: *Smithsonian Institution Annual Report, 1861.* 386-91.

Notes

Introduction

1. William Goetzmann, *Exploration and Empire: The Explorer and the Scientist in the Winning of the American West* (New York: Alfred A. Knopf, 1966), pp. x-xii.

2. Alvin M. Josephy, Jr., "Across the Mississippi," in *The Pioneer Spirit* (New York: American Heritage, 1959), p. 157.

3. Hiram M. Chittenden, *The American Fur Trade in the Far West,* 3 vols. (New York: F. P. Harper, 1902), 2: 570; Ray A. Billington, *Westward Expansion: A History of the American Frontier,* 4th ed. (New York: Macmillan Co., 1974), p. 378; Goetzmann, *Exploration and Empire,* p. 62.

4. John M. Tucker, "Major Long's Route from the Arkansas to the Canadian River, 1820," *New Mexico Historical Review* 38 (July 1963): 185; Richard H. Dillon, "Stephen Long's Great American Desert," *Proceedings of the American Philosophical Society* 111 (April 1967): 93; W. Eugene Hollon, *The Great American Desert, Then and Now,* (New York: Oxford University Press, 1966), p. 260.

5. Paul Wilhelm, *Travels in North America 1822-1824,* ed. Savoie Lottinville (Norman, Okla.: University of Oklahoma Press, 1973), p. xiv.

6. Ibid.

7. By the mid-1830s some of the Lewis and Clark findings were being used by contemporary scientists. See, for example, William R. Stanton, *The Leopard's Spots: Scientific Attitudes Toward Race in America 1815-59* (Chicago: University of Chicago Press, 1960), p. 26. Nevertheless, in his excellent study of Lewis and Clark as naturalists, Paul Cutright concedes that most of their significant findings lay hidden until nearly 1890. By then much of their information had been rediscovered and applied by others. See his *Lewis and Clark: Pioneering Naturalists* (Urbana, Ill.: University of Illinois Press, 1969), pp. vii-ix, 85.

8. John Livingston, "Colonel Stephen H. Long of the United States Army," *Portraits of Eminent Americans Now Living: With Biographical and Historial Memoirs of their Lives and Actions,* 4 vols. (New York: Cornish, Lamport & Co., 1853-54), 4: 488-89. Much of the material Livingston includes could have come only from Long himself, as, for example, the claim of distance traveled.

Chapter 1

1. Stephen Long to James Monroe, February 20, 1815, Records of the Adjutant General's Office, Letters Received, Record Group 94, National Archives, Washing-

ton, D.C., hereafter cited AGO, LR, RG 94.

2. Mrs. Chapin Hoskins of the New Hampshire Antiquarian Society provided some details of Long's early life; see also Richard G. Wood, *Stephen Harriman Long, 1784-1864: Army Engineer, Explorer, Inventor,* (Glendale, Calif.: Arthur Clark Co., 1966), pp. 22-27.

3. Wood, *Stephen Long,* pp. 30-32; *Dartmouth College Catalogue,* quoted in Leon B. Richardson, *History of Dartmouth College,* 2 vols. (Hanover, N.H.: Dartmouth College Publications, 1932), 1:376-77.

4. Wood, *Stephen Long,* pp. 31-32; Richardson, *History of Dartmouth,* 1:376-77.

5. Wood, *Stephen Long,* pp. 33-34.

6. Quoted in Ibid., pp. 35-36; John Livingston, "Colonel Stephen H. Long of the United States Army," in *Portraits of Eminent Americans Now Living: with Biographical and Historical Memoirs of Their Lives and Actions,* 4 vols. (New York: Cornish, Lamport & Co., 1853-54) 4:477.

7. Long to John Harris, June 10, 1811; September 28, 1811, Harris Papers, Dartmouth College Archives, Hanover, N.H.; Long to Harris, May 5, 1816, New Hampshire State Library, Concord; Wood, *Stephen Long*, pp. 35-36.

8. Long to Harris, April 18, 1811; September 13, 1811; September 28, 1811, Harris Papers.

9. Ibid., September 28, 1811, Harris Papers.

10. Ibid., February 2, 1812, Harris Papers.

11. Charles Redfeffer to Long, December 17, 1814, Stephen H. Long Letters, Miscellaneous, Pennsylvania Historical Society, Philadelphia.

12. Joseph G. Swift, *Memoirs of General Joseph Gardner Swift. . ., ed. Harrison Ellery (Worcester, Mass.: Press of F. S. Blanchard & Co., 1890), pp. 128, 204.*

13. Wood, *Stephen Long,* p. 37; Long to James Monroe, February 20, 1815, AGO, LR, RG 94.

14. Livingston, "Stephen Long," *Eminent Americans,* 4: 477; Swift, *Memoirs,* pp. 142, 177; Guy V. Henry, *Military Record of Civilian Appointments in the United States Army,* 2 vols. (New York: D. Van Nostrand, 1871-73), 1: 31; Wood, *Stephen Long,* pp. 37-38.

15. The recommendations from Swift and Roberdeau accompanied Long to the Secretary of War, April 26, 1816, AGO, LR, RG 94; see also Francis B. Heitman, Comp., *Historical Register and Dictionary of the United States Army, From Its Organization, September 29, 1789, to March 2, 1903,* 2 vols., (Washington, D.C., 1903), 1:640.

16. Long to William Crawford, June 14, 1816, Records of the Office of the Chief of Engineers, Miscellaneous File, Letters Received, Record Group 77, National Archives, Washington, D.C., hereafter cited as Engineers' Misc., LR, RG 77; Crawford to Long, June 18, 1816, Office of the Secretary of War, Letters Sent, Vol. 9, Record Group 107, National Archives, Washington, D.C., hereafter cited as SW, LS, RG 107; Crawford to Long, July 2, 1816, SW, LS, 9, RG 107.

17. Livingston, "Stephen Long," *Eminent Americans,* 4: 477-78; Long to Joseph Swift, September 15, 1816, Engineers Misc., LR, RG 77.

18. Wood, *Stephen Long,* p. 39.

19. Crawford to Long, July 2, 1816, SW, LS, 9, RG 107.

20. Long to Thomas A. Smith, September 15, 1816, Records of the Office of Secretary of War, Letters Received, RG 107, hereafter cited as SW, LR, RG 107; this letter is published in Richard G. Wood, "Stephen H. Long's Plan for a New Fort at Peoria," *Journal of the Illinois State Historical Society* 47 (Winter 1954): 417-21; Livingston, "Stephen Long," *Eminent Americans,* 4: 478.

21. Long to Smith, September 15, 1816, SW, LR, RG 107.

22. Ibid.

23. Ibid.; Long to George Graham, March 4, 1817, *National Register* (Washington, D.C.), March 29, 1817; Francis P. Prucha, *A Guide to the Military Posts of the United States, 1789-1895* (Madison, Wis.: State Historical Society of Wisconsin, 1964), p. 66; Henry P. Beers, *The Western Military Frontier, 1815-1846* (Philadelphia, Pa.: University of Pennsylvania Press, 1935), p. 52.

24. Long to Smith, September 15, 1816, SW, LR, RG 107.

25. Livingston, "Stephen Long," *Eminent Americans* 4: 478-79; Long to Graham, March 4, 1817, *National Register*, March 29, 1817; Long to Monroe, March 15, 1817, SW, LR, RG 107.

26. Long to Graham, March 4, 1817, *National Register*, March 29, 1817.

27. Ibid.

28. Ibid.

29. Ibid.

30. Ibid.

31. Ibid.

32. Ibid.

33. George Graham to Andrew Jackson, February 1, 1817, in Andrew Jackson, *Correspondence of Andrew Jackson*, ed. John S. Bassett, 7 vols. (Washington, D.C.: Carnegie Institution of Washington, 1926-35), 2: 275; Wood, *Stephen Long*, p. 43.

34. Wood, *Stephen Long,* pp 44-45.

35. John C. Calhoun to Henry Clay, December 28, 1819, abstract in *The Papers of John C. Calhoun*, ed. Robert L. Meriwether and W. Edwin Hemphill, 9 vols., (Columbia, S.C.: University of South Carolina Press, 1959-76), 4: 511-12; *American State Papers; Miscellaneous,* 2: 555-57; *National Register,* March 29, 1817.

Chapter 2

1. Orders, May 1, 1817, "Miscellaneous Treasury Accounts," Records of the General Accounting Office, Record Group 217, National Archives, Washington, D.C. John Livingston, *Eminent Americans Now Living: With Biographical and Historical Memoirs of Their Lives and Actions*, 4 vols. (New York: Cornish, Lamport & Co., 1853-54) 4: 479-80.

2. Stephen H. Long, "Voyage in a Six-Oared Skiff to the Falls of Saint Anthony

in 1817," *Collections of the Minnesota Historical Society* (St. Paul, Minn.: 1860-7), 2: 8; Livingston, *Eminent Americans*, 4: 479.

3. Long, "Voyage in a Skiff," p. 70; Livingston, *Eminent Americans,* 4: 479.

4. Long, "Voyage in a Skiff," p. 70; Francis P. Prucha, *Guide to the Military Posts of the United States, 1789-1895* (Madison, Wis.: State Historical Society, 1964), p. 57.

5. Livingston, *Eminent Americans,* 4: 479-80; Long, "Voyage in a Skiff," pp. 61-62.

6. Long, "Voyage in a Skiff," p. 9. A new edition of Long's journal describing this journey is Stephen H. Long, *The Northern Expeditions of Stephen H. Long: The Journals of 1817 and 1823 and Related Documents,* ed. Lucile M. Kane, Jane D. Holmquist, and Carolyn Gilman (Minneapolis, Minn.: Minnesota Historical Society Press, 1978).

7. Ibid., pp. 9-10; William H. Crawford to Long, June 18, 1816, Records of the Office of the Secretary of War, Letters Sent, Vol. 9, Record Group 107, National Archives, Washington, D.C.; Crawford to Long, July 2, 1816, Records of the Office of the Secretary of War, Letters Sent, Vol. 9, Record Group 107, hereafter cited SW, LS, RG 107.

8. Comments in his narrative indicate that he had the writings of these men with him. For example, see Long, "Voyage in a Skiff," pp. 27-28, 31, 35-36.

9. Ibid., pp. 13-14.

10. Ibid., pp. 14-15.

11. Ibid., p. 15.

12. Ibid., pp. 17-20; Joseph M. Street to Secretary of War, November 15, 1827, in U.S. Congress, House, *House Executive Document, No. 277,* 20th Cong., 1 sess., May 21, 1828, pp. 14-15.

13. Long, "Voyage in a Skiff," pp. 24-26, 30-31.

14. Ibid., pp. 29, 45.

15. Ibid., pp. 31-32; Jonathan Carver claimed to have traveled across Wisconsin and Minnesota during 1766-67. See Edward G. Bourne, "The Travels of Jonathan Carver," *American Historical Review* 11 (January 1906): 287-302.

16. Long, "Voyage in a Skiff," pp. 33-34.

17. Ibid., pp. 34-35, 40-42; Zebulon M. Pike, *The Journals of Zebulon Montgomery Pike with Letters and Related Documents*, ed. Donald Jackson, 2 vols. (Norman, Okla.: University of Oklahoma Press, 1966), 1: 202.

18. Long, "Voyage in a Skiff," pp. 42, 47, 50; Erna Risch, *Quartermaster Support of the Army: A History of the Corps, 1775-1939* (Washington, D.C.: Quartermaster Historian's Office, 1962), pp. 203-4; Allan Nevins, *Fremont, Pathmarker of the West* (New York: Longmans, Green and Co., 1955), pp. 353-68; John Bakeless, *Lewis and Clark, Partners in Discovery* (New York: William Morrow & Co., 1947), pp. 113-375 passim.

19. Long, "Voyage in a Skiff," pp. 46-47.

20. Ibid., 22, 27, 30.

21. Ibid., pp. 56-59.

22. Ibid., pp. 62-64.

23. Ibid., pp. 70, 75, 80-82.

24. Edwin C. Bearss and Arrell M. Gibson, *Fort Smith, Little Gibraltar on the Arkansas* (Norman, Okla.: University of Oklahoma Press, 1969), pp. 8-10, 12-14; Wood, *Stephen Long*, p. 52.

25. Bearss and Gibson, *Fort Smith*, pp. 14-16.

26. Richard Wood, "Stephen Harriman Long at Belle Point," *Arkansas Historical Quarterly* 13 (Winter 1954): 338-40; Long to Joseph Swift, Oct. 15, 1817, Records of the Office of the Chief of Engineers: Miscellaneous Letters Received, Record Group 77, National Archives, Washington, D.C.; *New York Columbian*, July 14, 1818.

27. Bearss and Gibson, *Fort Smith*, pp. 17-19; Wood, *Stephen Long*, pp. 52-53.

28. Bearss and Gibson, *Fort Smith*, pp. 22-24, 312-14; Henry Atkinson to William Bradford, December 15, 1819, Andrew Jackson Papers, Library of Congress, Washington, D.C.

29. Long to Smith, February 12, 1818, SW, LR, RG 107; Smith to Calhoun, February 14, 1818, SW, LR, RG 107; Long, "Report of the Country composing the 9th Military Department," May 12, 1818, Records of the Office of the Chief of Engineers, Engineers' Bulky File, Record Group 77, National Archives, Washington, D.C.

30. Long, "Report," RG 107.

31. Ibid.; General Orders, September 11, 1818, Records of the Office of the Adjutant General, Record Group 94, National Archives, Washington, D.C.; Roger L. Nichols, "Soldiers as Farmers: Army Agriculture in the Missouri Valley, 1818-1827," *Agricultural History* 44 (April 1970): 213-22.

32. Richard G. Wood, *Stephen Harriman Long, 1784-1864: Army Engineer, Explorer, Inventory* (Glendale, Calif.: Arthur Clark Co., 1966), p. 57; Livingston, *Eminent Americans*, 4: 479.

33. Edgar B. Wesley, "A Still Larger View of the So-Called Yellowstone Expedition," *North Dakota Historical Quarterly* 5 (July 1931): 219-21.

Chapter 3

1. Edgar B. Wesley, "A Still Larger View of the So-Called Yellowstone Expedition," *North Dakota Historical Quarterly* 5 (July 1931): 219-38.

2. John C. Calhoun to Thomas A. Smith, March 16, 1818, Records of the Office of Secretary of War, Letters Sent, Military Affairs, Vol. 10, Record Group 107, National Archives, Washington, D.C., hereafter cited SW, LS, RG 107.

3. John C. Calhoun to Jacob Brown, October 17, 1818, *The Papers of John C. Calhoun*, ed. Robert L. Meriwether and W. Edwin Hemphill, 9 vols. (Columbia, S.C.: University of South Carolina Press, 1959-76), 3: 214-16.

4. Henry P. Beers, *The Western Military Frontier, 1815-1846* (Philadelphia, Pa.: University of Pennsylvania Press, 1935), pp. 41-45; Roger L. Nichols, *General Henry Atkinson, A Western Military Career* (Norman, Okla.: University of Oklahoma Press, 1965), pp. 47-49.

5. Stephen Long to James Monroe, March 15, 1817, SW, LR, RG 107; Richard G. Wood, *Stephen Harriman Long 1784-1864: Army Engineer, Explorer, Inventor* (Glendale, Calif.: Arthur Clark Co., 1966), pp. 59-60.

6. Long to Joseph Swift, October 15, 1817, Records of the Office of the Chief Engineer, Engineers' Miscellaneous File Letters Received, Record Group 77, National Archives, Washington, D.C. Hereafter cited as Engineers' Misc., LR, RG 77.

7. Long to Smith, February 12, 1818, SW, LR, RG 107; Smith to Calhoun, February 14, 1818, SW, LR, RG 107; Smith to Calhoun, June 26, 1818, Engineers' Misc., LR, RG 77.

8. Long to Calhoun, August 31, 1818, SW, LR, RG 107; Calhoun to Swift, September 1, 1818, Engineers' Misc., LR, RG 77.

9. Louis C. Hunter, *Steamboats on the Western Rivers: An Economic and Technological History* (Cambridge, Mass.: Harvard University Press, 1949), p. 551; Cardinal L. Goodwin, "A Larger View of the Yellowstone Expedition, 1819-1820," *Mississippi Valley Historical Review* 4 (December 1917): 306-7.

10. Henry Atkinson to Thomas Jesup, February 23, 1819, Quartermaster General, Letters Received, Consolidated File, Record Group 92, National Archives, Washington, D.C.

11. Engineer Department to Long, September 2, 1818, Engineers' Letters Sent, Vol. 1, RG 77.

12. Titian R. Peale, Diary, May 3, 1819. The original diary is at the Library of Congress. For a published version, see A. O. Weese, ed., "Journal of Titian Ramsay Peale, Pioneer Naturalist," *Missouri Historical Review* 41 (January 1947): 147-63. The diary is quoted extensively in Jessie Poesch, *Titian Ramsay Peale, 1799-1885, And His Journals of the Wilkes Expedition. Memoirs,* No. 52 (Philadelphia, Pa.: American Philosophical Society, 1961); St. Louis, *Missouri Gazette,* May 26, 1819.

13. Hunter, *Steamboats on Western Rivers*, p. 150.

14. Wood, *Stephen Long,* pp. 62-63; Long to Calhoun, December 24, 1818, SW, LR, RG 107.

15. Quoted in Jeannette E. Graustein, *Thomas Nuttall, Naturalist: Explorations in America, 1808-1841* (Cambridge, Mass.: Harvard University Press, 1967), p. 130.

16. *Baltimore Niles Register*, October 10, 1818.

17. Calhoun to Long, December 15, 1818, SW, LS, Vol. 10, RG 107.

18. Long to Calhoun, December 24, 1818, SW, LR, RG 107.

19. *Washington* (D.C.) *Weekly Gazette,* September 30, 1818; *Cincinnati Inquisitor Advertizer,* July 13, 1819; Baldwin to William Darlington, October 9, 1818, in William Darlington, *Reliquiae Baldwinianae: Selections from the Correspondence of the late William Baldwin. . .and a Short Biographical Memoir* (Philadelphia, Pa.: Kimber and Sharpless, 1843), p. 286. Hereafter cited as *Baldwin Correspondence.*

20. Long to John Torrey, January 29, 1819, Stephen H. Long Letters, Miscellaneous Correspondence, Pennsylvania Historical Society, Philadelphia; Torrey to Amos Eaton, February 16, 1819, quoted in Andrew D. Rodgers, *John Torrey; a Story of North American Botany* (Princeton, N.J.: Princeton University Press, 1942), p. 47.

21. Long to Calhoun, December 24, 1818, SW, LR, RG 107.

22. These figures come from the material used in the biographical sketches of the expedition participants.

23. Long to Calhoun, December 24, 1818, SW, LR, RG 107.

24. *Baldwin Correspondence*, pp. 9-14; Henry R. Viets, S.V. "Baldwin, William," *Dictionary of American Biography.*

25. Wood, *Stephen Long,* p. 66; John H. Barnhart, S.V. "Torrey, John," *Dictionary of American Biography.*

26. Long to Calhoun, January 29, 1819, SW, LR, RG 107; Harry B. Weiss and Grace M. Ziegler, *Thomas Say, Early American Naturalist* (Springfield, Ill.: Charles C. Thomas, Publisher, 1931), p. 193; Wood, *Stephen Long,* p. 69.

27. Leland O. Howard, S.V. "Say, Thomas," Dictionary of American Biography; William J. Youmans, "Thomas Say," in William J. Youmans, ed., *Pioneers of Science in America; Sketches of Their Lives and Scientific Work* (New York: D. Appleton & Co., 1896), pp. 215-17; Weiss and Ziegler, *Thomas Say,* passim; Poesch, *Titian Peale,* pp. 20, 22-23.

28. Graustein, *Thomas Nuttall,* pp. 20-21, has an excellent description of Peale's Museum.

29. Quoted in Poesch, *Titian Peale,* p. 22; Horace W. Sellers, S.V. "Peale, Titian," Dictionary of American Biography.

30. Edwin James, comp., *Account of an Expedition from Pittsburgh to the Rocky Mountains. . .*, vols. 14-17, ed. Reuben G. Thwaites, *Early Western Travels,* 32 vols. (Cleveland, Ohio: Arthur Clark Co., 1904-7), 14: 42. Hereafter cited as James, *Account.* Peale, Diary, May 3, 1819; John F. McDermott, "Samuel Seymour: Pioneer Artist of the Plains and Rockies," *Smithsonian Report for 1950* (Washington, D.C.: Smithsonian Institution, 1951), pp. 497-509.

31. There is some confusion about Major Biddle's identity. R. G. Thwaites identified him as Major John Biddle and several scholars have accepted this error. See James, *Account,* 14: 39. Titian Peale's Diary, however, clearly identifies this man as Thomas Biddle, and he is the man who quit the expedition in 1819 to join the staff of Colonel Henry Atkinson. See Peale, Diary, May 3, 1819; Thomas Biddle to Adjutant General, August 5, 1819, Records of the Office of the Adjutant General, Letters Received, Record Group 94, National Archives, Washington, D.C.; Francis B. Heitman, comp. *Historical Register and Dictionary of the United States Army. . .1789 to 1903* (Washington, D.C.: Government Printing Office, 1903), 1: 217; Howard L. Cc nard, ed., *Encyclopedia of the History of Missouri* 8 vols. (St. Louis, Mo.: Southern History Co., 1901), 5: 96-97.

32. Heitman, *Historical Register,* 1: 468; George W. Cullum, *Biographical Register of the Officers and Graduates of the U.S. Military Academy. . .*, 8 vols. (Boston, Mass.: Houghton Mifflin & Co., 1891-1910), 1: 157-58; Carroll S. Alden, S.V. "Graham, James D.," Dictionary of American Biography.

33. Heitman, *Historical Register,* 1: 941; Cullum, *Biographical Register,* 1: 236; Thomas M. Spaulding, S.V. "Swift, William H." Dictionary of American Biography.

34. Fred W. Shipman, S.V. "O'Fallon, Benjamin," Dictionary of American Biography.

35. Long to Calhoun, April 20, 1819, SW, LR, RG 107.

36. Ibid., December 24, 1818, December 30, 1818, January 5, 1819, February 19, 1819.

37. Wood, *Stephen Long*, p. 72.

38. *Pittsburgh Gazette,* March 30, 1819, April 23, 1819; Long to Calhoun, April 20, 1819, SW, LR, RG 107.

39. Calhoun to Long, March 18, 1819, SW, LS, Vol. 10, RG 107; also quoted in James, *Account*, 14: 37-38; Calhoun to Robert Walsh, March 11, 1819, Stephen H. Long Papers, American Philosophical Society, Philadelphia; Walsh to Calhoun, March 30, 1819, April 8, 1819, SW, LR, RG 107; James, *Account*, 14: 36-37.

40. William Baldwin to William Darlington, May 1, 1819, *Baldwin Correspondence;* Peale, Diary, May 3-5, 1819; James, *Account*, 14: 43-44; *Baltimore Niles Register,* May 22, 1819.

Chapter 4

1. Titian R. Peale, Diary, May 3, 1819, Library of Congress, Washington, D.C.

2. *Baltimore Niles Register,* July 24, 1819; Peale, Diary, May 3, 1819.

3. *Baltimore Niles Register*, July 24, 1819.

4. Edwin James, comp., *Account of an Expedition from Pittsburgh to the Rocky Mountains. . . .,* vols. 14-17, ed. Reuben G. Thwaites, *Early Western Travels,* 32 vols. (Cleveland, Ohio: Arthur Clark Co. 1904-7), 14: 44; Peale, Diary, May 5, 1819.

5. James, *Account*, 14: 60-63; Peale, Diary, May 6-7, 1819.

6. James, *Account*, 14: 64; Peale, Diary, May 9, 1819.

7. William Baldwin to William Darlington, July 22, 1819 in William Darlington, *Reliquiae Baldwinianae: Selections from the Correspondence of the late William Baldwin. . .and a Short Biographical Memoir* (Philadelphia, Pa.: Kimber and Sharpless, 1843), pp. 320-21; hereafter cited as *Baldwin Correspondence*. Long to John C. Calhoun, May 27, 1819, Office of the Secretary of War, Letters Received, Record Group 107, National Archives, Washington, D.C.; hereafter cited as SW, LR, RG 107. Peale, Diary, May 9, 1819; *Cincinnati Western Spy*, May 15, 1819.

8. Peale, Diary, May 9 and 18, 1819; Baldwin to Darlington, May 27, 1819, *Baldwin Correspondence*, pp. 314-15; James, *Account*, 14: 65.

9. Denis Fitzhugh to John O'Fallon, May 22, 1819, O'Fallon Papers, Missouri Historical Society, St. Louis; Peale, Diary, May 23-27, 1819; James, *Account*, 14: 78-80.

10. Peale, Diary, May 28 and 30, 1819; James, *Account*, 14: 88.

11. Peale, Diary, May 30, 1819; James, *Account*, 14: 92-93.

12. Peale, Diary, June 1, 2, 5-7, 1819; James, *Account,* 14: 93, 95-96, 100, 106; Louis C. Hunter, *Steamboats on Western Rivers: An Economic and Technological History* (Cambridge, Mass.: Harvard University Press, 1949), pp. 263-64.

13. James, *Account*, 14: 108; O'Fallon to Fitzhugh, August 24, 1819, O'Fallon Papers; Peale, Diary, June 9, 1819; *St. Louis Missouri Gazette*, June 16, 1819.

14. Peale, Diary, June 9, 1819.

15. Henry Atkinson, Orders, June 8, 1819, Stephen W. Kearny Papers, Missouri Historical Society, St. Louis: *St. Louis Enquirer*, October 30, 1819.

16. James, *Account*, 14: 121-23; Peale, Diary, June 21 and 22, 1819.

17. James, *Account*, 14: 124.

18. O'Fallon to Thomas Smith, June 28, 1819, Thomas Smith Papers, State Historical Society of Missouri, Columbia.

19. Baldwin to Darlington, June 25, 1819, *Baldwin Correspondence*, p. 319; James, *Account*, 14: 126; Peale, Diary, June 25, 1819; Long to Calhoun, June 25, 1819, SW, LR, RG 107.

20. James, *Account*, 14: 127; Peale, Diary, June 26, 1819.

21. James, *Account*, 14: 129-30; Peale, Diary, June 26, 1819.

22. James, *Account*, 14: 130; Peale, Diary, June 26, 1819.

23. James, *Account*, 14: 131; Peale, Diary, June 27, 1819.

24. James, *Account*, 14: 131-32; Peale, Diary, June 28 and 29, 1819.

25. James, *Account*, 14: 134-36; Peale, Diary, June 30 and July 1, 1819.

26. Baldwin to Darlington, July 22, 1819, quoted in Susan D. McKelvey, *Botanical Exploration of the Trans-Mississippi West, 1790-1850* (Jamaica Plain, Mass.: Harvard University Press, 1955), p. 93; Peale, Diary, July 4, 1819.

27. James, *Account*, 14: 138-42; Peale, Diary, July 4 and 6, 1819.

28. James, *Account*, 14: 142; Peale, Diary, July 7, 1819.

29. James, *Account*, 14: 148; Peale, Diary, July 7-10, 12, 13, 1819.

30. John Gale, *The Missouri Expedition, 1818-1820. . .*, ed. Roger L. Nichols (Norman, Okla.: University of Oklahoma Press, 1969), p. 29.

31. Long to Calhoun, July 19, 1819, SW, LR, RG 107.

32. Calhoun to Joseph Swift, September 29, 1819, *The Papers of John C. Calhoun*, ed. Robert L. Meriwether and W. Edwin Hemphill, 9 vols. (Columbia, S.C.: University of South Carolina Press, 1959-76), 4:351; Calhoun to Long, September 1, 1819, SW, LS, Vol. 10, 365, RG 107.

33. Baldwin to Darlington, July 22, 1819, *Baldwin Correspondence*, pp. 320-21.

34. Baldwin to Long, July 18, 1819, SW, LR, RG 107; James, *Account*, 14: 153-56; *St. Louis Missouri Gazette*, November 24, 1819; *Baltimore Niles Register*, October 30, 1819.

35. James, *Account*, 14: 171-72, 183-84; Peale, Diary, July 25, 1819.

36. James, *Account*, 14: 185-87.

37. Ibid., 14: 187-88; Gale, *Missouri Expedition*, pp. 32-36.

38. James, *Account*, 14: 188-99.

39. Ibid., 14: 202-5; Thomas Biddle to Henry Atkinson, August 24, 1819, SW, LR, RG 107; John O'Fallon to Denis Fitzhugh, September 2, 1819, O'Fallon Papers.

40. The difference in figures comes because Biddle claimed that there were six soldiers, while James listed only five. Biddle to Atkinson, August 24, 1819, SW, LR, RG 107; James, *Account*, 14: 172.

41. Gale, *Missouri Expedition*, pp. 62-63; James, *Account*, 14: 205-9.

42. Gale, *Missouri Expedition*, p. 75; James, *Account*, 14: 215-21.

43. Quoted in James, *Account*, 14: 178n.

44. *St. Louis Missouri Gazette and Public Advertizer*, April 21, 1819.

Chapter 5

1. Edwin James, comp., *Account of an Expedition from Pittsburgh to the Rocky Mountains. . .*, vols. 14-17, ed. Reuben G. Thwaites, *Early Western Travels*, 32 vols. (Cleveland, Ohio: Arthur Clark Co., 1904-7), 14: 221-22, 229-30; John R. Bell, *The Journal of Captain John R. Bell. . .*, ed. Harlin M. Fuller and LeRoy M. Hafen, *The Far West and the Rockies Historical Series*, 15 vols. (Glendale, Calif.: Arthur Clark Co., 1954-61), 6: 87-88. Hereafter cited as Bell, *Journal*; Thomas Say to Benjamin Say, October 10, 1819, quoted in Harry B. Weiss and Grace M. Ziegler, *Thomas Say, Early American Naturalist* (Springfield, Ill.: Charles C. Thomas, Publisher, 1931), p. 73.

2. Thomas Biddle to Adjutant General, September 19, 1819, Records of the Office of the Adjutant General, Letters Received, Record Group 94, National Archives, Washington, D.C., hereafter cited as AGO, LR, RG 94; Long to John C. Calhoun, January 3, 1820, Records of the Office of the Secretary of War, Letters Received, Record Group 107, National Archives, Washington, D.C., hereafter cited as SW, LR, RG 107.

3. James, *Account*, 14: 248-49; Henry Atkinson, Orders, October 21, 1819, AGO, LR, RG 94.

4. James D. Graham to Long, November 20, 1819, Records of the Office of the Chief of Engineers, Miscellaneous File, Letters Received, Record Group 77, National Archives, Washington, D.C., hereafter cited as Engineers' Misc., LR, RG 77. Benjamin Edwards to Edwards, November 20, 1819, Stephen H. Long Letters, Miscellaneous Correspondence, Pennsylvania Historical Society, Philadelphia.

5. James, *Account*, 14: 263-64.

6. Ibid., 14: 270-71.

7. Robert C. Murphy, "The Sketches of Titian Ramsay Peale (1799-1885)," *Proceedings of the American Philosophical Society* 101 (December 1957): 523-31; Jessie Poesch, *Titian Ramsay Peale, 1799-1885, and His Journals of the Wilkes Expedition. Memoirs*, No. 52 (Philadelphia, Pa.: American Philosophical Society, 1961), pp. 27-30.

8. James, *Account*, 14: 256-57.

9. Paul R. Cutright, *Lewis and Clark: Pioneering Naturalists* (Urbana, Ill.: University of Illinois Press, 1969), p. 85; Meriwether Lewis and William Clark, *The Journals of the Expedition Under the Command of Capts. Lewis and Clark. . .*, ed. Nicholas Biddle (Philadelphia, Pa., 1814; reprint ed., New York: Heritage Press, 1962), p. 48. That Long's party had a copy of the journals may be seen from Long's orders quoted in James, *Account*, 14: 249.

10. James, *Account*, 14: 251-52, 257-58; J. Walker McSpadden, ed., *Animals of the World* (Garden City, N.Y.: Garden City Publishing Co., 1941), pp. 65-68.

11. John Torrey to William Darlington, August 10, 1826, quoted in Andrew D. Rodgers, *John Torrey. A Story of North American Botany* (Princeton, N.J.: Princeton University Press, 1942), pp. 52, 82; James De Kay, *Anniversary Address on the Progress of the Natural Sciences in the United States. . .*, quoted in Maxine Benson, "Edwin James: Scientist, Linguist, Humanitarian" (Ph.D. diss., University of Colorado, 1968), p. 61; Asa Gray, quoted in Susan D. McKelvey, *Botanical*

Exploration of the Trans-Mississippi West, 1790-1850 (Jamaica Plain, Mass.: Harvard University Press, 1955), p. 245. For a further discussion of this idea, see Chapters 8 and 11.

12. *St. Louis Enquirer*, October 30, 1819.

13. Long to Calhoun, October 28, 1819, SW, LR, RG 107.

14. Long to Calhoun, January 3, 1820, SW, LR, RG 107; Long to Darlington, February 3, 1820, Stephen H. Long Letters, Miscellaneous Correspondence, Pennsylvania Historical Society.

15. Long to Calhoun, January 3, 1820, SW, LR, RG 107.

16. Calhoun to Lewis Cass, January 14, 1820, *American State Papers: Indian Affairs,* 2: 319-20.

17. Long to Calhoun, January 22, 1820, SW, LR, RG 107.

18. Calhoun to Long, February 29, 1820, SW, LS, Vol. 11, RG 107.

19. John R. Bell to Calhoun, February 29, 1820, AGO, LR, RG 94.

20. L. H. Pammel, "Dr. Edwin James," *Annals of Iowa* 8 (October 1907, January 1908): 161-85, 277-95; Maxine Benson, "Edwin James: Scientist, Linguist, Humanitarian" (Ph.D. diss., University of Colorado, 1968), 6-24; Long to Calhoun, February 8, 1820, SW, LR, RG 107.

21. Bell, *Journal* p. 54.

22. Calhoun to Long, February 29, 1820, SW, LS, Vol. 11, RG 107; ibid., June 22, 1820, Bell, *Journal*, pp. 58-59.

23. Bell, *Journal*, pp. 59, 62.

24. James, *Account,* 15: 178.

25. Edwin James Diary, May 16, 1820, Special Collections, Butler Library, Columbia University, N.Y.; Bell, *Journal*, pp. 76-80.

26. Bell, *Journal,* pp. 85-86.

Chapter 6

1. Edwin James, comp., *Account of an Expedition from Pittsburgh to the Rocky Mountains. . .,* vols. 14-17, ed. Reuben G. Thwaites, *Early Western Travels,* 32 vols. (Cleveland, Ohio: Arthur Clark Co., 1904-7), 15: 38; Hiram M. Chittenden, *The American Fur Trade of the Far West*, 3 vols. (New York: F. P. Harper, 1902), 2:574-75; Richard G. Wood, *Stephen Harriman Long, 1784-1864: Army Engineer, Explorer, Inventor* (Glendale, Calif.: Arthur Clark Co., 1966), ch. 4.

2. Stephen W. Kearny, "Journal of Stephen Watts Kearny," ed. Valentine M. Porter, *Missouri Historical Society Collections* 3 (January 1908): 8-29; 3 (April 1908): 99-131.

3. Henry R. Schoolcraft, *Schoolcraft's Narrative Journal of Travels. . .to the Sources of the Mississippi River. . .,* ed. Mentor L. Williams (East Lansing, Mich.: Michigan State University Press, 1953), pp. 12-15; Susan D. McKelvey, *Botanical Exploration of the Trans-Mississippi West,. . .*(Jamaica Plain, Mass.: Harvard University Press, 1955), pp. 250-64. Max Meisel lists ten papers and one book as the publications that resulted from the Cass expedition. This is less than Long's

scientists wrote. See Meisel, *A Bibliography of American Natural History. . .*, 3 vols. (New York: Premier Publishing Co., 1924-29), 2: 400-44.

4. W. Randall Waterman, S.V. "Morse, Jedediah," *Dictionary of American Biography;* Jedediah Morse, *Report to the Secretary of War on Indian Affairs. . .*(New Haven, Conn.: S. Converse, 1822); John L. Allen, "An Analysis of the Exploratory Process. . .," *Geographical Review 62* (January 1972): 13.

5. John R. Bell, *The Journal of Captain John R. Bell. . .*, ed. Harlin M. Fuller and LeRoy R. Hafen, *The Far West and the Rockies Historical Series*, 15 vols. (Glendale, Calif.: Arthur Clark Co., 1957), pp. 58-62; Benjamin O'Fallon to William Clark, July 9, 1820, E. G. Voorhis Collection, Missouri Historical Society, St. Louis.

6. James, *Account*, 15: 191-92; Bell, *Journal*, pp. 90-91, 104; Wood, *Stephen Long*, pp. 94-95.

7. John Gale, *The Missouri Expedition*, 1818-1820. . ., ed. Roger L. Nichols (Norman, Okla.: University of Oklahoma Press, 1969), p. 86; James, *Account*, 15: 191-92; Bell, *Journal*, p. 104.

8. James, *Account*, 15: 191-92.

9. Ibid., 15: 191. Two other men, Joseph Bijou, guide and interpreter, and Abraham Ledoux, farrier and hunter, joined the explorers later. Long to Calhoun, February 8, 1821, Records of the Office of Secretary of War, Letters Received, Record Group 107, National Archives, Washington, D.C., hereafter cited as SW, LR, RG 107; also quoted in Bell, *Journal*, p. 104.

10. James, Account, 15: 190; Bell, *Journal*, p. 105.

11. James, *Account*, 15: 192-93; Bell, *Journal*, pp. 98, 103; Thomas Say to John F. Melsheimer, August 29, 1821, quoted in Harry B. Weiss and Grace M. Ziegler, *Thomas Say, Early American Naturalist* (Springfield, Ill.: Charles C. Thomas, Publisher, 1931), p. 84.

12. Bell, *Journal*, pp. 97-98.

13. James, *Account*, 15: 193; Say to Melsheimer, August 29, 1821, quoted in Weiss and Ziegler, *Thomas Say*, p. 84.

14. Long to Calhoun, June 2, 1820, SW, LR, RG 107.

15. William H. Goetzmann, *Exploration and Empire: The Explorer and the Scientist in the Winning of the American West* (New York: Alfred A. Knopf, 1966), p. 60; James, *Account*, 15: 198; Bell, *Journal*, pp. 104-5.

16. Wood, *Stephen Long*, p. 95; James, *Account*, 15: 193; Bell, *Journal*, p. 105.

17. James, *Account*, 15: 194, 197; Bell, *Journal*, p. 106.

18. James, *Account*, 15: 200-1; Bell, *Journal* p. 107.

19. Bell, *Journal*, pp. 106-7.

20. James, *Account*, 15: 202-3; Bell, *Journal*, p. 110.

21. Edwin James Diary, June 11, 1820, Special Collections, Butler Library, Columbia University, New York; James, *Account*, 15: 204; Bell, *Journal*, pp. 111-12.

22. James, *Account*, 15: 206-7; Bell, *Journal*, pp. 113-14.

23. James, *Account*, 15: 208.

24. Ibid., 15: 209-12; Bell, *Journal*, pp. 115-18.

25. Wood, *Stephen Long*, pp. 101-10; James, *Account*, 15: 213; Bell, *Journal*, pp. 104, 122-23.

26. Bell, *Journal,* pp. 123-25.

27. James, *Account,* 15: 225-27; Bell, *Journal,* pp. 126-27.

28. Bell, *Journal,* pp. 217-18.

29. James, *Account,* 15: 238-39, 246-47; Bell, *Journal,* pp. 127-29.

30. James, *Account,* 15: 247; William H. Emory, et al., *Notes of a Military Reconnaissance from Fort Leavenworth. . .to San Diego* (Washington, D.C.: Wendell and Van Benthuyson, printers, 1848), p. 11.

31. James, *Account,* 15: 249, 251; Bell, *Journal,* p. 143.

32. James, *Account,* 15: 259; Bell, *Journal,* pp. 137-38.

33. James, *Account,* 15: 264, 275, 285; Bell, *Journal,* pp. 142, 147.

34. Bell, *Journal,* p. 151.

35. Ibid., pp. 151-52, 154.

36. Ibid., pp. 159, 164-65.

37. Ibid., pp. 164, 166-67.

38. James, *Account,* 16: 14.

39. James, *Account,* 16: 19-21; Bell, *Journal,* pp. 167-68.

40. James, *Account,* 16: 16-19, 21-24; Maxine Benson, "Edwin James: Scientist, Linguist, Humanitarian," (Ph.D. diss., University of Colorado, 1968), p. 66.

41. Bell, *Journal,* p. 171.

Chapter 7

1. John R. Bell, *The Journal of Captain John R. Bell. . .,* ed. Harlin M. Fuller and LeRoy R. Hafen, *The Far West and the Rockies Historical Series,* 15 vols. (Glendale, Calif.: Arthur Clark Co., 1957), p. 178; Edwin James, comp., *Account of an Expedition from Pittsburgh to the Rocky Mountains. . .,* vols. 14-17, ed. Reuben G. Thwaites, *Early Western Travels,* 32 vols. (Cleveland, Ohio: Arthur Clark Co., 1904-7), 16: 43.

2. Bell, *Journal,* pp. 180-82; James, *Account,* 16: 55-56.

3. Bell, *Journal,* pp. 180-81; James, *Account,* 16: 56.

4. Bell, *Journal,* pp. 182, 184; James, *Account,* 16: 58.

5. A clear discussion and excellent map of this portion of the expedition is given in John M. Tucker, "Major Long's Route from the Arkansas to the Canadian River, 1820," *New Mexico Historical Review* 38 (July 1963): 184-219; Bell, *Journal,* p. 186; James, *Account,* 16: 63, 65.

6. James, *Account,* 16: 71.

7. Ibid., 16: 76.

8. Ibid., 16: 80-82.

9. Ibid., 16: 83.

10. Ibid., 16: 79, 84-85.

11. William H. Goetzmann, *Exploration and Empire: The Explorer and the Scientist in the Winning of the American West* (New York: Alfred A. Knopf, 1966), pp. 41-47; James, *Account,* 16: 66-76.

12. James, *Account,* 16: 87.

13. Ibid., 16: 87-89.

14. Ibid., 16: 90-92.

15. Ibid., 16: 93-94.

16. Ibid., 16: 94-95.

17. Ibid., 16: 96-97.

18. Ibid., 16: 99-100.

19. Ibid., 16: 100-3.

20. Ibid., 16: 106-9.

21. Ibid., 16: 110-11. John Bakeless, *Lewis and Clark: Partners in Discovery* (New York: William Morrow & Co., 1947), pp. 133-36.

22. James, *Account,* 16: 111-13.

23. Ibid., 16: 113-15, 118-21.

24. Ibid., 16: 123-24.

25. Ibid., 16: 140-46.

26. Ibid., 16: 173, 178.

27. Ibid., 16: 180-81.

28. Ibid.; Bell, *Journal*, pp. 280-81.

29. James, *Account*, 16: 186-87.

30. Ibid., 16: 193.

31. Bell, *Journal,* pp. 190-91, 193-97; James, *Account*, 16: 194-98.

32. Bell, *Journal*, p. 197.

33. James, *Account*, 16: 202-8, 209-11; Bell, *Journal*, p. 199.

34. James, *Account*, 16: 214-18; Bell, *Journal*, pp. 207-10.

35. James, *Account,* 16: 218-21; Bell, *Journal*, pp. 210-21.

36. James, *Account,* 16: 221, 224; Bell, *Journal*, pp. 212, 214-15.

37. James, *Account*, 16: 225-27; Bell, *Journal*, p. 217.

38. James, *Account*, 16: 232-33; Bell, *Journal,* pp. 223-24.

39. James, *Account*, 16: 234-36; Bell, *Journal*, pp. 224-26.

40. James, *Account*, 16: 241, 249-50, 255; Bell, *Journal*, pp. 238-40, 245-47.

41. James, *Account*, 16: 262-65; Bell, *Journal*, pp. 256-58.

42. James, *Account*, 16: 290-91; Bell, *Journal*, pp. 275-76.

43. Richard G. Wood, *Stephen Harriman Long, 1784-1864: Army Engineer, Explorer, Inventory* (Glendale, Calif.: Arthur Clark Co., 1966), pp. 110-11; James, *Account*, 17: 11-12, 84-85, 88; Bell, *Journal*, pp. 284, 289, 300, 304, 306.

44. Allan Nevins, *Fremont: Pathmarker of the West* (New York: Longmans, Green and Co., 1955), pp. 360-68; Wood, *Stephen Long*, pp. 121-41.

Chapter 8

1. John C. Calhoun to Long, November 24, 1820, Records of the Office of the Secretary of War, Letters Sent, 11: 119-20, Record Group 107, National Archives, Washington, D.C., hereafter cited as SW, LS (or LR for Letters Received), RG 107. Long to Calhoun, January 20, 1821, SW, LR; Calhoun to Long, February 23, 1821, SW, LS, 11: 155; Long to Adjutant General, February 25, 1821, Records of the

Office of the Adjutant General, Letters Received, Record Group 94, National Archives, Washington, D.C., hereafter cited as AGO, LR, RG 94.

2. Long to Calhoun, February 18, 1821, SW, LR, RG 107; Calhoun to Long, March 30, 1821, SW, LS, 11: 178-79; Richard G. Wood, *Stephen Harriman Long, 1784-1864: Army Engineer, Explorer, Inventor* (Glendale, Calif.: Arthur Clark Co., 1966), p. 112.

3. Maxine Benson, "Edwin James: Scientist, Linguist, Humanitarian," (Ph.D. diss., University of Colorado, 1968), pp. 81-89; Edwin James Diary, Special Collections, Butler Library, Columbia University, N.Y., p. 243; Wood, *Stephen Long,* p. 113.

4. Jessie Poesch, *Titian Ramsay Peale, 1799-1885, and His Journals of the Wilkes Expedition. Memoirs,* No. 52, (Philadelphia, Pa.: American Philosophical Society, 1961), pp. 36-37; Long to Christopher Vandeventer, February 18, 1821, SW, LR, RG 107.

5. Benson, "Edwin James," p. 89; Long to Calhoun, July 18, 1821, *The Papers of John C. Calhoun,* ed. Robert L. Meriwether and W. Edwin Hemphill, 9 vols. (Columbia, S.C.: University of South Carolina Press, 1959-76), 6:264-65.

6. Long to Calhoun, October 30, 1821, SW, LR, RG 107; Calhoun to Long, November 8, 1821, SW, LS, 11: 313, RG 107; Calhoun to Long, November 17, 1821, ibid., 11: 317.

7. *Washington* (D.C.) *National Intelligencer,* November 23, 1820; Wood, *Stephen Long,* p. 111n; Edwin James to Titian Peale, April 18, 1821, Stephen H. Long Letters, Pennsylvania Historical Society, Philadelphia.

8. Thomas Say to John Melsheimer, May 9, 1822, quoted in Harry B. Weiss and Grace M. Ziegler, *Thomas Say, Early American Naturalist* (Springfield, Ill.: Charles C. Thomas, Publisher, 1931), p. 86; Edwin James, comp. *Account of an Expedition from Pittsburgh to the Rocky Mountains. . .,* vols. 14-17, ed. Reuben G. Thwaites, *Early Western Travels* (Cleveland, Ohio: Arthur Clark Co., 1904-7), 14: 35.

9. Wood, *Stephen Long,* pp. 113-14; Carl I. Wheat, *Mapping the Trans-Mississippi West, 1540-1861* 5 vols. (San Francisco, Calif.: Institute of Historical Cartography, 1957-63), 2: 225; John F. McDermott, "Samuel Seymour: Pioneer Artist of the Plains and the Rockies," *Smithsonian Report for 1950* (Washington, D.C.: Smithsonian Institution, 1951), pp. 497-509; Benson, "Edwin James," pp. 94-95; Herman R. Friis, "Stephen Long's Unpublished Manuscript Map of the United States Compiled in 1820-1822 (?)," *The California Geographer* 8 (1967): 83-86.

10. Alexander Macomb to Long, June 15, 1822, Letters to Engineers, Records of the Office of the Chief of Engineers, 1: 327, Record Group 77, National Archives, Washington, D.C., hereafter cited as Eng LS, RG77; Long to Macomb, June 21, 1822, Eng LR, RG 77; Wood, *Stephen Long, p. 114; Long to Isaac Roberdeau, June 10, 1821, Eng LR, RG 77; Long to Roberdeau, October 10, 1822, Eng LR, RG 77; Long to Calhoun, December 21, 1822, SW, LR, RG 107.*

11. *Calhoun to Joseph Swift, September 29, 1819, Calhoun Papers,* 4: 351; Long to Calhoun, January 20, 1820, SW, LR, RG 107; Long to Calhoun, December 12, 1820, SW, LR, RG 107; William H. Goetzmann, *Exploration and Empire: The Explorer and the Scientist in the Winning of the American West* (New York: Alfred A. Knopf, 1966), p. 61.

12. Edwin James to Amos Eaton, December 8, 1820, quoted in Benson, "Edwin James," pp. 91-92; James, Diary, p. 268.

13. Weiss and Ziegler, Thomas Say, p. 88; Wood, Stephen Long, pp. 113, 115; Benson, "Edwin James," pp. 90-91; James, Diary, p. 268.

14. Reuben G. Thwaites, ed., preface to James, Account, 14: 18-19.

15. Baltimore Niles Register, February 8, 1823; Edward Everett, "Long's Expedition," North-American Review, 16 (April 1823): 242, 267.

16. Jared Sparks, "Major Long's Second Expedition," North American Review, 21 (July 1825): 178-79; London Quarterly 29 (April 1823): 15, quoted in Benson, "Edwin James," pp. 102-3; Henry R. Schoolcraft, "G. C. Beltrami, La Dé couverte des sources du Mississippi, et de la Riviére Sanglante," North American Review 27 (July 1828): 94-95.

17. Hiram M. Chittenden, The American Fur Trade of the Far West, 3 vols. (New York: F. P. Harper, 1902), 2: 574-75, 580; Ray A. Billington, Westward Expansion: A History of the American Frontier, 4th ed. (New York: Macmillan Co., 1974), p. 378.

18. Long, "A General Description of the Country Traversed by the Exploring Expedition," in James, Account, 17: 147. Richard Dillon mistakenly claims that Lieutenant William Swift, and not Long, was chiefly responsible for the desert label being attached to the Plains. However, Long had not yet completed drawing the map in June, 1821, months after Swift left Philadelphia for other duties. See Dillon, "Stephen H. Long's Great American Desert," Proceedings of the American Philosophical Society, 111: 95; Wood, Stephen Long, pp. 111, 113; Friis, "Stephen Long's Unpublished Map," The California Geographer, 8: 75-87. Friis demonstrates Long's authorship of both maps convincingly. See also Calhoun to Jedediah Morse, June 18, 1821, Calhoun Papers, 6: 199.

19. G. Malcolm Lewis, "Three Centuries of Desert Concepts in the Cis-Rocky Mountain West," Journal of the West 4 (July 1965): 457-77; Terry L. Alford, "The West as a Desert in American Thought Prior to Long's 1819-1820 Expedition," Journal of the West 8 (October 1969): 515-25; Ralph C. Morris, "The Notion of a Great American Desert East of the Rockies," Mississippi Valley Historical Review 13 (September 1926): 190-220.

20. James, Account, 16: 173-74; Bell, Journal, p. 178; Say to Melsheimer, August 29, 1821, quoted in Weiss and Ziegler, Thomas Say, p. 85.

21. John L. Allen, "Exploration and the Creation of Geographical Images of the Great Plains: Comments on the Role of Subjectivity" (Paper delivered at Images of the Plains Conference, Lincoln, Nebraska, April 1973), pp. 9-16. Merlin P. Lawson, "A Behavioristic Interpretation of Pike's Geographical Knowledge of the Interior of Louisiana," Great Plains-Rocky Mountain Geographical Journal 1 (1972): 58-64, considers the possibility of Pike's altering his description of the southern Plains to escape possible censure as an accomplice of General James Wilkinson. He suggests similar goals might have motivated other explorers, but this idea does not fit Long's 1820 actions.

22. Long to James Graham, March 4, 1817, Washington (D.C.) National Register, March 29, 1817; Douglas R. McManis, Initial Evaluation and Utilization of the Illinois Prairies, 1815-1840 (Chicago: University of Chicago Press, 1964), discusses attitudes of farmers toward prairie land; James, Account, 15: 247.

23. Walter P. Webb, "The American West, Perpetual Mirage," *Harper's Magazine* 214 (May 1957): 25-31, brought angry responses that he answered in "The West and the Desert," *Montana: The Magazine of Western History* 8 (January 1958): 2-12. For a longer discussion of technology and climate, see Webb, *The Great Plains*, (Boston: Ginn and Co., 1931), pp. 140-204; W. Eugene Hollon, *The Great American Desert, Then and Now* (New York: Oxford University Press, 1966), pp. 3-8, 33-69, 160-80. Two historical geographers have presented this idea convincingly within the past decade. See Martyn J. Bowden, "The Great American Desert and the American Frontier, 1800-1882: Popular Images of the Plains," in Tamara K. Hareven, ed., *Anonymous Americans* (Englewood Cliffs, N.J.: Prentice-Hall, 1971), pp. 48-79, discusses the existence of differing elite and folk images of the West and their impact on settlement. A second essay by G. Malcolm Lewis, "Regional Ideas and Reality in the Cis-Rocky Mountain West," *Transactions, Institute of British Geographers* 38 (1966): 135-50, notes that the desert idea was only one of several held about the West.

24. Kent L. Steckmesser, *The Westward Movement: A Short History* (New York: McGraw-Hill, 1969), pp. 172-73; William M. Malloy, comp., *Treaties. . .and Agreements Between the U.S.A. and Other Powers—1776-1909*, Senate Document No. 357, 61st Cong., 2d sess., 1910, 2: 1652-53.

25. Thomas D. Clark, *Frontier America* (New York: Charles Scribner's Sons, 1959), p. 652; Robert E. Riegel and Robert G. Athearn, *America Moves West*, 5th ed. (New York: Holt, Rinehart and Winston, Inc., 1971), p. 309; William H. Goetzmann, *Army Exploration in the American West, 1803-1863* (New Haven, Conn.: Yale University Press, 1959), p. 42.

26. Calhoun to Long, February 29, 1820, SW, LS, 11: 4-5, RG 107.

27. Goetzmann, *Exploration and Empire*, p. 62; Riegel and Athearn, *America Moves West*, p. 309. For a more complete discussion of the papers, articles, and books, see Appendix.

28. Andrew D. Rodgers, in his *John Torrey. A Story of North American Botany* (Princeton, N.J.: Princeton University Press, 1942), pp. 33-39, discusses the significance of personal correspondence in expanding scientific knowledge. Jessie Poesch, in *Titian Peale*, (pp. 16-19, 36-37), treats the intellectual climate in Philadelphia at the time. Jeannette E. Graustein (*Thomas Nuttall, Naturalist: Explorations in America, 1808-1841* [Cambridge, Mass.: Harvard University Press, 1967], pp. 18-30) describes the development of scientific knowledge during the early nineteenth century.

29. Weiss and Ziegler, *Thomas Say*, p. 81; J. Walker McSpadden, ed., *Animals of the World* (Garden City, N.Y.: Garden City Publishing Co., 1941), pp. 66, 68, 77, 183, 228, 310, 318.

30. Paul R. Cutright, *Lewis and Clark: Pioneering Naturalists* (Urbana, Ill.: University of Illinois Press, 1969), pp. vii-ix, 85; McSpadden, ed., *Animals of the World*, pp. 65-66.

31. John Torrey to William Darlington, August 10, 1826, quoted in Rodgers, *John Torrey*, pp. 52, 82; George E. Osterhout, "Rocky Mountain Botany and the Long Expedition of 1820," *Bulletin of the Torrey Botanical Club* 47 (December 1920): 557, quoted in Joseph A. Ewan, *Rocky Mountain Naturalists* (Denver, Col.: University of Denver Press, 1950), p. 15; Susan D. McKelvey, *Botanical Exploration*

of the Trans-Mississippi West, 1790-1850 (Jamaica Plain, Mass.: Harvard University Press, 1955), p. 245.

32. James, *Account*, 14; chs. 6-10; 15: chs. 1-6; 16: chs. 5, 13 include most of the ethnological material.

33. George P. Merrill, *The First One Hundred Years of American Geology* (New Haven, Conn.: Yale University Press, 1924), pp. 69-71; Goetzmann, *Army Exploration*, pp. 57-58; Benson, "Edwin James," p. 125.

34. Goetzmann, *Army Exploration*, p. 43; Thwaites, ed. preface to James, *Account*, 14: 24; Levette J. Davidson, "Colorado Cartography," *Colorado Magazine* 32 (July 1955): 186; Alice E. Smith, "Stephen H. Long and the Naming of Wisconsin," *Wisconsin Magazine of History* 26 (September 1942): 67-71; Wheat, *Mapping Trans-Mississippi* 2: 79-81.

35. Thwaites, ed. preface to James, *Account*, 14: 23; Wheat, *Mapping Trans-Mississippi,* 2: 78-80.

36. Erwin Raisz, "Land Forms of the United States," map, 6th ed. (New York: Ginn & Co., 1957).

37. Francis P. Prucha, "Indian Removal and the Great American Desert," *Indiana Magazine of History* 59 (December 1963): 299-322.

38. Goetzmann, *Army Exploration,* pp. 73-74.

39. James De Kay, *Anniversary Address*, quoted in Benson, "Edwin James," pp. 112-13.

40. Weiss and Ziegler, *Thomas Say,* pp. 88-89; Benson, "Edwin James," pp. 127-28.

41. Paul Wilhelm, *Travels in North America, 1822-1824,* trans. W. Robert Nitske, ed. Savoie Lottinville (Norman, Okla.: University of Oklahoma Press, 1973), pp. 128, 201n, 203, 396.

42. Ibid., p. xiv.

Chapter 9

1. Alexander Macomb to Long, March 8, 1823, Records of the Office of the Chief of Engineers, Letters to Engineers, 1: 393, Record Group 77, National Archives, Washington, D.C., hereafter cited as Letters to Engineers (or, when Long wrote Macomb as Engineers, Letters Received) RG 77.

2. William M. Malloy, comp., *Treaties. . .and Agreements Between the U.S.A. and Other Powers—1776-1909, Senate Document No. 357,* 61st Cong., 2d sess., 1910, 1: 632.

3. Edgar B. Wesley, "A Still Larger View of the So-Called Yellowstone *Expedition," North Dakota Historical Quarterly* 5 (July 1931): 219-22; Francis P. Prucha, *A Guide to the Military Posts of the United States, 1789-1895* (Madison, Wis.: State Historical Society of Wisconsin, 1964), p. 109; Thomas Forsyth, "Fort Snelling. Colonel Leavenworth's Expedition to Establish it, in 1819," *Minnesota Historical Society Collections* 3 (1880): 139-67.

4. Henry R. Schoolcraft, *Schoolcraft's Narrative Journal of Travels. . .to the*

Sources of the Mississippi River. . ., ed. Mentor L. Williams (East Lansing, Mich.: Michigan State University Press, 1953), pp. 10-12.

5. Long to John C. Calhoun, December 12, 1820, *The Papers of John C. Calhoun,* ed. Robert L. Meriwether and W. Edwin Hamphill, 9 vols. (Columbia, S.C.: University of South Carolina Press, 1959-76), 5: 478-80; Long to Christopher Vandeventer, February 18, 1821, ibid., 5: 635-36; Long to Vandeventer, February 1, 1823, ibid., 7: 452-55; William H. Keating, *Narrative of an Expedition to the Source of St. Peter's River. . .Performed in the Year 1823. . .*2 vols. (London, 1825), 1: 1. Reprinted with an introduction by Roy P. Johnson (Minneapolis, Minn.: Ross and Haines, 1959).

6. Long to Macomb, March 11, 1823, Engineers, Letters Received RG 77; Macomb to Long, March 17, 1823, Letters to Engineers, 1: 400, RG 77; Long to Macomb, March 19, 1823, Engineers, LR, RG 77.

7. Calhoun to Long, April 25, 1823, Letters to Engineers, 1: 414-16, RG 77; Special Orders No. 27, April 28, 1823, Special Orders, 1: 49, Office of the Adjutant General, Record Group 94, National Archives, Washington, D.C.

8. Wyndham D. Miles, "A Versatile Explorer: A Sketch of William H. Keating," *Minnesota History* 36 (December 1959): 297.

9. Ibid., pp. 297-99; John H. Frederick, S.V. "Keating, William H.," *Dictionary of American Biography.*

10. Stephen H. Long Topographical Journal, vol. 2, April 30-May 10, 1823 (this includes three volumes, numbered 2, 3, and 4; unpaged), Minnesota Historical Society, St. Paul; James E. Colhoun Diary, May 20, 1823, Minnesota Historical Society, St. Paul; Macomb to Long, May 3, 1823, Letters to Engineers, 1:419, RG 77.

11. Richard G. Wood, "Dr. Edwin James, a Disappointed Explorer," *Minnesota History* 34 (Autumn 1955): 284-86; Keating, *Narrative*, 1: 4-5, 46.

12. Roy P. Johnson, introduction William H. Keating, *Narrative of an Expedition. . .Performed in the Year 1823. . .*, 2 vols. (London, 1825; reprint ed., Minneapolis, Minn.: Ross and Haines, 1959), 1: xxiii.

13. Keating, *Narrative*, 1: 5-162; Long Journal, vol. 2, April 30-June 5, 1823; Long to Macomb, May 12, 1823, Engineers, LR, RG 77.

14. Keating, *Narrative*, 1: 165.

15. Ibid., 1: 175; Long to Macomb, June 10, 1823, Engineers, LR, RG 77; Long Journal, vol. 2, June 5-11, 1823.

16. Keating, *Narrative,* 1: 175, 192.

17. Ibid., 1: 193-94.

18. Ibid., 1: 194-218.

19. Long Journal, vol. 2, June 19, 1823; Keating, *Narrative*, 1: 218-20.

20. Keating, *Narrative*, 1: 220-41.

21. Long Journal, vol. 2, June 25, 1823; Long to Macomb, June 24, 1823, Engineers, LR, RG 77; Keating, *Narrative*, 1: 253-54.

22. Keating, *Narrative*, 1: 254.

23. Ibid., 1: 254-55.

24. Long Journal, Vol. 2, June 26-July 1, 1823; Colhoun Diary, July 1-2, 1823.

25. Keating, *Narrative*, 1: 259-61.

26. Ibid., 1: 273.

27. Ibid., 1: 278-79, 301.

28. Long Journal, vol. 2, July 2, 9, 1823; Colhoun Diary, July 3, 9, 1823; Keating, *Narrative*, 1: 304-5.

29. Long Journal, vol. 2, July 9, 1823; Colhoun Diary, July 9, 1823; Keating, *Narrative*, 1: 323-27; Gertrude W. Ackermann, "Joseph Renville of Lac Qui Parle," *Minnesota History* 12 (September 1931): 231-46.

30. Long Journal, vol. 2, July 9, 1823; Keating, *Narrative* 1: 327; Long to Macomb, July 9, 1823, Engineers, LR, RG 77; A. J. Hill, "Constantine Beltrami," *Minnesota Historical Society Collections* 2 (1860-67): 185-92; Theodore Christianson, "The Long and Beltrami Explorations in Minnesota One Hundred Years Ago," *Minnesota History Bulletin* 5 (November 1923): 249-64; Augusto P. Miceli, *The Man With the Red Umbrella: Giacomo Constantino Beltrami in America* (Baton Rouge, La.: Claitor's Publishing Division, 1974), pp. 69-71.

31. Giacomo C. Beltrami, *A Pilgrimage in Europe and America; Leading to the Discovery of the Sources of the Mississippi. . .*, 2 vols. (London: Hunt and Clarke, 1828), 2: 304-5; Miceli, *The Man With the Red Umbrella*, pp. 69-70.

32. Keating, *Narrative*, 1: 327; Long Journal, vol. 2, July 9, 1823.

33. Keating, *Narrative*, 1: 347-49; Long Journal, vol. 2, July 13, 1823; Colhoun Diary, July 11-13, 1823.

34. Keating, *Narrative*, 1: 349-50; Long to Macomb, July 15, 1823; Engineers, LR, RG 77.

35. Long to Macomb, July 15, 1823, Engineers, LR, RG 77; Keating, *Narrative*, 1: 350-56; Beltrami, *Pilgrimage*, 2: 324.

36. Keating, *Narrative*, 1:xxii, 354, 359.

37. Colhoun Diary, July 19, 1823; Beltrami, *Pilgrimage*, 2: 324; Keating, *Narrative*, 1: 360-61, 371; Miceli, *The Man With the Red Umbrella*, pp. 74-75.

38. Colhoun Diary, July 22, 1823; Keating, *Narrative*, 1: 377-79.

39. Keating, *Narrative*, 1: 378-80.

40. Colhoun Diary, July 22, 1823; Keating, *Narrative*, 1: 382-83.

41. Keating, *Narrative*, 1: 385-86; Beltrami, *Pilgrimage*, 2: 324-26.

42. Long Journal, vol. 3, July 28, 1823; Keating, *Narrative*, 2: 12-13.

43. Long Journal, vol. 3, July 28, 1823; Keating, *Narrative*, 2: 13-14.

44. Long Journal, vol. 3, July 28, 1823; Keating, *Narrative*, 2: 15-16.

45. Long Journal, vol. 3, July 28, 1823; Keating, *Narrative*, 2: 16-17, 32.

46. Keating, *Narrative*, 2: 32.

Chapter 10

1. William H. Keating, *Narrative of an Expedition. . .Performed in the Year 1823. . .*, 2 vols. (London, 1825; reprint ed., Minneapolis, Minn.: Ross and Haines, 1959), 2: 39-42.

2. Stephen H. Long Topographical Journal, vol. 3, August 7-8, 1823; James E. Colhoun Diary, August 7, 9, 1823 (this part of the diary is owned by Mr. Edwin B.

McDill of Greensboro, N.C., and is quoted with his permission); Long to Alexander Macomb, August 8, 1823, Records of the Office of the Chief of Engineers, Letters Received, Record Group 77, National Archives, Washington, D.C., hereafter cited as Engineers (or Letters to Engineers), LR, RG, 77; Keating, *Narrative*, 2: 42-43.

3. Keating, *Narrative*, 2: 54; John C. Calhoun to Long, April 23, 1823, Letters to Engineers, 1: 414-16, RG 77.

4. Long Journal, vol. 3, August 9, 1823; Richard G. Wood, *Stephen Harriman Long, 1784-1864: Army Engineer, Explorer, Inventor* (Glendale, Calif.: Arthur Clark Co., 1966), p. 129.

5. Colhoun Diary, July 22, August 8-9, 1823; Giacomo C. Beltrami, *A Pilgrimage in Europe and America, Leading to the Discovery of the Sources of the Mississippi. . .*, 2 vols. (London: Hunt and Clarke, 1828), 2: 368-70; Wood, *Stephen Long*, p. 129.

6. Long Journal, vol. 3, August 9, 1823; Beltrami, *Pilgrimage*, 2: 368-70; A. J. Hill, "Constantine Beltrami," *Minnesota Historical Society Collections* 2 (1860-67): 192.

7. Keating, *Narrative*, 2: 56-57.

8. Long Journal, vol. 3, August 9, 11-12, 14, 1823; Keating, *Narrative*, 2: 55-56.

9. Long Journal, vol. 3, August 17, 26-28, 1823; Keating, *Narrative*, 2: 72, 75-79, 82-101.

10. Long Journal, vol. 3, August 28, 31, September 1, 1823; vol. 4, October 11, 1823; Keating, *Narrative*, 2: 112-13.

11. Long Journal, vol. 3, August 31, September 1, 1823; vol. 4, October 11, 1823.

12. Wood, *Stephen Long*, pp. 134-35; Long Journal, vol. 3, September 2-3, 10-11, 1823; vol. 4, September 15, 1823; Keating, *Narrative*, 2: 113-24; John Tanner, *Narrative of the Captivity and Adventures of John Tanner. . .*, ed. Edwin James (New York: G. & C.H. Carvill, 1830), passim.

13. Keating, *Narrative*, 2: 93-94.

14. Ibid., 2: 138.

15. Ibid., 2: 139, 171-72; Long Journal, vol. 3, September 11, 1823; vol. 4, September 18, 1823.

16. Keating, *Narrative*, 2: 172-80; Long Journal, vol. 4, September 21, 1823.

17. Keating, *Narrative*, 2: 183-84.

18. Long Journal, vol. 4, September 23, 26-30, 1823; Keating, *Narrative*, 2: 184-90, 194-97.

19. Keating, *Narrative*, 2: 191-94.

20. Long Journal, vol. 4, October 1-5, 7-14, 17-27, 1823; Long to Macomb, October 18, 1823, Engineers, LR, RG 77; Keating, *Narrative*, 2: 200-1.

21. Macomb to Long, November 10, 1823, Letters to Engineers, 1: 481, RG 77; *Philadelphia Democratic Press*, October 30, 1823.

22. Long to Macomb, October 31, 1823, Engineers, LR, RG 77; Keating, *Narrative*, 1: xvii.

23. Keating, *Narrative*, 1: xix-xxiii; Wood, *Stephen Long*, pp. 138-40.

24. Thomas Say to John F. Melsheimer, November 30, 1823, quoted in Harry B. Weiss and Grace M. Zeigler, *Thomas Say, Early American Naturalist* (Springfield,

Ill.: Charles C. Thomas, Publisher, 1931), p. 103; Keating, *Narrative*, 1: 199.

25. Quoted in Susan D. McKelvey, *Botanical Exploration of the Trans-Mississippi West, 1790-1850* (Jamaica Plain, Mass.: Harvard University Press, 1955), pp. 279-80.

26. Keating, *Narrative*, 1: x.

27. Thomas Say, *The Complete Writings of Thomas Say on the Entomology of North America,* ed. John L. LeConte (New York: Bailliere Brothers, 1859); *The Complete Writings of Thomas Say on the Conchology of the United States,* ed. William G. Binney (New York: H. Bailliere, 1858); *Descriptions of Terrestrial Shells of North America, By Thomas Say*, ed. William G. Binney (Philadelphia: Childs and Peterson, 1856).

28. Wood, *Stephen Long,* pp. 139-40; Macomb to Long, May 14, 1824, Letters to Engineers, 2: 5; ibid., May 31, 2: 13, RG 77.

29. Keating, *Narrative*, 2: 224-26.

30. Ibid., 2: 227, 229.

31. Ibid., 2: 236.

32. Ibid., 2: 238.

33. Ibid.; Colhoun Diary, August 9, 1823.

34. Keating, *Narrative*, 2: 191.

35. Wyndham D. Miles, "A Versatile Explorer: A Sketch of William H. Keating," *Minnesota History* 36 (December 1959): 296 and n.

36. January 5, 1825, quoted in Harry B. Weiss and Grace M. Zeigler, *Thomas Say, Early American Naturalist* (Springfield, Ill.: Charles C. Thomas, Publisher, 1931), pp. 104-5.

37. Jared Sparks, "Major Long's Second Expedition," *North American Review* 21 (July 1825): 185.

38. Ibid., p. 189.

39. *Monthly Review* 108 (November 1825): 113-25, quoted in Miles, "Sketch of Keating," p. 296.

40. Max Meisel, *A Bibliography of American Natural History, The Pioneer Century, 1790-1865,* 3 vols. (Brooklyn, N.Y.: Premier Publishing Co., 1924-29), 2: 145-56, 244-60; Harry B. Weiss, *The Pioneer Century of Entomology* (New Brunswick, N.J.: privately printed, 1936), pp. 96-97.

41. Donald C. Peattie, *Green Laurels. The Lives and Achievements of the Great Naturalists* (New York: Garden City Publishing Co., 1936), p. 254; LeConte, ed., *Writings of Say on Entomology;* Binney, ed. *Writings of Say on Conchology;* Binney, ed., *Descriptions of Shells by Say.*

42. October 17, 1823, *Early Proceedings of the American Philosophical Society. . .1744-1838* (Philadelphia, 1884): 521-22.

43. Henry R. Schoolcraft, "Indians of North America," *North American Review* 22 (January 1826): 61-63; Joseph Sabin, *Bibliotheca Americana. A Dictionary of Books Relating to America from its Discovery to the Present Time,* 20 vols. (New York: Bibliographical Society of America, 1877), 9: 398, quoted in Miles, "Sketch of Keating," p. 297.

44. George P. Merrill, *The First One Hundred Years of American Geology* (New Haven, Conn.: Yale University Press, 1924), pp. 102-4.

45. Miles, "Sketch of Keating," pp. 296-97.

Chapter 11

1. See introduction, p. 5, William H. Goetzmann, *Exploration and Empire: The Explorer and the Scientist in the Winning of the American West* (New York: Alfred A. Knopf, 1966), pp. x-xii.

2. John L. Allen, "An Analysis of the Exploratory Process: The Lewis and Clark Expedition of 1804-1806," *Geographical Review* 57 (January 1972): 13-39.

3. John K. Wright, introduction to Sir Percy Sykes, *A History of Exploration* (New York: Harper Torchbooks, 1961), p. xvii.

4. Quoted in Richard G. Wood, *Stephen Harriman Long, 1784-1864; Army Engineer, Explorer, Inventor* (Glendale, Calif.: Arthur Clark Co., 1966), p. 111 and n.

Bibliography

This bibliography has been limited chiefly to items actually cited in the study, although a few sources that offered interesting and related ideas also have been included.

I. Primary Material: Archival and Manuscript Sources

Jacob Brown Letterbooks. Library of Congress, Washington, D.C.

James E. Colhoun Diary. Minnesota Historical Society, St. Paul.

James E. Colhoun Diary. Owned by Edwin B. McDill, Greensboro, North Carolina.

John Harris Papers. Dartmouth College Archives, Hanover, New Hampshire.

Andrew Jackson Papers. Library of Congress, Washington, D.C.

Edwin James Diary. Special Collections, Butler Library, Columbia University, New York.

Thomas S. Jesup Papers. Library of Congress, Washington, D.C.

Stephen W. Kearny Papers. Missouri Historical Society, St. Louis.

Stephen H. Long Letters. New Hampshire State Library, Concord.

Stephen H. Long Letters. Pennsylvania Historical Society, Philadelphia.

Stephen H. Long Papers. American Philosophical Society Library, Philadelphia.

Stephen H. Long Topographical Journals. 3 vols., Minnesota Historical Society, St. Paul.

John O'Fallon Papers. Missouri Historical Society, St. Louis.

Titian R. Peale Diary. Library of Congress, Washington, D.C.

Thomas A. Smith Papers. State Historical Society of Missouri, Columbia.

United States, Army Quartermaster Department Papers. Library of Congress, Washington, D.C.

United States, Records of the Office of the Adjutant General, Record Group 94. National Archives, Washington, D.C.

———. Records of the Office of the Chief of Engineers, Record Group 77. National Archives, Washington, D.C.

———. Records of the Office of Indian Affairs, Record Group 75. National Archives, Washington, D.C.

———. Records of the Office of the Quartermaster General, Record Group 92. National Archives, Washington, D.C.

———. Records of the Office of the Secretary of War, Record Group 107. National Archives, Washington, D.C.

———. Records of United States Army Continental Commands, Record Group 393. National Archives, Washington, D.C.

———. Records of the United States General Accounting Office, Record Group 217. National Archives, Washington, D.C.

E. G. Voorhis Collection. Missouri Historical Society, St. Louis.

II. Primary Material: Articles, Books, and Published Documents

Bell, John R. *The Journal of Captain John R. Bell, Official Journalist for the Stephen H. Long Expedition to the Rocky Mountains, 1820.* Edited by Harlin M. Fuller and LeRoy R. Hafen, vol. 6 in *The Far West and the Rockies Historical Series.* 15 vols. Glendale, Calif.: Arthur Clark Co. 1957.

Beltrami, Giacomo C. *A Pilgrimage in Europe and America Leading to the Discovery of the Sources of the Mississippi and Bloody River; with a Description of the Whole Course of the Former and of the Ohio.* 2 vols. London: Hunt and Clarke, 1828.

———. *To the Public of New York, and of the United States. The Author of "The Discovery of the Sources of the Mississippi, & &."* New York: J. Darke, 1825.

Calhoun, John C. *The Papers of John C. Calhoun.* 9 vols. Edited by Robert L. Meriwether and W. Edwin Hemphill. Columbia, S.C.: University of South Carolina Press, 1959-76.

Callan, John F., comp. *The Military Laws of the United States, Relating to the Army, Volunteers, Militia, and to Bounty Lands and Pensions from the Foundation of the Government to the Year 1863.* Philadelphia, Pa.: G. W. Childs, 1863.

Darlington, William. *Reliquiae Baldwinianae: Selections from the Correspondence of the late William Baldwin, M.D. Surgeon in the U.S. Navy, with occasional Notes, and a Short Biographical Memoir.* Philadelphia, Pa.: Kimber and Sharpless, 1843.

Emory, William H., et ·al. *Notes of a Military Reconnaissance from Fort Leavenworth in Missouri to San Diego in California, Including parts of the Arkansas, Del Norte, and Gila Rivers.* Washington, D.C.: Wendell and Van Benthuysen, printers, 1848.

Everett, Edward. "Long's Expedition." *North American Review* 16 (April 1823): 242-69.

Forsyth, Thomas. "Fort Snelling. Colonel Leavenworth's Expedition to Establish it, in 1819." *Minnesota Historical Society Collections* 3 (1880): 139-67.

Gale, John. *The Missouri Expedition, 1818-1820, The Journal of Surgeon John Gale with Related Documents.* Edited by Roger L. Nichols. Norman, Okla.: University of Oklahoma Press, 1969.

Harris, Gilbert Dennison, ed. "A Reprint of the Paleontological Writings of Thomas Say." Cornell University *Bulletin of American Paleontology* 5 (December 1896): 271-354.

Hubbell, William D. "The First Steamboats on the Missouri; Reminiscences of Captain W. D. Hubbell." Edited by Vivian K. McLarty. *Missouri Historical Review* 51 (July 1957): 373-81.

Jackson, Andrew. *The Correspondence of Andrew Jackson.* Edited by John S. Bassett. 7 vols. Washington, D.C.: Carnegie Institution of Washington, 1926-35.

James, Edwin, comp. *Account of an Expedition from Pittsburgh to the Rocky Mountains, Performed in the Years 1819 and '20, by Order of The Hon. J. C. Calhoun, Sec'y. of War: Under the Command of Major Stephen H. Long.* Vols. 14-17 in *Early Western Travels.* 32 vols. Edited by Reuben G. Thwaites. Cleveland, Ohio: Arthur Clark Co., 1905.

Kearny, Stephen W. "Journal of Stephen Watts Kearny." Edited by Valentine M. Porter. *Missouri Historical Society Collections* 3 (January-April 1908): 8-29, 99-131.

Keating, William. H. *Narrative of an Expedition to the Source of St. Peter's River, Lake Winnepeek, Lake of the Woods, &c.*

Performed in the Year 1823, By Order of the Hon. J. C. Calhoun, Secretary of War, Under the Command of Stephen H. Long, U.S.T.E. 2 vols. London: Geo. B. Whittaker, 1825. Reprint. Introduction by Roy P. Johnson, Minneapolis, Minn.: Ross and Haines, 1959.

Lewis, Meriwether and William Clark. *The Journals of the Expedition Under the Command of Capts. Lewis and Clark to the Sources of the Missouri, thence Across the Rocky Mountains and down the River Columbia to the Pacific Ocean. Performed During the Years 1804-5-6.* 2 vols. Edited by Nicholas Biddle. Philadelphia, Pa.: Bradford and Inskeep, 1814. Reprint. New York: Heritage Press, 1962.

Livingston, John. "Colonel Stephen H. Long of the United States Army." In *Portraits of Eminent Americans Now Living: With Biographical and Historical Memoirs of Their Lives and Actions.* 4 vols. New York: Cornish, Lamport & Co., 1853-54.

Long, Stephen H. *The Northern Expeditions of Stephen H. Long: The Journals of 1817 and 1823 and Related Documents.* Edited by Lucile M. Kane, June D. Holmquist, and Carolyn Gilman, St. Paul, Minn.: Minnesota Historical Society Press, 1978.

―――. "Voyage in a Six-Oared Skiff to the Falls of Saint Anthony in 1817." *Collections of the Minnesota Historical Society.* 17 vols. St. Paul, Minn., 1860-1920. Vol. 2: 8-88.

Morse, Jedediah. *A Report to the Secretary of War of the United States, on Indian Affairs, Comprising a Narrative of a Tour Performed in the Summer of 1820, under a Commission from the President of the United States, for the Purpose of Ascertaining, for the use of the Government, the Actual State of the Indian Tribes in our Country.* New Haven, Conn.: S. Converse, 1822.

Peale, Titian R. "Journal of Titian Ramsay Peale, Pioneer Naturalist." Edited by A. O. Weese. *Missouri Historical Review* 41 (January 1947): 147-63.

Pike, Zebulon M. *The Journals of Zebulon Montgomery Pike with Letters and Related Documents.* 2 vols. Edited by Donald Jackson. Norman, Okla.: University of Oklahoma Press, 1966.

Poesch, Jessie. *Titian Ramsay Peale, 1799-1885, and His Journals of the Wilkes Expedition. Memoirs,* No. 52. Philadelphia, Pa.: American Philosophical Society, 1961.

Raisz, Erwin. "Land Forms of the United States." Map, 6th ed. New York: Ginn & Co., 1957.

Say, Thomas. *The Complete Writings of Thomas Say on the Conchology of the United States.* Edited by William G. Binney. New York: H. Bailliere, 1858.

———. *The Complete Writings of Thomas Say on the Entomology of North America.* Edited by John L. LeConte. New York: Bailliere Brothers, 1859.

———. *Descriptions of Terrestrial Shells of North America, By Thomas Say.* Edited by William G. Binney. Philadelphia, Pa.: Childs and Peterson, 1856.

Schoolcraft, Henry R. "G. C. Beltrami, *La De couverte des Sources du Mississippi, et de la Riviere Sanglante." North American Review* 27 (July 1828): 89-114.

———. "Indians of North America." *North American Review* 22 (January 1826): 53-119.

———. *Schoolcraft's Expedition to Lake Itasca: The Discovery of the Source of the Mississippi.* Edited by Philip P. Mason. East Lansing, Mich.: Michigan State University Press, 1958.

———. *Schoolcraft's Narrative Journal of Travels Through the Northwestern Regions of the United States, Extending from Detroit Through the Great Chain of American Lakes to the Sources of the Mississippi River in the Year 1820.* Edited by Mentor L. Williams. East Lansing, Mich.: Michigan State University Press, 1953.

Silliman, Benjamin. "Expedition of Major Long and party, to the Rocky Mountains." *American Journal of Science and Arts* 6 (1823): 374-75.

Sparks, Jared. "Major Long's Second Expedition." *North American Review* 21 (July 1825): 178-89.

Swift, Joseph G. *Memoirs of Gen. Joseph Gardner Swift, LL.D., U.S.A., First Graduate of the United States Military Academy, West Point, Chief Engineer U.S.A. from 1812 to 1818. 1800-1865.* Edited by Harrison Ellery. Worcester, Mass.: F. S. Blanchard & Co., 1890.

Tanner, John. *A Narrative of the Captivity and Adventures of John Tanner (U.S. Interpreter at the Saut de Ste. Marie) During Thirty Years Residence among the Indians in the Interior of North America.* Edited by Edwin James. New York: G. & C. H. Carvill, 1830.

Wilhelm, Paul. *Travels in North America, 1822-1824.* Translated by W. Robert Nitske. Edited by Savoie Lottinville. Norman, Okla.: University of Oklahoma Press, 1973.

Williams, J. F. "Memoir of Capt. Martin Scott." *Minnesota Historical Society Collections* 3 (1870-80): 181-83.

Wood, Richard G. "Exploration by Steamboat." *Journal of Transport History 2* (November 1955): 121-23.

———. "Stephen Harriman Long at Belle Point." *Arkansas Historical Quarterly* 13 (Winter 1954): 338-40.

———. "Stephen Harriman Long's Plan for a New Fort at Peoria." *Journal of the Illinois State Historical Society* 47 (Winter 1954): 417-21.

III. Primary Material: Newspapers and Contemporary Periodicals

Inquisitor Advertizer (Cincinnati), 1819.

Missouri Gazette and Public Advertizer (St. Louis), 1819-22.

Missouri Republican (St. Louis), 1822-24.

National Intelligencer (Washington, D.C.), 1815-25.

The National Register (Washington, D.C.), 1817.

New York Columbian, 1817.

Niles Weekly Register (Baltimore), 1815-25.

North American Review (Boston), 1815-25.

Pittsburgh Gazette, 1819.

St. Louis Enquirer, 1819-24.

Weekly Gazette (Washington, D.C.), 1818.

Western Spy (Cincinnati), 1819.

Western Sun and General Advertizer (Vincennes, Indiana), 1815-25.

IV. Primary Material: U.S. Government Publications

American State Papers: Indian Affairs. 2 vols. Washington, D.C., 1832-34.

American State Papers: Military Affairs. 7 vols. Washington, D.C., 1832-61.

American State Papers: Miscellaneous. 2 vols. Washington, D.C. 1834.

Carter, Clarence E. and John Porter Bloom, ed. *The Territorial Papers of the United States.* 27 vols. Washington, D.C. 1934—.

Heitman, Francis B. Comp. *Historical Register and Dictionary of the United States Army, From Its Organization, September 29, 1789, to March 2, 1903.* 2 vols. Washington, D.C.: Government Printing Office, 1903.

Hodge, Frederick W., ed. *Handbook of American Indians North of Mexico.* 2 vols. *Bureau of American Ethnology Bulletin* 30. Washington, D.C. 1907-10.

Kappler, Charles J., comp. *Indian Affairs: Laws and Treaties.* 5 vols. Washington, D.C., 1903-41.

Malloy, William M., comp. *Treaties, Conventions, International Acts, Protocols and Agreements Between the United States of America and Other Powers, 1776-1909. Senate Document No. 357.* 61st Cong., 2d sess., 1910.

Risch, Erna. *Quartermaster Support of the Army: A History of the Corps, 1775-1939.* Washington, D.C. Quartermaster Historian's Office, 1962.

United States Congress. House of Representativs. "Hostile Disposition of Indian Tribes on the Northwestern Frontier," *House Executive Document, No. 277,* 20th Cong., 1 sess. May 21, 1828.

V. Secondary Material: Articles and Essays

Ackerman, Gertrude W. "Joseph Renville of Lac Qui Parle." *Minnesota History,* 12 (September 1931): 231-46.

Alden, Carroll S. s.v. "Graham, James D." *Dictionary of American Biography.*

Alford, Terry L. "The West as a Desert in American Thought

Prior to Long's 1819-1820 Expedition." *Journal of the West* 8 (October 1969): 515-25.

Allen, John L. "An Analysis of the Exploratory Process: The Lewis and Clark Expedition of 1804-1806." *Geographical Review* 62 (January 1972): 13-39.

———. "Exploration and the Creation of Geographical Images of the Great Plains: Comments on the Role of Subjectivity." Paper read at Images of the Plains Conference, April 1973, at Lincoln, Neb.

———. "Geographical Knowledge & American Images of the Louisiana Territory." *Western Historical Quarterly* 2 (April 1971): 151-70.

Baker, James H. "The Sources of the Mississippi, Their Discoveries, Real and Pretended." *Minnesota Historical Society Collections* 6 (1894): 1-28.

Barnhart, John. s.v. "Torrey, John." *Dictionary of American Biography.*

Beers, Henry P. "A History of the U.S. Topographical Engineers, 1813-1863." *Military Engineer* 34 (June-July 1942): 287-91, 358-62.

Bourne, Edward G. "The Travels of Jonathan Carver." *American Historical Review* 11 (January 1906): 287-302.

Bowden, Martyn J. "The Great American Desert and the American Frontier, 1800-1882: Popular Images of the Plains." In *Anonymous Americans,* edited by Tamara K. Hareven. Englewood Cliffs, N.J.: Prentice-Hall, Inc., 1971.

———. "The Perception of the Western Interior of the U.S., 1800-1870; A Problem in Historical Geosophy." *Proceedings of the Association of American Geographers* 1 (1969): 16-21.

Brendel, Frederick. "Historical Sketch of the Science of Botany in North America from 1635 to 1840." *American Naturalist* 13 (December 1879): 754-71.

Brower, Jacob B. "The Mississippi River and Its Source." *Minnesota Historical Society Collections* 7 (1893).

Christianson, Theodore. "The Long and Beltrami Explorations in Minnesota One Hundred Years Ago." *Minnesota History Bulletin* 5 (November 1923): 249-64.

Davidson, Levette J. "Colorado Cartography." *Colorado Magazine* 32 (July 1955): 178-90.

Dillon, Richard. "Stephen Long's Great American Desert." *Proceedings of the American Philosophical Society* 111 (April 1967): 93-108.

Fernald, Merritt L. "Some Early Botanists of the American Philosophical Society." *Proceedings of the American Philosophical Society* 86 (September 1943): 63-71.

Frederick, John H. s.v. "Keating, William H." *Dictionary of American Biography.*

Friis, Herman, R. "Stephen Long's Unpublished Manuscript Map of the United States Compiled in 1820-1822 (?)." *The California Geographer* 8 (1967): 75-87.

Goodwin, Cardinal L. "A Larger View of the Yellowstone Expedition, 1819-1820." *Mississippi Valley Historical Review* 4 (December 1917): 299-313.

Hill, A. J. "Constantine Beltrami." *Minnesota Historical Society Collections* 2 (1860-67): 183-96.

Howard, Leland O. s.v. "Say, Thomas." Dictionary of American Biography.

Hunter, Louis C. "The Invention of the Western Steamboat." *Journal of Economic History* 3 (November 1943): 201-20.

Josephy, Alvin M., Jr. "Across the Mississippi." In *The Pioneer Spirit.* Edited by Richard M. Ketchum. New York: American Heritage, 1959.

Kelly, Howard A. "William Baldwin." In *Some American Medical Botanists Commemorated in our Botanical Nomenclature.* New York: D. Appleton and Company, 1929.

Lawson, Merlin P. "A Behavioristic Interpretation of Pike's Geographical Knowledge of the Interior of Louisiana." *Great Plains-Rocky Mountain Geographical Journal* 1 (1972): 58-64.

Lewis, G. Malcolm. "Early American Exploration and the Cis-Rocky Mountain Desert, 1803-1823." *Great Plains Journal* 5 (Fall 1965): 6-9.

———. "Regional Ideas and Reality in the Cis-Rocky Mountain West." *Transactions, Institute of British Geographers* 38 (1966): 135-50.

———. "Three Centuries of Desert Concepts in the Cis-Rocky

Mountain West." *Journal of the West* 4 (July 1965): 457-77.

McDermott, John F. "Samuel Seymour: Pioneer Artist of the Plains and the Rockies." *Smithsonian Report for 1950,* Washington, D.C.: Smithsonian Institution, 1951: 497-509.

Miles, Wyndham D. "A Versatile Explorer: A Sketch of William H. Keating." *Minnesota History* 36 (December 1959): 294-99.

Morris, Ralph C. "The Notion of a Great American Desert East of the Rockies." *Mississippi Valley Historical Review* 13 (September 1926): 190-200.

Murphy, Robert C. "The Sketches of Titian Ramsay Peale, (1799-1855). *Proceedings of the American Philosophical Society* 101 (December 1957): 523-31.

Muszynska-Wallace, E. Sotteris. "The Sources of the Prairie." *American Literature* 21 (May 1949): 191-200.

Nichols, Roger L. "Soldiers as Farmers: Army Agriculture in the Missouri Valley, 1818-1827." *Agricultural History* 44 (April 1970): 213-22.

Osterhout, George E. "Rocky Mountain Botany and the Long Expedition of 1820." *Bulletin of the Torrey Botanical Club* 47 (1920): 555-62.

Pammel, L. H. "Dr. Edwin James." *Annals of Iowa* 8 (October 1907: 161-85; January 1908): 277-95.

Prucha, Francis P. "Indian Removal and the Great American Desert." *Indiana Magazine of History* 59 (December 1963): 299-322.

Rau, Albert G. s.v. "von Schweinitz, Lewis David." *Dictionary of American Biography.*

Sellers, Horace S. s.v. "Peale, Titian." *Dictionary of American Biography.*

Shipman, Fred W. s.v. "O'Fallon, Benjamin." *Dictionary of American Biography.*

Smith, Alice, E. "Stephen H. Long and the Naming of Wisconsin." *Wisconsin Magazine of History* 26 (September 1942): 67-71.

Spaulding, Thomas M. s.v. "Swift, William H." *Dictionary of American Biography.*

Tucker, John M. "Major Long's Route from the Arkansas to the

Canadian River, 1820." *New Mexico Historical Review* 38 (July 1963): 184-219.

Viets, Henry R. s.v. "Baldwin, William." *Dictionary of American Biography*.

Waterman, W. Randall. s.v. " Morse, Jedediah." *Dictionary of American Biography*.

Webb, Walter P. "The American West, Perpetual Mirage." *Harper's*, (May 1957): 25-31.

———. "The West and the Desert." *Montana: The Magazine of Western History* 8 (January 1958): 2-12.

Wesley, Edgar B. "A Still Larger View of the So-Called Yellowstone Expedition." *North Dakota Historical Quarterly* 5 (July 1931): 219-38.

Wheat, Carl I. "Mapping the American West, 1540-1857, A Preliminary Study." *American Antiquarian Society Proceedings* 64 (1954): 19-194.

Wood, Richard G. "Dr. Edwin James, a Disappointed Explorer." *Minnesota History* 34 (Autumn 1955): 284-86.

Wright, John K. Introduction to *A History of Explorations,* by Percy Sykes. New York: Harper Torchbooks, 1961.

———. "Terrae Incognitae: The Place of Imagination in Geography." *Annals of the Association of American Geographers* 37 (March 1947): 1-15.

Youmans, William J. "Thomas Say." In *Pioneers of Science in America; Sketches of Their Lives and Scientific Work,* edited by William J. Youmans. New York: D. Appleton & Co., 1896.

VI. Secondary Material: Books and Theses

Bakeless, John. *Lewis and Clark, Partners in Discovery*. New York: William Morrow & Company, 1947.

Bearss, Edwin C. and Arrell M. Gibson. *Fort Smith, Little Gibralter on the Arkansas*. Norman, Okla.: University of Oklahoma Press, 1969.

Beers, Henry P. *The Western Military Frontier, 1815-1846*. Philadelphia, Pa.: University of Pennsylvania Press, 1935.

Benson, Maxine. "Edwin James, Scientist, Linguist, Humanitarian." Ph.D. dissertation, University of Colorado, 1968.

Billington, Ray A. *Westward Expansion, A History of the American Frontier.* 4th ed. New York: Macmillan Company, 1974.

Chittenden, Hiram M. *The American Fur Trade of the Far West.* 3 vols. New York: F. P. Harper, 1902.

Clark, Thomas D. *Frontier America.* New York: Charles Scribner's Sons, 1959.

Conard, Howard L., ed. *Encyclopedia of the History of Missouri, a Compendium of History and Biography for Ready Reference.* 8 vols. St. Louis, Mo.: Southern History Company, 1901.

Cullum, George W. *Biographical Register of the Officers and Graduates of the United States Military Academy at West Point, N.Y.* 8 vols. Boston: Houghton Mifflin and Co., 1891-1910.

Cutright, Paul R. *Lewis and Clark: Pioneering Naturalists.* Urbana, Ill.: University of Illinois Press, 1969.

Ewan, Joseph A. *Rocky Mountain Naturalists.* Denver, Colo.: University of Denver Press, 1950.

Goetzmann, William H. *Army Exploration in the American West, 1803-1863.* New Haven, Conn.: Yale University Press, 1959.

———. *Exploration and Empire: The Explorer and the Scientist in the Winning of the American West.* New York: Alfred A. Knopf, 1966.

Graustein, Jeannette E. *Thomas Nuttall, Naturalist: Explorations in America, 1808-1841.* Cambridge, Mass.: Harvard University Press, 1967.

Hall, E. Raymond and Keith R. Kelson. *The Mammals of North America.* 2 vols. New York: Ronald Press Co., 1959.

Halley, Patrick L. "The Western Enterprises of Major Stephen H. Long, 1816-1821." Ph.D. dissertation. University of Oklahoma, 1951.

Harshberger, John W. *The Botanists of Philadelphia and Their Work.* Philadelphia, Pa.: T. C. Davis & Son, 1899.

Henry, Guy V. *Military Record of Civilian Appointments in the United States Army.* 2 vols. New York: D. Van Nostrand, 1871-73.

Hollon, W. Eugene. *The Great American Desert, Then and*

Now. New York: Oxford University Press, 1966.

Hunter, Louis. *Steamboats on the Western Waters: An Economic and Technological History.* Cambridge, Mass.: Harvard University Press, 1949.

Lawson, Merlin P. "The Climate of the Great American Desert: Reconstruction of the Climate of Western Interior United States, 1800-1850." Ph.D. dissertation, Clark University, 1973.

McKelvey, Susan D. *Botanical Exploration of the Trans-Mississippi West, 1790-1850.* Jamaica Plain, Mass.: Harvard University Press, 1955.

McManis, Douglas R. *Initial Evaluation and Utilization of the Illinois Prairies, 1815-1840.* Department of Geography Monograph No. 93. Chicago: University of Chicago Press, 1964.

McSpadden, J. Walker, ed. *Animals of the World.* Garden City, N.Y.: Garden City Publishing Co., 1941.

Meisel, Max., *A Bibliography of American Natural History, The Pioneer Century, 1790-1865.* 3 vols. Brooklyn, N.Y.: Premier Publishing Co., 1924-29. Includes valuable discussion of explorers, development of scholarly societies, as well as the bibliography.

Merrill, George P. *The First One Hundred Years of American Geology.* New Haven, Conn.: Yale University Press, 1924.

Miceli, Augusto P. *The Man With the Red Umbrella: Giacomo Constantino Beltrami in America.* Baton Rouge, La.: Claitor's Publishing Division, 1974.

Nevins, Allan. *Fremont, Pathmarker of the West.* New York: Longmans, Green and Co., 1955.

Nichols, Roger L. *General Henry Atkinson: A Western Military Career.* Norman, Okla.: University of Oklahoma Press, 1965.

Overland, Orm. *The making and meaning of an American classic: James Fenimore Cooper's The Prairie.* New York: Humanities Press, 1973.

Peattie, Donald C. *Green Laurels. The Lives and Achievements of the Great Naturalists.* New York: Garden City Publishing Co., 1936.

Prucha, Francis P. *A Guide to the Military Posts of the United States, 1789-1895.* Madison, Wis.: State Historical Society of Wisconsin, 1964.

Richardson, Leon B. *History of Dartmouth College.* 2 vols. Hanover, N.H.: Dartmouth College Publications, 1932.

Riegel, Robert E. and Robert G. Athearn. *America Moves West.* 5th Ed. New York: Holt, Rinehart and Winston, Inc., 1971.

Rodgers, Andrew D. *John Torrey: A Story of North American Botany.* Princeton, N.J.: Princeton University Press, 1942.

Sabin, Joseph. *Bibliotheca Americana. A Dictionary of Books Relating to America from its Discovery to the Present Time.* 20 vols. New York: Bibliographical Society of America, 1868-1936.

Stanton, William R. *The Leopard's Spots: Scientific Attitudes Toward Race in America 1815-59.* Chicago: University of Chicago Press, 1960.

Steckmesser, Kent L. *The Westward Movement: A Short History.* New York: McGraw-Hill, 1969.

Webb, Walter P. *The Great Plains.* Boston, Mass.: Ginn and Co., 1931.

Weiss, Harry B. *The Pioneer Century of Entomology.* New Brunswick, N.J.: Privately printed, 1936.

——— and Grace M. Zeigler. *Thomas Say, Early American Naturalist.* Springfield, Ill.: Charles C. Thomas, Publisher, 1931.

Wesley, Edgar B. *Guarding the Frontier: A Study of Frontier Defense from 1815-1825.* Minneapolis, Minn.: University of Minnesota Press, 1935.

Wheat, Carl I. *Mapping the Transmississippi West, 1540-1861.* 5 vols. San Francisco, Calif.: Institute of Historical Cartography, 1957-63.

Wiltse, Charles M. *John C. Calhoun: Nationalist, 1782-1828.* Indianapolis, Ind.: Bobbs-Merrill Co., 1944.

Wood, Richard G. *Stephen Harriman Long, 1784-1864: Army Engineer, Explorer, Inventor.* Glendale, Calif.: Arthur Clark Co., 1966.

Index